Building and Managing a Cloud Using Oracle Enterprise Manager 12c

Madhup Gulati
Adeesh Fulay
Sudip Datta

New York Chicago San Francisco
Lisbon London Madrid Mexico City Milan
New Delhi San Juan Seoul Singapore Sydney Toronto

Cataloging-in-Publication Data is on file with the Library of Congress

McGraw-Hill Education books are available at special quantity discounts to use as premiums and sales promotions, or for use in corporate training programs. To contact a representative, please e-mail us at bulksales@mcgraw-hill.com.

Building and Managing a Cloud Using Oracle Enterprise Manager 12c

1 2 3 4 5 6 7 8 9 0   QFR QFR   1 0 9 8 7 6 5 4 3

ISBN   978-0-07-176322-6
MHID   0-07-176322-8

Sponsoring Editor Meghan Manfre	**Copy Editor** William McManus	**Illustration** Cenveo Publisher Services
Editorial Supervisor Patty Mon	**Proofreader** Carol Shields	**Art Director, Cover** Jeff Weeks
Project Manager Raghavi Khullar, Cenveo® Publisher Services	**Indexer** Ted Laux	**Cover Designer** Pattie Lee
Acquisitions Coordinator Stephanie Evans	**Production Supervisor** George Anderson	
Technical Editors Mark Carlson Pramod Chowbey	**Composition** Cenveo Publisher Services	

Dedicated to our sons, Maanye, Ruhaan, Aritro, and Oishik

About the Authors

Madhup Gulati is a Principal Product Manager at Oracle. He specializes in Infrastructure-as-a-Service and Virtualization solutions. He engages actively in new product development as well as in customer adoption of existing product offerings globally. Madhup has been a speaker at various conferences, expos, and briefings. Previously, Madhup has worked in the Oracle Fusion Middleware and Oracle E-Business Suite divisions within Oracle. He has a Master of Science in Computer Science with Distinction in Research from Stanford University.

Adeesh Fulay is a Consulting Product Manager for Oracle System Management products. He possesses extensive hands-on experience in consulting, training, and development in a product environment. Currently, Adeesh is the Product Management Lead for Database-as-a-Service features within Oracle Enterprise Manager. Prior to joining Oracle, Adeesh traveled extensively on consulting assignments to various customer sites, thus gaining extensive knowledge about datacenter management and automation.

Sudip Datta is the Vice President of Product Management for Oracle Systems Management products. He heads up product management for Cloud Management and Data Center Automation solutions. He has extensive experience spanning 20 years, working with enterprise customers and partners such as Dell, Boeing, Verizon, AT&T, GE, and Telstra, to name a few. Sudip has a Bachelor in Electronics and Telecommunication Engineering and an MBA.

About the Technical Editors

Mark A. Carlson, Principal Cloud Strategist at Oracle, has more than 30 years of experience with Networking and Storage development and more than 15 years of experience with Java technology. Mark was one of the authors of the CDMI Cloud Storage standard. He has spoken at numerous industry forums and events. He is the chair of the SNIA Cloud Storage, NDMP, and XAM SDK technical working groups, chairs the DMTF Policy working group, serves on the SNIA Technical Council, and represents Oracle on the DMTF Technical Committee and serves as DMTF VP of Alliances.

Pramod Chowbey is Director, Strategic Customer Programs for Systems Management at Oracle. He is responsible for all aspects of the Strategic Customer Program worldwide. Pramod has been with Oracle since 1994, holding various management positions in consulting, sales consulting, and product development. Pramod holds an MBA from University of North Carolina, Chapel Hill.

Contents

Foreword

Things change over time. When I joined Oracle in August 1993, version 6 of Oracle Database was still a production release, and version 7.0 was the new Database version just being adopted. Back then, a DBA had at most a handful of databases to manage. The size of those databases was trivial compared to the size of databases today. The number of end users for each database was typically very small—remember, those were client-server days, before Internet deployments were possible. Also, a database application most times had its own resources—machine resources, such as its own computer, disk drives, memory, and so on. The need to be available 24×7 was far more rare than today. (In 1993, when you went home from work, you actually went home—you did not go home to go back to work at home! We had maintenance windows.) In short, the challenges we faced in 1993 were very different from those we face today.

Today, a DBA might have hundreds, if not thousands, of databases, application servers, and systems in general to manage. These databases are typically "huge" in size, and they support a massive user community in most cases. The size of today's applications is many orders of magnitude larger than applications of the past, and today's applications are far more complex. Availability concerns are dominant; security concerns are overwhelming. Managing and monitoring these systems is paramount.

To meet these challenges, IT has returned to its roots in the 1980s and earlier when it worked predominantly with mainframe-based systems: centralized management and pooling of resources. It is an "old new" way to manage our infrastructure, and to accomplish this, we need a different approach from what was used in the past. Today, we call this approach "the cloud."

Enter Oracle Enterprise Manager, the systems management tool for managing your Oracle ecosystem—from the operating system, to the middle tier, to the database itself. This book describes how to utilize this core piece of your management infrastructure to manage, patch, monitor, and charge back for resources used in your cloud environment. Written by people who helped to write the product, this book gives you the details necessary to configure and be successful with Oracle Enterprise Manager. It will take you through topics such as planning your cloud management implementation, implementing and utilizing a self-service paradigm, and implementing, managing, and monitoring Infrastructure as a Service, Platform as a Service, and Database as a Service. Then it moves into an important topic in a shared resource implementation such as the cloud: resource usage monitoring and capture, which enables you to implement a fair chargeback scheme. Lastly, this chapter presents a series of real-life case studies so that you can see how others have implemented their cloud infrastructure.

All in all, this book covers the topics you need to be aware of in order to be successful with Oracle Enterprise Manager.

Thomas Kyte
http://asktom.oracle.com

Acknowledgments

We would like to thank everyone who helped turn our thoughts and ideas into this book. Special mention goes to Lisa McClain and Meghan Manfre for approaching us with this project and driving it to completion. Thanks to Stephanie Evans for answering our questions throughout the writing and publishing process. We would also like to thank experts who helped us refine the content: Jagan Athreya, for insights into Consolidation Planner, Mark McGill, for his contribution to the Metering and Chargeback chapter, and Dhruv Gupta, for expert advice on Middleware as a Service. Special thanks to Sushil Kumar, Vice President of Product Management and Strategy, for his leadership in making the Oracle Enterprise Manager 12c release a success that goes far beyond the features outlined in this book.

We are grateful to Mark Carlson and Pramod Chowbey for accepting to be the technical editors for this book. Their dedication in reviewing the content in a timely manner and providing invaluable feedback is what made this book possible.

We would also like to extend our thanks to various members of Engineering at Oracle, who are too many to be named individually, but for whose tireless efforts the features, and hence this book, would not be possible.

Last but not least, we want to thank our families for being supportive and encouraging of this endeavor.

Introduction

There are times when a secondary meaning of a particular word surpasses the primary meaning, in terms of usage. "Cloud" is one such (buzz) word that has been in vogue lately, especially in Information Technology circles. While the broad definition of cloud connotes any infrastructure, platform, or application accessed over the Internet, the definition becomes more focused when we talk about enterprise IT. IT administrators in enterprises traditionally have been buried in requests for new servers, databases, and applications and have had little time to plan a consolidated infrastructure or a platform for providing those services. Lack of standardization and consolidation has fueled the problem further, and administrators are spending an inordinate amount of time just servicing new requests and "keeping the lights on."

Cloud offers the precise model that enables IT to be in the business of service enablement and fulfillment without resorting to manual, error-prone tasks for each request. When it comes to enterprise IT, cloud becomes a service delivery platform for enterprise applications that encompasses self-service, showback, and elasticity without compromising on high availability, scalability, security, and so forth.

As members of the Oracle Enterprise Manager product development team, we meet hundreds of administrators—Oracle DBAs, middleware administrators, SOA administrators, and others. Most have warmed up to the notion of cloud, but many still have more questions than answers. There are various use cases, from getting a host for an upcoming project, to getting a database for functional testing, to getting a platform for hosting a Java application. These use cases carry different nuances, and administrators are often left pondering what is the right model and what are the right considerations for each model. Certain enterprises have resorted to a VM-based approach, which has yielded immediate returns but has also created more sprawl and compliance challenges as the enterprises started venturing into more complicated use cases. There are similar nuances associated with monitoring, showback, compliance, and so on.

This book is our humble attempt to respond to all those questions. As readers may know, Oracle Enterprise Manager 12<i>c</i>, released in 2011, is Oracle's flagship offering for cloud management. It comes with an out-of-the-box Self Service Portal, supplemented by APIs and features to manage the operational aspects of cloud. Ever since the release of Oracle Enterprise Manager 12<i>c</i>, we have received an overwhelming response from customers and service providers, several of which are on track to implement cloud. The most interesting aspect that we have witnessed is that customers have varied requirements, from Database as a Service on Exadata, to Application as a Service for Siebel on Oracle VM. Oracle Enterprise Manager 12<i>c</i> is a great confluence of these cloud-enabling technologies, and we have endeavored to describe those reference implementations in this book.

As we continue to get inquiries, we see that the need for this book is greater than we expected. This book covers the planning, architecture and setup, self-service provisioning, showback, and ongoing operational management of a cloud. (It does not cover Oracle's public cloud solution at this point.) This book is intended for IT architects and administrators who are involved in cloud projects. It provides real-life examples and points to deeper Oracle Technology Network documentation for additional details. The content of the book is current as of Oracle Enterprise Manager 12<i>c</i>, Release 2.

Happy reading!

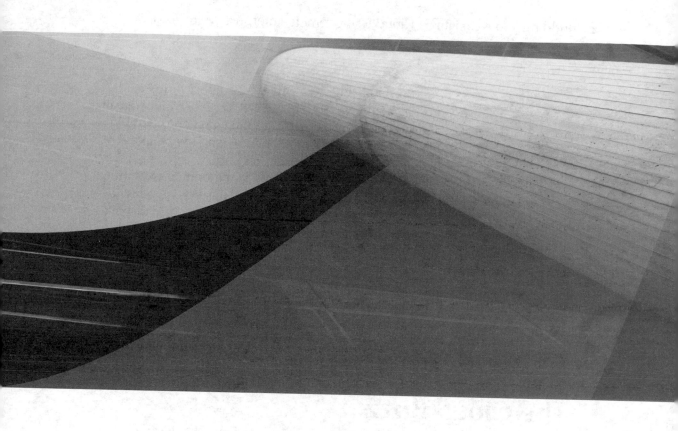

CHAPTER
1

Introduction

loud computing has become one of the latest industry buzzwords. Industry watchers, analysts, bloggers, and media all seem to be talking about cloud computing, and considerable IT investments are being made to adopt and reap the benefits of cloud computing. As Oracle pushes forward to deliver products and solutions to lead this transformation, the Oracle community is exploring ways to take advantage of this opportunity. As you read this book, you will gain a better understanding of Oracle's role in cloud computing and discover new ways to leverage Oracle offerings for building and managing a cloud.

This first chapter provides an overview of the key cloud computing concepts and introduces Oracle's offerings in this space. Chapter 2 discusses business and technical considerations for adopting the right cloud model and reference architectures using Oracle's product portfolio. Subsequent chapters drill down into how you can leverage Oracle's product functionality, especially in the Oracle Enterprise Manager 12*c* area, to deploy and manage various aspects of a cloud.

The Cloud Buzz

In October 2009, IDC released its "IT Cloud Services Forecast: 2009-2013" (http://blogs.idc.com/ie/?p=543), which estimated that of the approximately $400 billion customers would spend on IT in 2009, $17.4 billion would be consumed as cloud services. It also estimated that by 2013, customer spending on IT cloud services would grow almost threefold, to $44 billion. With an estimated five-year annual growth rate of 26 percent—over six times the rate of traditional IT offerings—the growth rate for cloud computing remains strong.

Government, too, seems to have bought into the paradigm. Vivek Kundra, former chief information officer (CIO) of the U.S. Office of Management and Budget (OMB), gave a keynote address on the U.S. government's cloud computing policy on April 7, 2010 at the Brookings Institution. In his speech, titled "The Economic Gains of Cloud Computing," Kundra noted that "agencies across the government have already begun shifting to the cloud." As examples, Kundra reported that, at the time of his speech, the U.S. Department of Health and Human Services (HHS) was leveraging cloud computing to support implementation of Electronic Health Records (EHR) systems; the U.S. Department of Interior was migrating 80,000 e-mail boxes to the cloud; NASA had recently announced that it was reevaluating its enterprise data center strategy and had halted future requests for a proposal that would have been up to $1.5 billion in data center contracts; and the U.S. Department of Energy was investing $32 million on its cloud computing Magellan project.

In citing benefits of cloud computing, Kundra stated, "By using cloud services, the Federal Government will gain access to powerful technology resources faster and at lower costs. This frees us to focus on mission-critical tasks instead of purchasing, configuring, and maintaining redundant infrastructure."

What Is Cloud Computing?

The growing interest in cloud computing has led to efforts by vendors, analysts, and government agencies to try to agree on a single definition of cloud computing, as a means to provide a common ground for discussing how best to leverage this new paradigm. For purposes of this book, the term *cloud computing* refers to a style of computing where dynamically and massively scalable—and often virtualized—resources are provided as a service over the Internet. The services can be of any type or complexity. They can range from complete applications that are available as a service on a subscription basis, such as applications for customer relationship management (CRM), HR, billing and invoicing, document management, accounting, project management, and collaboration, to infrastructure services that are billed on a usage basis, such as servers, storage, network, and backup and recovery platforms. Figure 1-1 graphically demonstrates how cloud computing works from the customers' perspective. The term "cloud" is sometimes used as a metaphor for the Internet, based on how the Internet is depicted in computer network diagrams such as this, and is an abstraction for the complex underlying infrastructure.

The cloud service provider maintains a *seemingly unlimited* pool of resources that consumers can tap into on demand and pay for, based on usage a service model that is similar to how traditional utilities such as power, water, and telephone services are delivered, consumed, and paid for. Cloud consumers do not need to have knowledge of, expertise in, or control over the technology infrastructure "in the cloud" that supports them. A cloud provider makes services available to cloud consumers at agreed service levels and costs. The provider manages the technical infrastructure

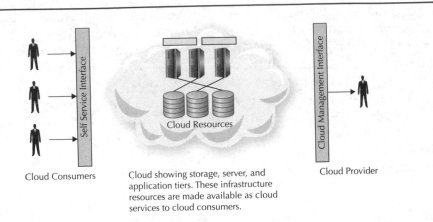

Cloud Consumers   Cloud showing storage, server, and   Cloud Provider
                         application tiers. These infrastructure
                         resources are made available as cloud
                         services to cloud consumers.

FIGURE 1-1.   *Cloud computing*

required for providing the services and provides billing and other reports to consumers.

Cloud consumers—organizations or individuals—contract for services with cloud providers and then use those services. Cloud consumers are responsible for selecting the appropriate services, arranging payment for the services, and performing the administration necessary to use those services, such as managing user identities.

Cloud Computing Definition

If you want an official definition of cloud computing from the U.S. government, look no further than "The NIST Definition of Cloud Computing" (Special Publication 800-145), from the National Institute of Standards and Technology. NIST defines cloud computing as "a model for enabling ubiquitous, convenient, on-demand network access to a shared pool of configurable computing resources (e.g., networks, servers, storage, applications, and services) that can be rapidly provisioned and released with minimal management effort or service provider interaction."

Cloud Computing Characteristics

The formal definition of cloud computing from the National Institute of Standards and Technology has gained broad support from the industry. It describes the following five essential characteristics:

- **On-demand self-service**   Self-service is the most visible part of a cloud to its consumers. Users are able to manage, request, and decommission cloud services without manual intervention by an IT administrator.

- **Broad network access**   Computing services are delivered over (as in build on top of) standard networks and heterogeneous devices.

- **Rapid elasticity**   IT resources are able to scale out and in quickly and on an as-needed basis, giving the perception of unlimited cloud resources to the cloud consumer.

- **Resource pooling**   IT resources are shared across multiple applications and consumers in a nondedicated manner, which encourages sharing and, thus, higher utilization of cloud resources.

- **Measured service**   IT resource utilization is tracked for each application and consumer, typically for public cloud billing or private cloud chargeback.

Cloud Computing vs. Grid Computing

Cloud computing is sometimes confused with grid computing, but distinct differences exist between the models. First, let's look at the similarities between grid computing and cloud computing. Much like a grid, the cloud consists of large pools of networked computers that work together to fulfill user requests. Instead of dedicating servers and storage for each request, infrastructure resources are shared among requests, resulting in greater flexibility, reduced costs, power efficiency, scalability, and availability. Both computing models involve multi-tenancy and multitasking, meaning that many users can submit different tasks at the same time.

Both grid computing and cloud computing can be the basis for utility computing, where users pay only for what they use on shared server pools, similar to how they would pay only for the resources they use for a public utility such as electricity, gas, and so on. Both grid and cloud models can provide service-level agreements (SLAs) for guaranteed uptime availability. If the service slides below the level of the guaranteed uptime service, users get service credit for receiving data late.

The major difference between grid computing and cloud computing is in the type of relationship that IT shares with its consumers, the end users, in the context of these two computing paradigms.

Traditionally, most efforts to increase efficiency in the use of datacenter resources have been focused on putting in place software and processes to enable IT to optimize the use of datacenter resources and run its operations more efficiently. This allowed IT to manage larger deployments and support growing businesses at reduced cost. Automation that came with grid computing helped this trend. With grid computing, computer resources are pooled together to run shared services. Sophisticated job-scheduling algorithms for parallel processing and workload management are used to automate the allocation of these resources to fulfill requests. This architecture creates a fault-tolerant environment that is highly scalable and allows IT to serve user requests with minimum downtime. Although this greatly increases IT efficiency, the focus is not on fundamentally changing the way IT serves business. End users still submit service requests to IT and wait for IT to fulfill those requests. Moreover, there's rarely a formal contract between IT and business that spells out the details of how and when the services will be provisioned and the quality of service that the users should expect.

Cloud computing goes a step further—it empowers end users to access IT resources as services and procure the resources as required with no intervention from IT administrators. IT acts as an enabler of the cloud model by optimizing the production and management of these services. Resources are provisioned (not just allocated) on demand. This removes the need to overprovision in order to meet the demands of hundreds of users. Cloud computing brings a business-centric approach to IT. By aligning the performance levels and cost structures with business priorities, it enables the *IT as a Service (ITaaS)* model and transforms IT from being a cost center to a center of strategic importance.

In summary, cloud computing encapsulates and extends the behavioral characteristics of grid computing and utility computing and introduces a platform that unifies the benefits associated with both. Figure 1-2 shows how application deployment environments have evolved from being dedicated silos to a grid and then to a cloud.

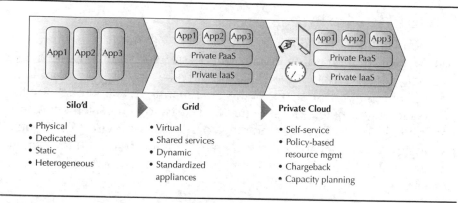

FIGURE 1-2. *Evolution from siloed to grid and then to cloud computing*

Benefits of Cloud Computing

One of the main reasons that the cloud model has gained such widespread popularity is that it is seen as a way to realize many of the long-cherished goals of having agile, elastic, cost-effective, and more egalitarian computing environments. In particular, the cloud is seen not only as a solution for making IT environments more flexible and responsive, thereby enabling them to fulfill dynamic and transient business needs, but also as a means to reduce operational and capital expenditure.

Agility

Agility is a key benefit of cloud computing, especially from an enterprise perspective. Centralized IT organizations often are not equipped to respond to dynamic user demands in a timely fashion, which could impact go-to-market speed and lead to missed business opportunities. The cloud solves this problem by enabling users to provision resources on demand.

Elasticity

The cloud provides the required elasticity for web applications that need to scale up and down dynamically based on workload. It is often very difficult to predict how popular a website or a web application is going to be, which in turn makes capacity planning very difficult. Applications deployed in the cloud are able to provision more resources on demand so as to maintain an acceptable performance level.

Cost Effectiveness

The cloud helps users reduce costs associated with running their own data center. Consumption is billed on a utility basis (resources consumed, like electricity) or subscription basis (time based, like a newspaper) with little or no upfront cost. Other benefits of this time sharing style approach are low barriers to entry, shared infrastructure and costs, low management overhead, and immediate access to a broad range of applications. Users can generally terminate the contract at any time (thereby avoiding return on investment risk and uncertainty), and the services are often covered by SLAs with financial penalties.

Cloud Service Delivery Models

As mentioned earlier, a cloud is basically pools of resources exposed as services to cloud consumers, who can tap into those services on demand and pay for them on a utility basis. These pools of resources may be infrastructure pools, where storage, network, and server hardware resources are made available as a service to consumers, or they may be pools of software services that users intend to share. Depending on what is exposed as a service through the cloud interface to the consumer, different delivery models exist. The most common classification divides them into three broad categories: Software as a Service (SaaS), Platform as a Service (PaaS), and Infrastructure as a Service (IaaS).

There are subcategories of PaaS, such as Development as a Service (DaaS), Testing as a Service (TaaS), Database as a Service (DBaaS), Middleware as a Service (MWaaS), and others. The first few chapters of the book cover cloud service delivery through self-service provisioning for IaaS and PaaS. Subsequent chapters discuss the operational aspects of managing a cloud environment.

Software as a Service (SaaS)

Software as a Service refers to applications delivered as a service to end users through a browser. Some are commercial SaaS applications delivered by public cloud providers over the Internet, while others are commercial and custom SaaS applications delivered by enterprise IT to internal business users. Oracle Cloud, Oracle CRM On Demand, Salesforce.com, and NetSuite are some of the well-known public SaaS providers.

Software as a Service comes in two distinct models:

- **Simple multi-tenancy**   In this model, each SaaS consumer has its own resources in the cloud that are segregated from those of other consumers. This allows multiple customer environments to be isolated from each other, providing complete segregation of consumer application deployments and data. It amounts to a relatively inefficient form of multi-tenancy, but offers the highest level of security.

- **Fine-grain multi-tenancy**   This model also offers a high level of segregation but is far more efficient than the simple multi-tenancy model. Cloud infrastructure resources are shared, but customer data and access capabilities are segregated within the application.

Platform as a Service (PaaS)

Platform as a Service is the delivery of a computing platform and application development stack as a service. PaaS facilitates development and deployment of applications without the cost and complexity of buying and managing the underlying infrastructure, providing entirely via the Internet all of the facilities required to support the complete life cycle of building and delivering web applications and services. PaaS offerings include workflow facilities for application design, application development, testing, deployment, and hosting, as well as application services such as team collaboration, web service integration, database integration, security, scalability, storage, persistence, state management, application versioning, application instrumentation, and developer community facilitation. These services are provisioned as an integrated solution over the Web. Oracle Cloud, Google App Engine, Force.com (Salesforce.com's PaaS offering), and Microsoft Azure are some examples of PaaS offerings.

Depending on what the platform is offering as a service, PaaS can be classified further. For example, if a database is offered as a shared resource, it is called Database as a Service (DBaaS). If an application container, such as Oracle WebLogic Platform, is offered as a service, it is called Middleware as a Service (MWaaS). Sometimes a development environment or tools might be offered as shared cloud resources to multiple application developers, in which case PaaS might be termed Development as a Service (DaaS) or Testing as a Service (TaaS).

Infrastructure as a Service (IaaS)

Infrastructure as a Service is the delivery of datacenter infrastructure (server, storage, and other resources) as a service, typically based on some form of virtualization. It is an evolution of traditional hosting that does not require any long-term commitment and allows users to provision servers or storage on demand. For example, a test engineer may request a few Linux machines through a cloud self-service interface for setting up a test environment. Unlike a PaaS provider, an IaaS provider does very little application stack management other than keep the data center operational. Users receive barebones machines and must deploy and manage the software services themselves—just the way they would in their own data center. Amazon Web Services (AWS) is representative of this class of service.

Amazon Web Services

The following are some of the key services offered by Amazon Web Services (http://aws.amazon.com/products):

- **Elastic Compute Cloud (EC2)**   Allows users to rent virtual machines (VMs) by the hour, with prices ranging from $0.10 to $0.80 per hour depending on the size of the VMs.

- **Elastic Block Storage (EBS)**   Persistent storage for EC2. EC2 VMs by default come with local storage that does not persist beyond the life of the VMs and thus, may not be suitable for running any application that requires data persistence (for example, databases). Using EBS, users can request persistent storage volumes and attach them to any of their EC2 VMs. This is a priced offering on top of EC2 ($0.10 per GB of allocated storage per month).

- **Simple Storage Service (S3)**   A simple file store for storing data such as website images, documents, and backups. This service is accessed using simple HTTP GET and PUT commands. This service can be used independently of EC2.

Cloud Computing and Enterprises

Generally, enterprises recognize that cloud computing offers some compelling business benefits, but many enterprises have been finding cloud adoption to be somewhat of a challenge, particularly for PaaS and IaaS services. While some enterprises have gradually become more comfortable with the idea of SaaS—as reflected by the success of players like Oracle On Demand, Salesforce.com, and NetSuite—large scale adoption of public cloud services still remains slow due to a number factors, which are discussed in this section.

Compliance Risks and Lack of Control

Using a public cloud is not an option for many enterprises because they have to comply with regulations that often require IT to pinpoint the actual location of data and maintain tight control over how the data is accessed. Most public cloud providers like Amazon provide very limited control over where the computing and storage resources reside and how those resources are shared across multiple customers.

Lack of Enterprise-Class Service-Level Agreements

The public cloud vendors offer few to no service-level guarantees, which makes hosting any critical applications a very risky proposition.

Platform Lock-in

Most PaaS providers—including Google App Engine and Force.com—require developers to code to a proprietary stack and proprietary APIs. The purported benefit, as proclaimed by the cloud service providers, is simplicity and speed of development. However, it also means that the developers have to learn a new set of skills to build applications on top of these platforms. Also, in view of the proprietary nature of PaaS offerings, applications written on top of one PaaS offering can't be ported to a different PaaS platform or brought in-house.

Previous Investments

Most enterprises have already made substantial investments in their captive data centers and thus, have plenty of capacity in-house to meet all their needs.

However, these resources can't be as dynamically provisioned as in the cloud, which constrains the IT organization's ability to meet end-user demand quickly. As such, what the enterprises actually need is a solution that helps transform their existing IT infrastructure into the cloud and delivers them its benefits without ceding control or incurring additional costs.

Capital Expense vs. Operational Expense

One of the key benefits often highlighted by the cloud service providers is that the cloud service allows customers to convert some of their capital expenses to operational costs. While this is certainly appealing to startups, small and medium-sized businesses (SMBs), and even some enterprise customers, many big enterprises prefer the capital expense characterization because of the tax advantages associated with accelerated depreciation.

In summary, enterprise adoption of publicly available IaaS and PaaS services has been limited to early-stage experimentation. Although the cloud service providers are gradually beefing up their offerings to address some of the concerns of enterprises outlined in the previous sections, and although moves toward standardization have been made in the industry, it is fair to say that enterprises will continue to face these concerns in the near term and will find it difficult to adopt the publicly available cloud in a significant way. The industry in general seems to have realized this and has consequently coined a new phrase, *private cloud.*

Private Cloud vs. Public Cloud

To put it simply, the private (or internal) cloud concept implies running a service hosted in an in-house data center that emulates some of the behavioral characteristics of the IaaS and PaaS services (referred to here as "public cloud" to denote a publicly shared infrastructure), such as self-service, on-demand provisioning, resource consumption tracking, and chargeback. In other words, enterprises want to transform their existing IT infrastructure to provide these capabilities so that they can satisfy user demands without compromising security or compliance and without giving up control. This idea is gaining increasing acceptance among large enterprises. According to a 2010 Forrester Research, Inc. survey, more than 40 percent of 269 enterprise hardware decision makers surveyed reported interest in deploying some type of private cloud. Figure 1-3 shows the results of the survey.

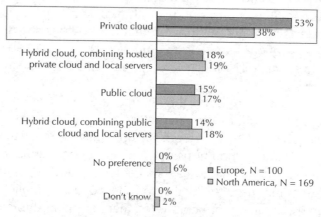

"Which type of cloud computing IaaS deployment approach are you most interested in?"

Private cloud — 53% / 38%

Hybrid cloud, combining hosted private cloud and local servers — 18% / 19%

Public cloud — 15% / 17%

Hybrid cloud, combining public cloud and local servers — 14% / 18%

No preference — 0% / 6%

Don't know — 0% / 2%

■ Europe, N = 100
□ North America, N = 169

Base: 269 North American and European enterprise and SMB hardware decision-makers
(percentages may not total 100 due to rounding)

FIGURE 1-3. *Private clouds gaining momentum. Reprinted, by permission, from Forrester Research, Inc., European Cloud Infrastructure-As-A-Service (IaaS) Outlook, fig. 4.*

There is an argument over whether the term "cloud" can really be used in the context of internal IT. Some public cloud vendors argue that this is just a ploy by enterprise IT vendors to hold onto their existing revenue stream. Among their most cited reasons is the fact that internal IT infrastructure has limited resources and, thus, can't provide the illusion of unlimited capacity that a public cloud does. However, this argument misses the point that, for enterprises, unlimited scaling is not necessarily the biggest issue. Unlike an Internet startup, the enterprise workload generally does not increase 500 percent overnight. Most enterprises see a gradual and often predictable increase in workload.

What really excites enterprises about cloud computing is the fact that it allows them to serve their users in a more dynamic and agile way—something that they have not been able to do in the past, compelling their users to look for public cloud alternatives to meet their needs. Also, the inability of enterprises to meet this need is not necessarily because of a lack of hardware resources; rather, the challenge is more operational in nature, such as fragmentation and underutilization of resources, lack of standardization and automation, and so forth.

Hardware now represents a relatively small chunk of the IT budget. Similarly, power and cooling, which does get a lot of industry press, is also still a relatively small part of spending within most IT organizations. It is operations, and specifically manpower, that dominate costs. Automating more of these operations using cloud management tools enables an even more agile and scalable IT infrastructure, adding to the cost savings for the customer.

The private cloud, thus, helps the enterprise to evolve their existing IT infrastructure and make it more responsive, efficient, and cost effective.

As appealing as the concept of a private cloud may be to larger corporations, the reality is that some corporations may encounter occasional demands for resources that exceed the enterprise data center capacity. For such situations, some corporations may need to link their private cloud to a public cloud and tap into its resources, but in a more controlled manner than is typical of public cloud usage. This concept is often referred to as "cloud bursting," which implies a controlled interaction of private and public clouds. "Hybrid cloud" and "federated cloud" are some other terms that are used to describe this interlinking of public and private clouds. Figure 1-4 shows how enterprises will eventually evolve into using a hybrid cloud.

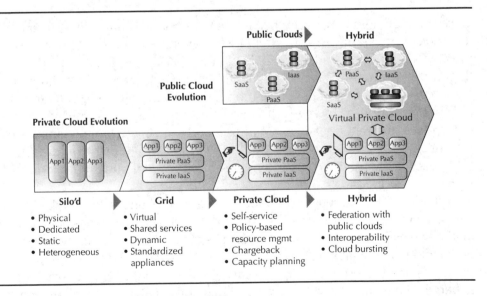

FIGURE 1-4. *Evolution to hybrid cloud*

Oracle and Cloud Computing

Cloud computing in not new to Oracle. Oracle was one of the pioneers of SaaS and has a number of SaaS offerings today in the form of Oracle On Demand services. And though it might appear that Oracle's presence in the PaaS and IaaS space is somewhat new based on its product offerings, Oracle has been a leader in many of the technologies, such as grid computing and virtualization, that form the foundation for PaaS and IaaS.

Oracle's overall cloud computing strategy rests on two main objectives. The first is to ensure that its cloud computing products provide enterprise-grade functionality to enable enterprise adoption. Enterprise-grade functionality means the products offer high performance, scalability, availability, and security, and are based on standards to ensure portability and interoperability. The second objective is to support both public and private cloud computing to give customers choices. To meet these objectives, Oracle has employed three strategies:

- **Offer public SaaS and PaaS (Oracle On Demand and Oracle Cloud)** For enterprises looking to move the cost of hosting and managing Oracle investments from a capital expense to an operating expense, Oracle offers the Oracle On Demand service. This is a "hosted and managed applications" model wherein Oracle hosts and/or manages the Oracle environment for its customers. In addition, Oracle recently announced the availability of Oracle Cloud for customers who are looking to access Oracle products on a subscription basis. Oracle Cloud provides Oracle Fusion CRM Cloud Service, Oracle Fusion HCM Cloud Service, and Oracle Social Network as SaaS, and provides Oracle Database Cloud Service and Oracle Java Cloud Service as PaaS.

- **Give customers the choice to deploy Oracle technologies in either their own private cloud or a public cloud** Not only can customers license Oracle technologies such as Oracle Database 11g, Oracle Fusion Middleware 11g, and Oracle Enterprise Manager 12c for use in their internal customer data center environment, but they can also now use their existing software licenses on third-party public clouds such as Amazon EC2 with no additional license fees.

■ **Provide enabling technologies to cloud providers** Oracle provides a rich portfolio of software and hardware products to enable customers and partners to build, deploy, and manage public and private SaaS, PaaS, and IaaS environments. These technologies are enterprise grade, well tested, certified for large-scale deployment, and backed by 24/7 Oracle support, so enterprises can confidently move important workloads to public or private clouds.

The following sections discuss each of these offerings in detail.

Oracle Service Offerings

Oracle On Demand is the name of a wide spectrum of service offerings from Oracle that allows customers various choices for deploying and managing Oracle environments. Customers can choose to deploy either on premises in their own data centers or in Oracle's data centers. Customers can choose to manage these environments themselves or allow Oracle to manage them. These "hosted and managed application" options allow customers to move the cost of hosting and managing their Oracle investments from a capital expense to an operating expense, thus freeing up more capital dollars for revenue-generating (or strategic) projects. Figure 1-5 shows the various

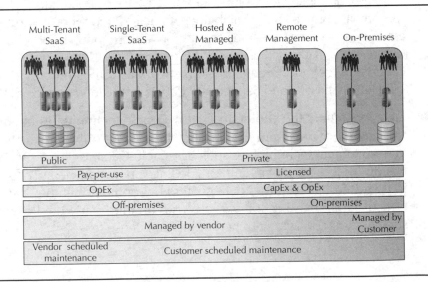

FIGURE 1-5. *Oracle On Demand deployment options*

combinations of managed and hosted deployment models available in the Oracle On Demand portfolio. These models, from right to left in Figure 1-5, are as follows:

- **On-premises**   This is the traditional software license and onsite deployment model where the customer licenses the software and deploys and manages it themselves in their own data centers.

- **Remote management**   Oracle manages the software for the customer, but the software is still deployed in the customer's own data centers.

- **Hosted & managed**   Oracle hosts and manages the deployment at Oracle's data centers. In this model, the customer buys a perpetual license and annual maintenance, and pays Oracle a fee to provide hosting/management services.

- **Single-tenant SaaS**   The customer pays per use of the software—like a rental or longer-term lease—and gets a dedicated system that can be optimized for the customer and for which the customer has some degree of control (for example, specifying when maintenance gets done).

- **Multi-tenant SaaS**   The customer pays per use of the software and shares resources with other customers, so the cost is lower, but the vendor must treat the group of customers exactly the same in order to get the cost efficiencies.

The availability of these different models means Oracle On Demand customers get to choose how they want to deploy their Oracle software based on their specific needs and budget requirements.

Oracle Product Offerings

In addition to allowing customers to access some of its products as public cloud services in the form of Oracle On Demand and Oracle Cloud services, Oracle makes existing products licensable, supported, and easily deployable on third-party public clouds—the fundamental objective of which is to ensure that a customer who wants to use another public cloud for any reason should not have to look beyond Oracle technologies.

The adoption of public PaaS and IaaS services currently is predominately among developers and independent software vendors (ISVs), the key attractions being reduced capital expense, no need to operate their own data center, and utility pricing. These cloud services have therefore become very popular among developers, startups, and even enterprise developers who are tired of waiting on IT. As the developers gravitate toward the cloud, they may be forced to use the stack provided by the public cloud provider, because most PaaS vendors (such as Google and Salesforce.com) do not provide any flexibility to developers to use the stack of their choice. With support for Oracle technologies in public clouds, developers can continue to use Oracle's open standards-based application development stack even if they choose to do it on a third-party public cloud.

Oracle announced new cloud licensing policy and support for the Amazon Web Services platform at Oracle Open World 2008. As a part of this announcement, Oracle also made available a set of preconfigured virtual machine images (called Amazon Machine Images, or AMIs) for database and middleware products, thus enabling Amazon cloud consumers to provision a fully functional and ready-to-use Oracle development environment in a matter of minutes.

More recently, in early 2011, Oracle and Amazon announced support for Oracle VM, Oracle's server virtualization technology, on Amazon EC2. All products certified on the Oracle VM, including enterprise applications such as Oracle E-Business Suite, Oracle's PeopleSoft Enterprise, Oracle's Siebel CRM, Oracle Fusion Middleware, Oracle Database, and Oracle Linux, automatically become certified to run on Amazon EC2 using Oracle VM. Customers can now apply standard Oracle partitioned licensing models to software running on Amazon EC2 without restrictions. This allows customers who power their businesses with Oracle software to fully leverage the scalability, reliability, and utility-based pricing model of Amazon Web Services for *production* workloads with support from Oracle and Amazon.

Oracle also extends generic product capabilities to leverage some of the unique functionality of clouds. The first step in this direction was the introduction of *Oracle Secure Backup Cloud Module for Amazon S3*, a new product that allows Oracle databases to be backed up on Amazon S3, the storage cloud.

Enterprises have traditionally relied on tapes for offsite backups. However, new disk economics and the compelling price point offered by the storage cloud vendors have presented new opportunities to make offsite backups more accessible and reliable. Oracle's cloud backup functionality provides the following advantages over traditional tape-based, offsite backups:

- **Continuous accessibility**   Backups stored in the cloud are always accessible, much in the same way local disk backups are. As such, there is no need to call anyone and no need to ship or load tapes before a restore can be performed. Administrators can initiate restore operations using their standard tools (Oracle Enterprise Manager, scripts, and so forth) just as if the offsite backup was stored locally. This can help make restores faster and reduce downtime from days to hours or minutes in many cases.

- **Better reliability**   Storage clouds are disk based and, thus, inherently more reliable than tapes. Additionally, the cloud vendors typically keep multiple redundant copies of data for availability and scalability purposes.

- **Cost savings**   Cloud backup functionality lowers or eliminates upfront capital expenditures, as well as tape backup licensing and offsite storage costs.

Oracle Technologies for Cloud Computing

Oracle provides a comprehensive portfolio of technology products to build and manage cloud environments; see Figure 1-6 for the complete offering. These can be used by customers or partners to build enterprise private cloud environments and by providers of public clouds.

To build an IaaS offering, Oracle infrastructure components such as Oracle VM for virtualization, Oracle Linux and Oracle Solaris operating systems, Oracle Sun SPARC and x86 servers, and Oracle Sun storage can be used. Oracle Enterprise Manager 12c provides complete lifecycle management for provisioning, delivering, and operating the IaaS cloud services. This is discussed in detail in Chapter 4.

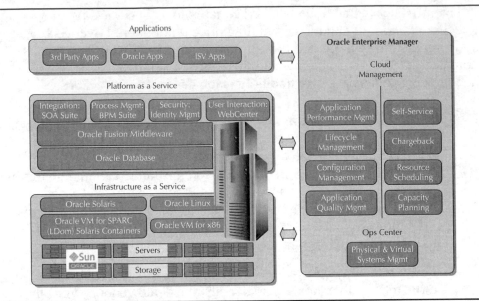

FIGURE 1-6. *Oracle technologies for cloud computing*

A cloud provider can augment the infrastructure stack with platform components and build a foundation for offering PaaS. This could be a DBaaS offering based on Oracle Database and grid technologies such as Oracle Real Application Clusters (RAC) and Automatic Storage Management (ASM), or it could be an MWaaS offering based on Oracle Cloud Application Foundation technologies such as Oracle WebLogic Server, Oracle Coherence in-memory data grid, and the JRockit Java Virtual Machine (JVM). Oracle Enterprise Manager 12*c* provides complete lifecycle management for a PaaS cloud. This is discussed in detail later in the context of PaaS.

As more businesses become attracted to the SaaS cloud model for application delivery because of its promise of faster adoption and minimal impact and cost to internal IT, new and existing ISVs are under pressure to offer their applications in the hosted model—either by hosting existing applications or by rewriting to a new architecture for SaaS. Oracle provides all the key capabilities to build and deliver on-demand applications. In addition to the infrastructure and platform components discussed earlier, SaaS cloud providers can leverage components such as Oracle SOA Suite, Oracle BMP Suite, Oracle Identity Management, Oracle WebCenter, Oracle

Business Intelligence (BI) Suite, and Oracle JDeveloper to provide rich, UI-driven custom applications backed by customizable business processes and shared business services.

The following sections describe the various technologies that Oracle provides for enabling cloud environments.

Storage

Oracle's Sun Open Storage products combine open source software with industry-standard hardware to deliver an open, scalable storage platform that can be optimized to provide public or private cloud storage services at scale. Indeed, Oracle's groundbreaking Sun Fire X4500 Server helped the industry see the benefits of combining server and storage technology in the same system. Oracle delivers virtual networking for large-scale computing through InfiniBand to massive-scale compute grids with the Sun Datacenter Switch 3456, scaling up to 13,834 nodes.

Providing a glimpse of what synergies are possible when software and hardware are designed together, Oracle Exadata Storage Servers also feature software intelligence, but with a particular affinity with the Oracle Database. Oracle Exadata Storage Servers combine Oracle's smart storage software and Oracle's industry-standard Sun hardware to deliver the industry's highest performance database storage.

Oracle Exadata Storage Servers use a massively parallel architecture to dramatically increase data bandwidth between the database server and storage. In addition, smart storage software offloads data-intensive query processing from Oracle Database 11g servers and does the query processing closer to the data. The result is faster parallel data processing and less data movement through higher-bandwidth connections. This massively parallel architecture also offers linear scalability and mission-critical reliability and renders itself very well as a building block for cloud infrastructure.

Servers and Operating Systems

The modern enterprise data center is a highly optimized, complicated engine that drives and defines how a business functions. The most popular vision of cloud computing has everything running on farms of blade servers. While this vision is becoming more and more viable, there remains broad demand for servers of varying sizes and configurations that are optimal for certain particular application requirements.

Oracle offers Sun server product lines (Netra, Blade Servers, SPARC Enterprise, X64, and so forth) and support for industry-standard operating systems (Solaris, Linux, Windows), which will continue to provide a wide range of physical infrastructure optimized for the highly virtualized and distributed nature of cloud implementations.

For operating systems that power the cloud, there is a fundamental requirement of enterprise-class security, performance, and reliability. Oracle has a long track record of investment and leadership in the development and support of Linux with Oracle Enterprise Linux and Unbreakable Linux Support. Oracle has also supported the Linux community by providing code for a clustered file system, data integrity, optimized I/O, and virtualization that has been accepted into the mainline Linux kernel. Oracle remains focused on continuing to enhance and extend the enterprise-class capabilities of Linux.

The added dimension of offering the best UNIX technology with Oracle Solaris provides numerous key benefits for those wanting to build cloud infrastructure. The many Solaris innovations in networking, security, clustering and failover, file system, virtualization, and self-diagnostics directly contribute to a high-performance cloud-computing implementation.

Virtualization

The combination of Sun and Oracle virtualization products offers an unparalleled portfolio that enables users to virtualize from the desktop to the data center.

Server Virtualization　By isolating the software from the hardware, virtualization offers tremendous opportunity to add agility to IT processes. It permits rapid software deployment using prepackaged application environments with minimal to no provisioning required for physical hardware, thus dramatically reducing the time necessary to get applications up and running. Software environments can be migrated across virtualized physical hardware for high availability and maximum consolidation. With key enabling characteristics such as low system overhead for optimum performance and integrated management capabilities, server virtualization can be used as a foundation for building dynamic cloud environments. Oracle offers various server virtualization technologies.

Oracle VM is a hypervisor technology that installs on a bare-metal server and allows multiple operating system environments to be hosted on it. Oracle VM offers support for both x86 and SPARC architectures, making it possible to deploy in a heterogeneous cloud environment. Customers can leverage Oracle VM to consolidate servers, rapidly deploy software, recover quickly from system failure, and match resource capacity to workloads.

SPARC Logical Domains (LDoms) is now rebranded as Oracle VM Server for SPARC and continues to provide a highly efficient hypervisor for Sun SPARC Chip Multithreading (CMT) servers and enables multiple, independent Solaris instances on a single server. Oracle VM Server for SPARC technology is still included as part of Oracle Solaris. Oracle also supports Solaris, along with Linux and Windows, as a guest operating system on top of Oracle VM Server for x86.

The virtualization capabilities of Solaris Containers enable customers to safely consolidate multiple Solaris applications onto one operating system and increase utilization rates with the advanced functionality of Solaris 11. This enables customers to host up to thousands of applications on a single system, with a single OS instance. This hardware-independent virtualization can dynamically adjust to business goals and uses less than 1 percent system overhead. Solaris containers can start and restart in seconds and are easy to create, replicate, rename, and clone, which can greatly simplify and accelerate cloud administration.

System administrators can use the cloning capability to quickly provision a new Solaris container based on changes in workload demand or type. They can also move containers from system to system or disk to disk within the same system as capacity or configuration needs change using the attach/detach features.

Oracle VM Templates and Oracle Virtual Assemblies   Rapid application deployment in cloud environments requires highly automated, mature application packaging and provisioning capabilities. There is a need to quickly manipulate applications, to deploy, grow, shrink, move, and clone them.

Oracle VM Templates are guest VM images containing preinstalled and preconfigured enterprise software that can be used to develop, package, and distribute applications for faster deployment on Oracle VM Server for x86 environments. Oracle VM Templates can speed and simplify application deployments and help reduce the risk of errors in production, development, or test environments. Each VM Template is essentially a software appliance because, just like hardware appliances, it is prebuilt and very easy to deploy.

The next level of this type of application packaging is the concept of Oracle Virtual Assemblies. While software appliances are useful, enterprise applications are not always self-contained, single-VM entities; sometimes they are complex, multitier applications spanning multiple VMs. There might be multiple VMs in the web tier, other VMs in the middle tier, and other VMs in the database tier. There needs to be a way for these multi-VM applications to be packaged for easy deployment.

Oracle Virtual Assembly Builder (OVAB) is a tool that takes such a multitier, distributed application and packages it up into an assembly that can be reused in a way similar to the way appliances are used. The assembly, like an appliance virtual image, is essentially a file that contains the images of the constituent appliances as well as metadata about appliance configuration, connections, and startup sequence. This technology will be a critical element for creating a library of applications and shared services in either public or private cloud environments.

Database and Storage Grid

On top of the Oracle technology stack for IaaS are the higher-level software components that are needed to build modern platforms for cloud environments. A highly optimized PaaS layer requires high-performance database and middleware services delivered as quickly and seamlessly as physical and virtual cloud infrastructure.

Oracle Database has offered grid computing capabilities since the release of Oracle Database 10*g* in 2003. Since then, Oracle has continued to enhance the grid capabilities of the database in the areas of clustering with Oracle RAC, storage virtualization and manageability with ASM, and database performance with Oracle In-Memory Database Cache.

When lighter-weight database services are needed, Oracle Berkeley DB and MySQL are also possible options that are actively developed and supported by Oracle.

Even after ten years since the introduction of Oracle RAC, none of the other database vendors offers a database product with equivalent capabilities such as predictable performance, scalability, and availability in a database cluster. RAC is unique in database technologies in its support of grid architecture. Particularly relevant to the cloud is the ability of RAC to provide a single view of the database even though the number of compute nodes in the RAC cluster might be going up or down. Multiple database instances can be running on a single RAC cluster, all consuming the same shared resources. This elasticity and virtualization at the database tier can be used as the foundation for building a database cloud on physical (non-server virtualized) hardware.

Oracle RAC is supported on all Oracle operating systems and virtualization platforms and features online addition and removal of cluster nodes without needing to halt the database or the application. The ability to run database (and, as discussed a bit later, middleware) clusters on either physical or virtual cluster nodes gives the ultimate in choice of deployment options in a cloud environment.

Another new RAC innovation that is relevant to cloud implementations is *Oracle RAC One Node*. Oracle RAC One Node is a one-node version of Oracle RAC that enables customers to standardize on a single deployment model for all their database needs. It enables the consolidation of multiple databases into a single cluster with minimal overhead while providing the high-availability benefits of failover protection, rolling upgrades, and so forth.

ASM creates a grid of storage for a database that can also be adjusted dynamically and automatically. It has become the most common method of deploying storage under Oracle RAC and provides significant manageability and productivity gains for DBAs. This simplified administration is also ideal for those wishing to offer database services in a cloud.

Oracle In-Memory Database Cache enables certain tables, rows, and columns from Oracle Database to be cached in the memory of the middle-tier servers, delivering very low latency and high throughput. Data remains synchronized with Oracle Database and is accessed through a standard SQL interface. Oracle In-Memory Database Cache also supports clustering for elastic scalability and high availability.

Oracle Cloud Application Foundation

Of the key characteristics of cloud computing identified earlier, elastic capacity is often a high priority for many applications. Having an infrastructure automatically adapt to the evolving needs of various applications means the IT shop can do more with less: It can provide better performance against application SLAs across the enterprise without having each application individually provisioned for its own worst-case workload.

Similar to the grid architecture in Oracle Database and storage, Oracle Fusion Middleware also supports robust grid functionality in the middle tier with a group of products called Oracle Cloud Application Foundation. It is built on standards-based technologies for portability, efficiency, and ease of integration.

Oracle Cloud Application Foundation brings together key industry-leading technologies: Oracle Exalogic Elastic Cloud, the world's best foundation for cloud computing, Oracle WebLogic Server for Java EE, Oracle Tuxedo for C/C++/COBOL, Oracle Coherence in-memory data grid, Oracle JRockit and Hotspot Java SE solutions, Oracle Enterprise Manager 12*c*, Oracle Virtual Assembly Builder, and Oracle Traffic Director.

Oracle WebLogic Server is the core Java EE application server technology within Oracle Fusion Middleware and the overall market leader among application servers. Its clustering capabilities, with support for automated load balancing and failover as well as dynamic addition and removal of nodes, serves as the fundamental mechanism for adjusting capacity. WebLogic Server clustering supports both console- and script-based automation of capacity adjustment, providing flexibility for a wide range of needs while maximizing ease of use. WebLogic Server clustering management easily plugs into the Oracle Enterprise Manager 12*c* framework, enabling unified management of the entire private cloud infrastructure from a single console.

WebLogic Server is complemented and enhanced by Oracle Coherence for an in-memory data grid cache for Java, .NET, and C++ objects. Coherence significantly increases performance, reliability, and scalability of data-intensive transaction processing or analytical applications by caching data—potentially very large amounts of data—in memory, accessing that data at memory speeds rather than disk access speeds. This provides the obvious benefit of performance improvement due to the memory access speed, but it has additional performance benefits based on the ability to parallelize computation across the data grid and additional reliability benefits deriving from the way objects are replicated in the grid, eliminating single points of failure. Coherence automatically "repartitions," or redistributes, data objects optimally across the data grid as nodes are added to or removed from the grid, again supporting the elastic capacity requirement of cloud computing. Management of this mechanism also plugs cleanly into Oracle Enterprise Manager 12*c*.

WebLogic Server and Coherence are packaged with additional components, such as the JRockit JVM, in an offering called WebLogic Suite. With the automatable, dynamic clustering mechanisms of WebLogic Server and Coherence managed by Oracle Enterprise Manager 12c, consolidation of applications onto a centralized, shared application platform is one of the key steps on the path to private cloud computing.

Service-Oriented Architecture and Business Process Management

A PaaS cloud offering doesn't have to stop at providing database or middleware services in the cloud. The more reusable components a cloud platform builds upon, the greater the value it provides to the cloud consumers. For instance, application developers may want to consume preconfigured application development platforms as a cloud service where they can deploy and test their applications. Service-oriented architecture (SOA), with its approach of modularizing applications into reusable components accessible through standardized interfaces using XML, SOAP, and the various web services (WS-*) specifications, is an obvious starting point.

Oracle SOA Suite provides a comprehensive yet easy-to-use basis for creating the reusable components at the heart of your PaaS private cloud. Rich drag-and-drop SOA component features in JDeveloper and the Service Component Architecture designer enable rapid creation of components and subsequent composition of those components into applications. Oracle Service Bus provides a simple way to make components available to department application creators using your PaaS cloud. End-to-end instance tracking and Oracle Business Activity Monitoring (BAM) provide a range of metrics visualizations supporting both the central IT function charged with keeping the PaaS up and running and the departmental application owners concerned with business-level performance indicators.

In addition to SOA components, many enterprises will want to include business process components managed within a unified Business Process Management (BPM) framework as part of PaaS. Oracle BPEL Process Manager provides the federation capability to create Business Process Execution Language (BPEL) process components out of new and legacy assets while also supporting the flexibility to enable multiple departments to incorporate PaaS-based BPEL components into their respective workflows.

User Interaction

Like SOA and BPM components, standard and shared user interface (UI) components are great candidates for inclusion in an enterprise's PaaS. A centrally managed library of UI components can give department application owners a great head start in composing their solutions and can also give the central IT function a desirable level of control over consistency across the enterprise's UIs. At the same time, a robust, standards-based UI framework can give the departments the flexibility they need to accommodate their specific functionality, customization, and personalization needs for applications and portal solutions.

UI technologies play an additional role in a PaaS environment as the basis of the self-service interface for the cloud. In many cases this will be a fairly extensive portal that must work closely with an identity management system to authenticate users, filter their access based on roles, and present the platform's shared components for application development and composition.

Oracle WebCenter Suite provides a number of portal and user interaction capabilities that are ideal for creating reusable UI components as part of a PaaS. Themes and skins provide powerful facilities for tailoring the look and feel of applications in a tiered way—for an entire web interface or for portions of a web interface associated with a department. This enables consistency in look and feel while consolidating deployment. The Advanced Personalization Framework provides the ability to further tailor the usage of the UI and the information delivered to the UI based on users' activities. Powerful mashup integration capabilities enable business users to further personalize the information they want to see while maintaining enterprise information security. Common enterprise metadata services provide a revolutionary way to store and manage all look-and-feel changes, personalizations, and mashups via uniform metadata that enables in-place customizations at runtime and insulates the UI from changes to the base application.

Identity and Access Management

A high-priority concern for many enterprises in moving to cloud computing is identity and access management. Particularly for organizations in domains with a high level of regulation and/or sensitive customer data, cloud computing's self-service model can be a significant challenge. Balancing rich mechanisms for identity and access management with convenience features such as single sign-on is a must for cloud environments.

Implementing PaaS with a high degree of self-service or implementing SaaS where multiple subscribers access the same application in a security-critical environment requires an approach where security pervades the entire architecture rather than being bolted on as an afterthought. An important strength of Oracle Fusion Middleware is that, in addition to each of the products having best-of-breed security in their respective categories, its security mechanisms are well integrated, enabling ease of deployment, ease of change, and high reliability.

Oracle Identity and Access Management Suite provides an ideal facility for managing access and security in a cloud environment. Within the suite, Oracle Access Manager supports corporate directories and single sign-on. Oracle Entitlements Server provides centralized access-control policies for a cloud environment that has various decentralized components.

Oracle Identity Manager is a best-in-class user-provisioning and administration solution that automates the process of adding, updating, and deleting user accounts from applications and directories. It improves regulatory compliance by providing granular reports that attest to who has access to what. Oracle Identity Federation (OIF) provides a self-contained and flexible multiprotocol federation server that can be rapidly deployed with your existing identity and access management systems. With its support for leading standards-based protocols, OIF ensures the interoperability to securely share identities across vendors, customers, and business partners without the increased costs of managing, maintaining, and administering additional identities and credentials.

Cloud Management

Cloud computing succeeds or fails based on the quality of the cloud management engine that enables and manages it. A cloud setup requires highly sophisticated automation in order to provision, de-provision, and balance the utilization of the vast amount of computing power, huge data sets, and highly virtualized IT services. With the availability of Oracle Enterprise Manager Cloud Control 12c, Oracle now has the industry's most comprehensive solution for setting up, delivering, and managing cloud services. Figure 1-7 shows Oracle Enterprise Manager 12c capability for managing the complete life cycle of a cloud.

Oracle Enterprise Manager Cloud Control 12c offers a single, integrated console for testing, deploying, operating, monitoring, diagnosing, and troubleshooting today's complex IT environments. It offers a simple,

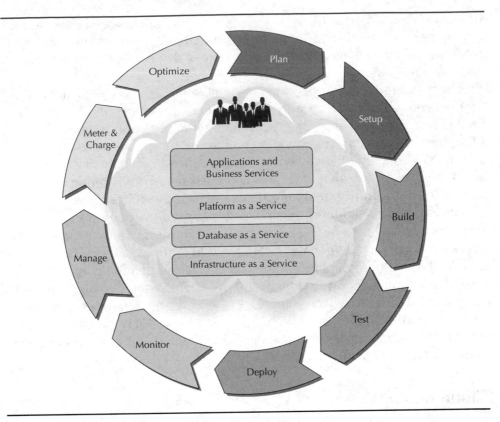

FIGURE 1-7. *Cloud management using Oracle Enterprise Manager 12*c

scalable solution for running the Oracle stack, from applications to disk, in cloud environments. It manages everything in your data center—from the hypervisor to the operating system, database, and application tiers.

Plan and Setup   Some cloud projects are considered *greenfield*, meaning the enterprise wants to start a fresh cloud project with brand new hardware, new software, and, in some cases, even a new data center. Other projects are *brownfield* in nature. The enterprise is concerned with transforming existing assets into a cloud environment. It is therefore important to plan out the cloud deployment model, beginning with the discovery and baselining of existing assets. Oracle Enterprise Manager 12*c* provides automated discovery capabilities that can find existing assets and manage them. It also offers a Consolidation Planner feature, which can provide Physical to Physical (P2P), Physical to Virtual (P2V), and Physical to Exalogic or Exadata (P2E) advisories based on both technical and functional constraints (such as production to test systems cannot be co-located).

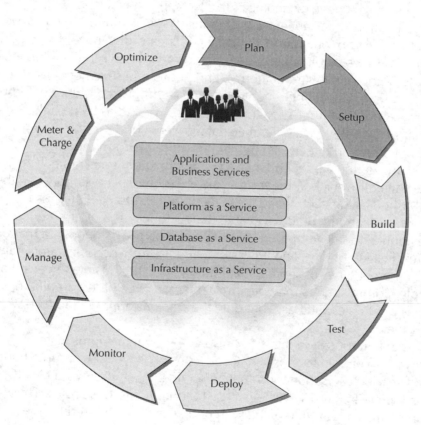

After the planning comes the actual setup of the cloud. This is a very significant part of the process, especially given that cloud computing is not about islands of automation on existing scripts, but requires a comprehensive architecture that cuts across various infrastructure and application components.

Oracle Enterprise Manager 12*c* provides a very rich cloud resource model that can be used to tie in various technologies from storage to applications running on both physical and virtual infrastructure, so that enterprises can maximize the gain from their IT investments. Oracle Enterprise Manager 12*c* offers capabilities such as bare-metal provisioning of hypervisors, setting up of server and storage pools, and grouping the pools into zones based on functional or QoS characteristics. Oracle Enterprise Manager 12*c* can also leverage Storage Connect technology in the virtualization layer to allow clouds to be built on top of best-of-breed storage technologies like Netapp, Hitachi, and Fujitsu.

Oracle Enterprise Manager 12*c* is industry's first solution that has the ability to model not only IaaS but also PaaS, including DBaaS, from a single console. It allows administrators to define standardized service templates for databases and middleware platforms, and publish these as services. These services can represent single-tier templates or complex, multitier enterprise platforms. Oracle Enterprise Manager 12*c* uses OVAB to help package a multitier platform into a single, metadata-driven cloud service. Using OVAB, platform architects can model the entire platform topology graphically, define all dependencies and deployment constraints, and deliver the entire stack in the form of an assembly. This assembly can then be published to the centralized software library in Oracle Enterprise Manager 12*c*, and be made available to developers as a cloud service—an entire application development stack that can be provisioned in a matter of minutes, instead of days and weeks of manual effort! Administrators can create different types of services depending upon the business needs. For example, administrators may offer a database service based on different versions of Oracle Database, but only the versions approved for use within the business.

Oracle Enterprise Manager 12*c* also comes with a sophisticated framework to enable role-driven access control as well as resource limits for the self-service users that consume the service. Integration with LDAP allows Oracle Enterprise Manager 12*c* to inherit enterprise roles. The resource limits are implemented with quotas that are tailored for the specific service type (IaaS, PaaS, or DBaaS). This prevents rogue usage of a service while also preventing a few users from devouring the majority of the resources in the cloud.

Build, Test, and Deploy   Deploying an application in the cloud poses interesting challenges. The traditional model has been to deploy various components of the application individually and then manually wire them together. The problem gets aggravated by other deployment constraints, such as different network segments for each application tier.

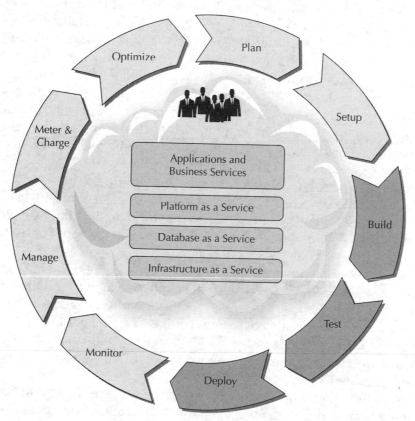

Oracle Enterprise Manager 12*c* is unique in addressing this challenge. Leaning again on the notion of assemblies, it allows entire applications or components thereof to be packaged and published to the cloud as services. This paradigm dramatically expedites application development and provisioning processes within an organization. For example, developers can publish utility components and applications in the form of assemblies to each other, and build a library of best practices to enrich their cloud. Similarly, making applications available as assemblies allows QA users, business analysts, and production teams to deploy prebuilt applications in a few clicks. No more software installation, configuration, and patching is necessary—QA can focus on testing instead of complex installations!

Once you build an application, you need to test it. Oracle Enterprise Manager 12*c* carries a complete testing portfolio that allows users to test both application configuration changes and the changes at the database or at a lower layer in the application stack. A very unique aspect of the testing solution is the ability to capture a production load and replay it in a test environment, so that the results are predictable. The testing solution also leverages the deep diagnostic capabilities built into the technology layers and provides prescriptions for remediation.

Oracle Enterprise Manager 12*c* comes with an out-of-the-box yet customizable self-service application that lets end users deploy a wide range of these services. End users can choose to provision application assemblies, along with databases and platforms, all in on-demand fashion. For each request, users can specify the amount of underlying resources (CPU, memory, and so on) that they require for each component. Oracle Enterprise Manager 12*c* automatically provisions the requested service and the appropriate resources. The self-service application also lets users define policies to scale out or scale back resources based on schedule or performance metrics. For example, a user can set a policy to elastically scale out a web server if the processor load on existing web servers exceeds a certain threshold value.

Thus, Oracle Enterprise Manager 12*c* enables a layer of abstraction that hides the underlying complexities of the application from the end user. This abstraction is delivered via a self-service interface, both in graphical (GUI) and programmatic (API) variants.

Monitor and Manage   Once a cloud has been commissioned, it has to be monitored and managed.

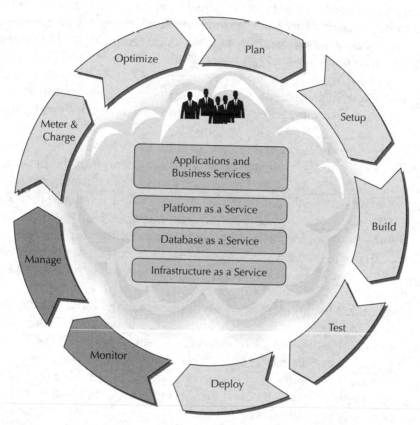

Over the years, the industry has witnessed superficial service level monitoring and fragmented management of individual components. Oracle Enterprise Manager 12*c* fundamentally transforms this by following anapplication-to-disk management paradigm, which not only monitors all components through a single pane of glass, but also provides deep, out-of-the-box capabilities that are instrumented in the base product and proven to reduce problem resolution time by more than 50 percent. The ultimate manifestation of the application-to-disk management paradigm comes in the form of management of engineered systems such as Exadata and Exalogic.

In a cloud, the monitoring framework has to scale to thousands of servers, databases, and middleware targets. Oracle Enterprise Manager 12*c* provides the ability to collate the targets into groups for better manageability. The new Administration Group feature lets administrators define monitoring settings, compliance standards, and cloud policies through templates and organize each target in multiple hierarchies, such as Line of Business and Lifecycle status. Oracle Enterprise Manager 12*c* also comes with an in-built incident management system that can manage by exceptions. Administrators can review, suppress, escalate, and remediate the events as needed, and also integrate the system with ticketing systems.

Oracle Enterprise Manager 12*c* has the ability to define contractual SLAs that govern the contract between the application owner and the provider of the cloud. Administrators as well as users can also define management policies that automatically adjust the service resources to ensure that SLAs are met. Also, while most tools focus only on the stack management aspects of cloud infrastructure, Oracle Enterprise Manager 12*c* also provides user experience management and business transaction management. Bolstered by acquired technologies in these areas, Oracle Enterprise Manager 12*c* is the leading solution for ensuring application performance in the cloud.

A management requirement often overlooked in the cloud context is that of configuration management. The agility and elasticity (such as VM Migration) in a cloud demand real-time discovery of and synchronization with fast-changing system topologies, thereby rendering traditional configuration management deficient. Unlike these solutions, Oracle Enterprise Manager 12*c* configuration management capabilities are optimized for cloud environments. It can monitor vast numbers of configurations continuously, discover changes, measure drifts, pinpoint configuration errors, and offer insight into system topologies, all within a single pane of glass!

Finally, the cloud management capabilities are also integrated with My Oracle Support. This integration delivers facilities such as patch advisories, service request management, and knowledge management right on premises and in context of the overall cloud.

Meter, Charge, and Optimize   Shared services and clouds bring some additional challenges for IT. As different tenants start sharing the same piece of platform or infrastructure, they need to be accountable for their respective usage; otherwise, a few individuals might consume the majority of the resources. Also, the very ease of self-service provisioning may lead to overprovisioning of resources, and result in a sub-optimal utilization of IT resources. To mitigate this, organizations must meter the usage and optionally chargeback (also known as showback) the tenants. Though money may not trade hands, this provides IT as well as the Lines of Business with cost transparency on an ongoing basis.

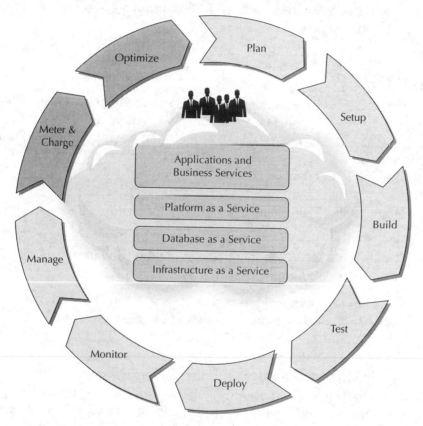

Oracle Enterprise Manager 12c is equipped with sophisticated and flexible metering and chargeback mechanisms. Unlike existing chargeback tools that solely focus on basic compute metrics like CPU, memory, and storage usage, IT can define pricing models based on application usage, database usage, and middleware-level metrics. Also, they can extend pricing models to account for fixed costs, configurations, administrative expenses, people costs, energy utilization, or a combination of these. These capabilities enable enterprises to account for actual usage versus representative usage.

Cloud management also entails an ongoing optimization of resources as well as processes to make sure the service levels are persistent. Oracle Enterprise Manager 12*c* is rich in features that help IT rediscover assets, reevaluate the performance, rebalance the cloud, and fine-tune the provisioning process. The tuning capabilities in the operating system, database, and middleware layers aid in continuous optimization and subsequent improvement.

Summary

In this chapter you were introduced to cloud computing concepts, including the key characteristics, benefits, and challenges. You learned about the IaaS, PaaS, and SaaS cloud service delivery models and how they apply to public and private clouds. You also now understand the following about Oracle's leading role in cloud computing:

- Oracle delivers enabling technologies for building and managing clouds.

- Oracle technology product licenses can be used in private clouds or third-party public clouds such as Amazon EC2.

- Oracle offers public cloud services: Oracle On Demand offers application hosting/management and Oracle Cloud provides subscription-based SaaS and PaaS.

In the following chapters we will discuss business and technical considerations for cloud computing and explore best practices for building and managing clouds. We will focus on one aspect of cloud management in each chapter and discuss how Oracle Enterprise Manager 12*c* addresses that aspect.

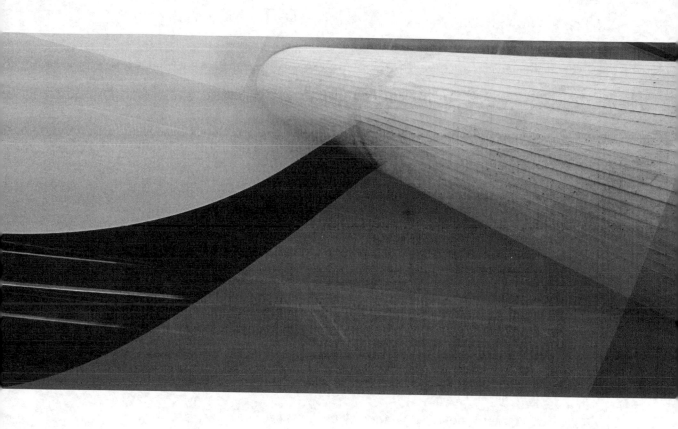

CHAPTER
2

Cloud Planning
and Architecture

s an IT organization, you may have recently decided to move to the cloud and now need to plan how to do so. Or perhaps your business has already begun its cloud migration by moving to public clouds, but now you are looking to avoid the risk of noncompliance by providing comparable services in an internal cloud. In both cases, adequately planning and designing the appropriate cloud architecture is key to providing a successful implementation that meets the demands of your internal customers while also reducing costs.

Cloud Planning

There could be multiple reasons why your organization is considering moving to a private cloud. Typical motivations include the following:

- Consolidating infrastructure and streamlining operations

- Reducing capital expenditure (capex) in lieu of increasing operational expenditure (opex)

- Faster time in delivering key business services

Having well-defined goals and articulating them in a cloud plan ensures that the technology decisions address the right problems, stakeholders have the right expectations, and the cloud implementation goes ahead smoothly. Various people need to get involved in the cloud project planning from both IT and business organizations to make the cloud project successful.

Determining Stakeholders and Responsibilities

Deploying a cloud requires stakeholders to agree on an architecture that transforms the IT environment to take advantage of the IT as a service paradigm. This may require not only repurposing existing software and hardware resources into well-defined services, but also making shifts in organizational processes. For example, a cloud architecture that supports Database as a Service (DBaaS) may require the database administrators and storage administrators to agree on standard software configurations and common automation workflow for provisioning the services.

Cloud Architects

Cloud architects understand and know how to leverage public and private cloud computing technologies to form business solutions. Cloud architects understand how to configure IT assets to enable services that meet the needs of the business. Generally, cloud architects should be familiar with the concepts, architecture, and other aspects of the cloud and how to map them to the business needs.

Cloud Infrastructure Administrators

Cloud infrastructure administrators are responsible for putting together the initial physical cloud infrastructure and determining the physical and logical partitioning of cloud resources based on IT and business constraints. These individuals are also responsible for the ongoing cloud operations for managing the elastic cloud capacity, managing performance and configuration, administering cloud infrastructure and deprovisioning the physical infrastructure, including server, storage, and networking. These individuals may come from multiple disciplines, such as

- System administrators
- Network administrators
- Storage administrators

Tasks performed by the cloud infrastructure administrators include

- Setting up and pooling the overall physical infrastructure (servers, storage, and networks).

- Gauging cloud infrastructure requirements and making physical infrastructure available for those requirements. The cloud infrastructure administrator may or may not be aware of the services that will consume the infrastructure.

- Ongoing monitoring and management of the cloud infrastructure.

Cloud Self-Service Administrators

One of the tenets of cloud computing is to allow cloud consumers to request cloud resources in a self-service manner. This allows for a pay-as-you-go model where consumers view the cloud as having unlimited resources from which they can request what they need, and pay for what they consume. Organizations must establish clear operating agreements between the providers and consumers of cloud services. Both sides need to understand the details and consequences of areas such as change management, financial chargeback, and problem resolution. Cloud self-service administrators define these governance policies for the cloud self service users.

Tasks performed by the cloud self-service administrators include

- Defining access boundaries for cloud self-service users/consumers. For example, self-service users may be restricted to provision resources in a specific network, from a specific location, or from a predefined resource pool, or they may be restricted to select among only certain images during deployment.

- Setting up quotas for self-service users in terms of the aggregate amount of infrastructure (server, storage, network) resources they are allowed to request.

- Publishing cloud services in a self-service catalog for the users and controlling their access.

- Setting up unit charges and, optionally, payment terms for the users.

- Establishing maintenance windows, SLAs, and support services.

A single individual may act as the self-service administrator for an organization and perform all the preceding tasks, or a group of administrators may take up the various responsibilities. For example, a separate chargeback administrator may be responsible for setting up charge plans.

Cloud Users/Application Teams

The application teams are generally the de facto "users" or "consumers" of the cloud. In many cases, the cloud infrastructure administrators will belong to central IT, whereas the cloud users will be testers and developers in the application teams from the line of business side of the house. These users have access to a self-service interface or portal application. They can browse a service catalog to select a service for deployment. The users have no visibility into the underlying cloud infrastructure that hosts that service.

Tasks performed by the cloud users include

- Requesting resources (virtual machines, databases, middleware, and so on) from the cloud

- Monitoring and administering requested resources

- Scaling out and scaling back existing deployments in the cloud

- Reviewing charges accrued for the cloud services consumed

Discovering and Assessing Existing Assets and Current Workloads

As discussed in Chapter 1, a cloud project, especially a private cloud project, may be considered either *greenfield* or *brownfield*. As a reminder, a greenfield project is one that involves new infrastructure, including, in some cases, a new data center. A brownfield project is one where existing assets are consolidated and transformed into a cloud. For the brownfield projects, it is important to discover existing assets (technology portfolio), make them manageable by Oracle Enterprise Manager 12c, and then baseline their performance for consolidation.

As part of planning for the cloud, the process of discovery and assessment looks for the software and hardware assets in the environment along with the relationships among them. Many companies do not have an accurate, current inventory of both their physical and virtual environments. As the first step to developing a plan for the new cloud environment, it is important to take a correct inventory of the current technology portfolio. Companies may choose to rationalize all the assets in their IT environment in one project, but this "boil the ocean" approach can introduce significant risks. A more practical approach is to develop a strategy that involves multiple projects, each focusing on rationalizing only the assets that support a horizontal or vertical "slice" of business functionality, and is aligned with a business goal or objective.

TIP
*For easier transition to the cloud, select the part
of the IT environment that is not organizationally
or technically complex and where there is
opportunity for short-term savings, via license or
support savings. Near-term success and payback
will help justify continued investment.*

Rationalizing the technology portfolio involves two steps:

1. Capturing the existing technology portfolio. This can be done either manually, with spreadsheets, or with automated tools such as Oracle Enterprise Manager 12*c*. Typical information captured includes: asset name and description, owner, location, department, number of users, packaged/custom, hardware, operating system, and database.

2. Mapping the technology portfolio to the business capabilities. Once the inventory is complete, the organization must map the assets to either capabilities or business processes within the business architecture. This makes it easy to identify redundancies and gaps. Completing such an inventory and mapping exercise will usually reveal many overlapping and duplicate assets that are candidates for consolidation. When a recommendation for an asset is not obvious, a more detailed evaluation may be required.

Oracle Enterprise Manager can be used to discover and collect information about datacenter assets either one time or on an ongoing basis. To do automatic host discovery, Oracle Enterprise Manager uses an agentless Nmap (Network Mapper) protocol. Nmap can discover hosts only for a subnet, so the process has to be repeated for every subnet. For each subnet, Nmap is executed as a job from one host where the agent is already deployed. Figure 2-1 shows the process of automatic discovery.

In automatic host discovery, a single Oracle Enterprise Manager Agent is tasked to scan the entire network based on IP address ranges that the administrator specifies. It then returns a list of "unmanaged" host machines—that is, host machines that do not yet have the Oracle Enterprise Manager Agent installed—with a list of ports in use that match

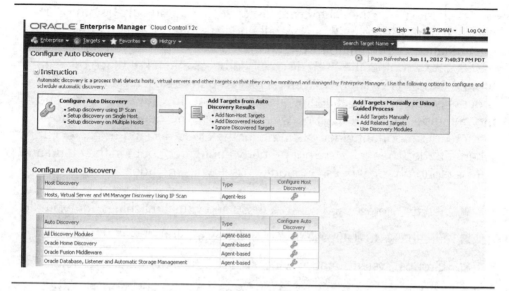

FIGURE 2-1.   *Automatic discovery in Oracle Enterprise Manager*

the ranges specified. The name of the service using each port is also returned.

By looking at the list of services and ports, an administrator should be able to determine what types of Oracle components have been discovered. For example, if a host is returned with port 7001 in use, the administrator can reasonably assume that this port is associated with an Oracle WebLogic Server domain that can be promoted to managed target status. Similarly, a host returned with port 1521 in use would indicate a database server.

The next step is to deploy Oracle Enterprise Manager Agents to the hosts if the administrator wants to promote the host to a managed status. The Agent Push application is integrated with the discovery flow, so that the agent is pushed into the hosts. Once an Oracle Enterprise Manager Agent is deployed to the host, any Oracle components running on the host will be discovered and reported as potential targets. These components can then be promoted to managed target status, enabling them to be managed and monitored by Oracle Enterprise Manager Cloud Control 12c.

To be most effective, automatic discovery should ideally be run by a network administrator with an overall understanding of which Oracle components are running on which ports.

Let's now look at the deep discovery process that takes place once the Oracle Enterprise Manager Agent is placed on the host. The discovery process is automated, cataloging all the elements in your data center and the dependencies that exist between systems. The dependencies are particularly important when planning for the cloud, as failures can occur when interdependencies are not properly configured, both in the cloud and across cloud/physical lines. Supported asset types include

- Servers, storage, and network (hosts and virtual machines, for example)

- Databases (a database instance, for example)

- Groups, systems, and services (a database system, for example)

- Middleware (application deployments, WebLogic Servers, and WebLogic Domains, for example)

- Business applications (such as Oracle Fusion Applications, Oracle Siebel, Oracle E-Business Suite, etc.)

The discovery process is thorough in detecting software and targets through multiple means. However, if for some reason a target is not discovered, Oracle Enterprise Manager provides a guided, manual flow to add the target.

Oracle Enterprise Manager 12*c* supports a group of metrics and compliance rules to be applied to the newly discovered or created targets in the form of Monitoring Templates. For example, there could be different Monitoring Templates for monitoring production and test databases. When the targets get promoted, the Monitoring Templates for subsequent management can be automatically applied, thereby making the targets manageable from the onset.

Figure 2-2 shows the Inventory and Usage Details page of Oracle Enterprise Manager Cloud Control 12*c*, which provides a summary view of the discovered targets and allows you to drill down to view details about each target. Configuration information that is periodically collected is stored in the Oracle Enterprise Manager's Repository, allowing you to view, save, track, compare, search, and customize up-to-date configuration information for your entire enterprise.

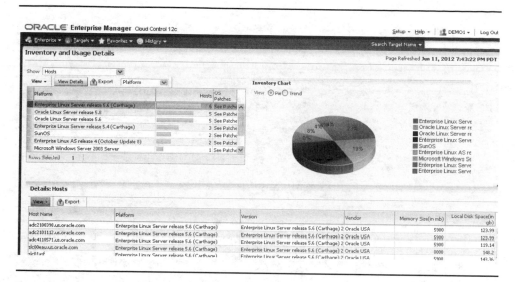

FIGURE 2-2. *Oracle Enterprise Manager asset inventory*

Administrators can segregate the targets into Administration Groups, which greatly simplify the process of setting up targets for management in Oracle Enterprise Manager by automating the application of management settings such as monitoring settings or compliance standards. Typically, these settings are manually applied to individual target, or perhaps semi-automatically using custom scripts. However, by defining Administration Groups, Oracle Enterprise Manager uses specific target properties to direct the target to the appropriate Administration Group and then automatically apply the requisite monitoring and management settings. This level of automation simplifies the target setup process and also enables a data center to easily scale as new targets are added to Oracle Enterprise Manager for management. Administrators can also store with each target additional target attributes, like Cost Center, Location, Lifecycle Status, and so forth, for better reporting and decision making. Figure 2-3 demonstrates the typical Administration Group workflow.

The first step involves setting a target's Lifecycle Status property when a target is first added to Oracle Enterprise Manager for monitoring. At that time, you determine where in the prioritization hierarchy that target belongs, with

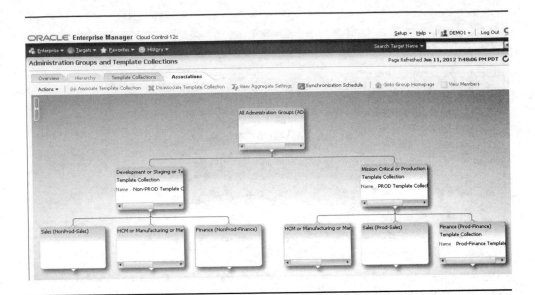

FIGURE 2-3.   *A typical Administration Group*

the highest level being "mission critical" and the lowest being "development."
Target Lifecycle Status prioritization consists of the following levels:

- Mission Critical (highest priority)
- Production
- Staging
- Test
- Development (lowest priority)

As shown in the second tier of Figure 2-3, once Lifecycle Status is set,
Oracle Enterprise Manger uses it to determine which Administration Group
the target belongs to.

To prevent different monitoring settings from being applied to the same
target, Administration Groups were designed to be mutually exclusive with

other Administration Groups in terms of group membership. Administration Groups can also be used for hierarchically classifying targets in an organization. For example, Figure 2-3 shows an Administration Group hierarchy consisting of two subgroups, Production targets and Test targets, with each subgroup having its own Template Collection. In this example, targets in the Production subgroup inherit monitoring settings from Monitoring Template A while targets in the Test subgroup inherit monitoring settings from Monitoring Template B.

Consolidation Planning

The discovery and assessment process results in the identification of targets, after which their workloads are monitored to determine if they are suitable for moving to the cloud. Depending on the procurement cycle or the specific hardware vendor agreement in effect, enterprises may acquire different types of server hardware and operating systems for building the cloud, inadvertently creating a confusing array of systems that administrators must manage, administer, patch, and upgrade. This, in turn, increases labor costs and ongoing maintenance and support costs against IT budgets. Hence, it is important to find a way to migrate existing, often disparate hardware and workloads to standardized operating systems and hardware in the cloud, with the ultimate goal of reducing costs.

Before delving deeper into the Oracle Enterprise Manager 12c Consolidation Planner, let us understand how Oracle Engineered Systems and server virtualization technologies can function as consolidated platform for the cloud.

Oracle Engineered Systems and Server Virtualization Technologies

Engineered systems are hardware and software that are pre-integrated to reduce the cost and complexity of IT infrastructures while increasing productivity and performance. Oracle's engineered systems contain software components such as the operating system, middleware, database, and so forth that are optimized for performance, reliability and scalability. Typically, customers can house tens and thousands of application components in a relatively dense configuration to save on data center floor space, power and cooling costs. That is why engineered systems are often the preferred building blocks for a consolidated cloud platform. Examples of engineered systems include Oracle Exadata Database Machine, Oracle Exalogic Elastic Cloud, Oracle SPARC SuperCluster, and Oracle Database Appliance.

Enterprises are also increasingly investigating server virtualization technologies, such as Oracle VM, as a foundation for clouds. Server virtualization masks physical server resources such as processors, memory and storage from applications running on the server. The server administrator uses a virtualization software called the hypervisor to divide one physical server into multiple isolated virtual environments. The virtual environments are also known as guests, instances, containers, or emulations, depending on the platform. This makes it possible to use the shared hardware infrastructure while getting the benefits of isolation that virtualization provides. Guest virtual machines running on Oracle VM Server can be configured to use one of the following virtualization modes:

- **Paravirtualized mode (PVM)** In this mode, the kernel of the guest operating system is modified to distinguish that it is running on a hypervisor instead of on the bare-metal hardware. As a result, I/O actions and system clock timers in particular are handled more efficiently, as compared with nonparavirtualized systems where I/O hardware and timers have to be emulated in the operating system. Oracle VM supports PV kernels for Oracle Linux and Red Hat Enterprise Linux, offering better performance and scalability.

- **Hardware virtualized mode (HVM) or fully virtualized mode** When support for hardware virtualization (Intel VT-x or AMD-V) is available in the host server hardware, the guest operating system may run unmodified and depend on the hardware features to ensure proper operation in a virtualized environment. However, HVM can introduce additional overhead since it relies on binary translation and device emulation. But it brings the benefits of compatibility: largely, any "unmodified" operating system image such as Linux, Solaris, or Windows that is not virtualization-aware can run as an HVM guest without any changes, making it easy to consolidate existing physical server images, leaving them essentially untouched. With the recent development in Intel and AMD processors, in some scenarios, hardware-assisted virtualization will also provide performance benefits.

■ **Hardware virtualized mode using paravirtualized drivers (PVHVM)**   This mode is identical to HVM, but with additional paravirtualized I/O drivers installed in the guest's operating system to improve virtual machine performance. This allows the operating system to essentially run unmodified, but uses PV drivers that have been modified specifically to execute I/O commands efficiently in a virtualized environment to minimize overhead. Oracle provides PV drivers for Microsoft Windows. PV drivers are provided as part of the operating system for Oracle Linux and Oracle Solaris. HVM works with all CPUs featuring the AMD-V (SVM) extension. Intel Virtualization Technology requires a computer system with an enabled Intel processor, BIOS, virtual machine monitor (VMM), and, for some uses, certain platform software enabled for it.

Depending on whether the cloud infrastructure will be physical or virtualized, the workloads are potential P2V (physical to virtual) or P2P (physical to physical) migration candidates. P2E (physical to engineered systems) can be considered to be another variant of consolidation planning. Consolidating applications, systems, or data centers reduces costs and simplifies operations.

Consolidation, however, could result in a case of putting more eggs in a single basket. To consolidate successfully, you need to ensure that you have a "stronger basket." The principles of virtualization, standardized processes, and management automation help to ensure that IT operations and systems are more robust. There are many other aspects of resiliency, such as security and disaster recovery, that also need to be enhanced. By consolidating, however, you can afford the investments needed to implement more robust technologies and processes, and thus the consolidated systems can indeed be made stronger.

Oracle Enterprise Manager 12*c* Consolidation Planner

Oracle Enterprise Manager 12*c* Consolidation Planner enables you to map servers you want to consolidate to the generic physical machines, Oracle Exadata or Exalogic engineered systems, or Oracle VM servers on which they can be consolidated. By leveraging metric and configuration data collected from servers managed by Oracle Enterprise Manager, Consolidation Planner helps you to determine the optimum consolidation scenarios that will produce the maximum cost benefits for the risk you are willing to take.

The goal of consolidation is to identify underutilized servers and find a way to consolidate them, enabling the enterprise to free up as many servers as possible while continuing to maintain service levels. Since servers have different levels of CPU capacity, Consolidation Planner uses computer benchmark data to normalize the CPU usage for a given hardware in the consolidation process. Specifically, Consolidation Planner uses the SPECint2006 benchmark, published by Standard Performance Evaluation Corporation (SPEC), for the different classes of hardware. More information on this benchmark is available on the SPEC website (www.spec.org).

Let us look at how workload characteristics can be taken into account when consolidating into a cloud environment.

Identifying the Right Workloads   Source servers are existing servers in your data center that are candidates for consolidation based on existing workload. Effective consolidation must also take into account the nature of the workload and the supporting technologies. For example, you may want to consolidate the databases of two different applications. If the applications currently run on different versions of the database, you may decide to keep each software stack pristine, and use CPU virtualization to simply consolidate the applications onto a pool of hardware servers. In this case, the historical data stored in the Oracle Enterprise Manager repository for the CPU resource consumption by the database workloads is used for consolidation (see Figure 2-4).

Destination servers are either existing servers or yet-to-be-purchased servers that source servers will be consolidated to. These may be individual machines or an integrated system such as Oracle Exadata or Oracle Exalogic.

Consolidation Project   A consolidation project is created for each consolidation effort, and then individual consolidation scenarios are created and executed within the scope of the project. A consolidation project defines the scope of consolidation in terms of the following:

■ The type of consolidation. In Oracle Enterprise Manager 12 *c*, two types of consolidation schemes are supported:

   ■ **P2V**   From physical source servers to Oracle VM destination servers

   ■ **P2P**   From physical source servers to physical destination servers

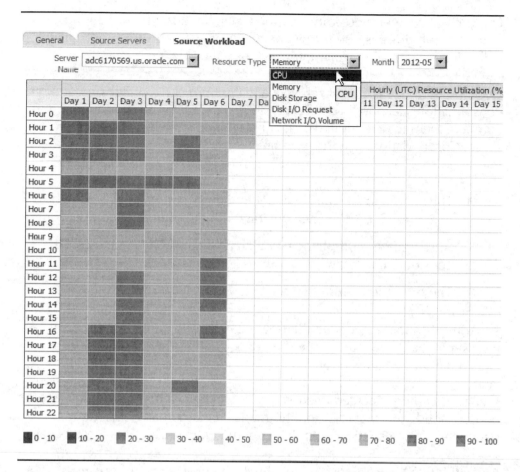

FIGURE 2-4.   *Oracle Enterprise Manager's Consolidation Planner*

- The preliminary set of candidate source servers to consider consolidating from.

- The preliminary set of candidate destination servers to consider consolidating to.

- The duration over which resource usage data will be collected for the workloads on the source servers. This data is used to create consolidation scenarios.

After the project is defined, an Oracle Enterprise Manager job is executed to bring the historical performance data for the source servers from the Oracle

Enterprise Manager repository into the Consolidation Planner application. Once the job finishes, the project becomes an active project, and data collection happens on regular intervals—usually once a day.

Consolidation Scenario   Each consolidation project contains one or more consolidation scenarios. You can create and execute scenarios and then compare them to determine which consolidation strategy makes the most sense. Consolidation scenarios can be created by providing the following information:

- The metrics to take into account for consolidation. These could be one or more of CPU, memory, disk I/O, network I/O, and disk storage.

- Any business, compliance, or technical constraints that must be considered.

- The list of destination servers.

Administrators can create their own custom scenarios that best suit their situation. Alternatively, they can choose from a set of preconfigured consolidation scenarios provided in the product, representing conservative, aggressive, and medium consolidation schemes. Once created, the various scenarios can be executed and the results can be evaluated to choose the best consolidation strategy. Administrators can also change the various parameters in a scenario, rerun the scenario, and view the new results.

Consolidation Constraints   Consolidation constraints are business, corporate, or technical constraints that must be taken into account when consolidating. The constraints represent the restrictions placed on the consolidation process for business, legal, or compliance reasons. There may be constraints on the way in which workloads on the source servers can be combined, or there may be constraints on the way in which destination servers can be used as targets for consolidation.

For source servers, there are two categories of constraints: inclusive and exclusive. Inclusive constraints bring potential consolidation candidates into the consolidation scope based on target properties. Exclusive constraints exclude servers from the consolidation scope based on target properties. Some examples of exclusive constraints are

- **Location**   Laws or regulations may mandate that specific servers must remain within a specific location, such as a particular datacenter location or within a specific geographical area. Sometimes, country-specific regulations or data privacy rules may dictate that resources must remain within the national boundaries.

- **Lifecycle status**   Test and production servers should not be consolidated on common hardware.

- **Application**   For businesses that host applications for several customers, there may be contractual obligations to keep separate the servers and data for those customers.

- **Security**   Certain machines may have specific security requirements.

For destination servers, there are three categories of consolidation constraints: utilization, related, and exclusiveness. Utilization constraints limit the amount of server resources that may be utilized. Related constraints dictate that some servers are associated and therefore should be consolidated in the same server pool or server zone. Exclusiveness constraints prevent certain source servers from being consolidated on the same destination server due to compliance and technical reasons. The following are some examples of scenarios where servers should not be consolidated on the same destination server:

- **Department**   Broker and dealer systems should be on different machines.

- **Lifecycle status**   Servers utilized within different stages of the application lifecycle, such as testing and production should not be mixed together.

- **Affinity**   Servers used for the middleware and database tiers should be consolidated separately.

- **Topology**   Database Real Application Cluster nodes should not be on the same physical server because doing that will not provide fault tolerance against physical server failure.

- **High availability** Machines with specific HA requirements, such as multiple web servers or application servers, should not be on the same physical machine.

- **Disaster recovery** Machines supporting disaster recovery strategies or other application-level availability features should not be placed with other regularly used systems.

- **Security** Servers in different security zones should not be mixed together.

Choosing the Best Consolidation Strategy You can define new scenarios and rerun existing scenarios with new input parameters and compare the results. This iterative process helps you to obtain the optimized consolidation scenario that is generated by comparing various factors and weighing different trade-offs. For each scenario that's executed, Oracle Enterprise Manager provides the following information:

- **Destinations** The list of destination servers to which the source servers will be consolidated. Resource configuration and calculated utilization are shown for each destination server.

- **Ratio** The ratio of source servers to destination servers. By default, the Consolidation Planner tries to "fit" source servers into as few destination servers as possible.

- **Confidence** The percentage of the data collected for source servers that meets the source server usage requirements defined in the scenario. This value is aggregated for all source servers defined with the project.

- **Violations** The number of violations of technical or business constraints defined in the scenario.

- **Exclusions** The number of source servers that do not have a qualified mapping to a destination server. These are source servers that exceed the capacity of available destination servers. This metric is applicable only if auto-mapping of source servers to destination servers is used.

A different set of constraints may result in a different optimal scenario. You can modify the constraints to come up with different scenario results. Comparing various results lets you determine the consolidation strategy that best meets your requirements. These strategies include:

- Matching source server workload requirements with destination servers to achieve required application performance after consolidation

- Fitting source server requirements with each destination server's available resources as tightly as possible, so you can get maximum usage of destination server capacity

- Balancing the source server workload across all available destination servers

In summary, Oracle Enterprise Manager 12c Consolidation Planner helps you with the cloud planning process by allowing you to explore various options for reusing existing physical hardware, leveraging server virtualization, and procuring new hardware such as Oracle Exadata or Oracle Exalogic. If done correctly, consolidation, as a first step to building a cloud architecture, can go a long way toward providing improved performance, ease of management, improved technology, and lower costs. Once the technology portfolio for the cloud is identified, the hardware and software components need to be modeled into a cloud architecture that addresses key business requirements.

Cloud Architecture

Without an optimized architecture that is built on a standardized portfolio, with standardized interfaces, the cloud provider will not be able to effectively provide at an attractive price the quality of service (QoS) and the level of agility required to keep its cloud consumers happy. Conversely, a cloud consumer of shared services doesn't need to know about the underlying cloud infrastructure, but should be aware of the available services and the resource model exposed in the GUI or API.

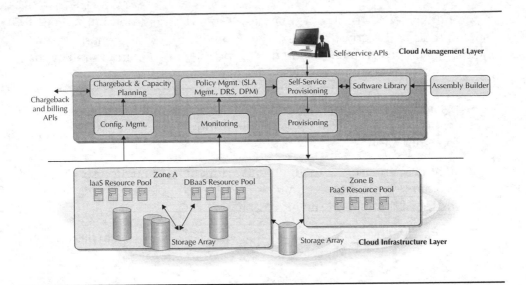

FIGURE 2-5. *Oracle Enterprise Manager cloud components*

Figure 2-5 depicts the high-level cloud schematic, which consists of two layers. The upper layer, the cloud management layer, is responsible for handling user interactions with the cloud. The lower layer, the cloud infrastructure layer, deals with virtual and physical resource management. The Oracle Enterprise Manager Cloud Control 12*c* Virtualization Plug-in provides the underlying resource management for Oracle VM today.

Cloud Management Layer Components

Oracle Enterprise Manager handles cloud user authentication, user/role management, software library management, provisioning requests, policy definition and enforcement, monitoring and reporting, and other aspects of managing the cloud. In addition, you can use a client-side tool such as Oracle VM Template Builder or Oracle Virtual Assembly Builder (OVAB) to build and modify Oracle VM Templates or Oracle Virtual Assemblies.

Following is a brief description of various components included in cloud management:

- **Self-Service Provisioning**   As the name indicates, this component allows authorized end users (developers, testers, and so forth) to provision applications and resources on demand in the cloud. In addition to a self-service portal GUI, a web services API is available to allow integration of external applications. To supplement self-service provisioning, the cloud management layer includes the following:

  - **Oracle VM Template Builder/Oracle Virtual Assembly Builder**   These tools can be used to design and bundle various services to be published and deployed in the cloud. An *Oracle VM Template* is a package that comprises an operating system and other application components that can be deployed as a single virtual machine. An *Oracle Virtual Assembly* extends that concept. A Virtual Assembly is a collection of virtual appliances that comprises a multitier application that can be deployed across several virtual machines (for example, a web application with a web server, an application server, and a database server). Assembly Builder can be used to modify the prepackaged Virtual Assemblies shipped by Oracle. It also integrates with Oracle Enterprise Manager Software Library so that Virtual Assemblies can be staged within the Software Library directly from Assembly Builder.

  - **Software Library**   This is the repository for managing all prepackaged and user-defined Oracle VM Templates and Virtual Assemblies, provisioning profiles (in case of physical servers), and associated scripts. The Software Library can be co-located either within the same infrastructure as the management server or remotely, closer to the end targets of the cloud.

- **Chargeback and Capacity Planning**   This component is responsible for providing chargeback, trending, and other information related to resource consumption and can integrate with external billing systems.

- **Policy Management**   This component is responsible for enforcing user-defined policies. These policies could be as simple as determining initial placement of VMs or reserving capacity to meet a future need (VM reservation), or could be as sophisticated as dynamically scaling applications up or down to maintain a certain level of business service. This includes Dynamic Resource Scheduling (DRS) and Dynamic Power Management (DPM) capabilities.

■ **Monitoring, Configuration Management, and Compliance Management** These components provide comprehensive post-deployment operations management, such as performance and configuration management solutions for the cloud.

Cloud Infrastructure Layer Components

The cloud infrastructure layer consists of hardware and software components that are used to build the cloud environment. This includes the various software, server, storage, and networking components organized into resource pools and cloud zones. As discussed earlier, Oracle Enterprise Manager's Consolidation Planner can help an administrator identify the right resources to be consolidated for use in the cloud.

The cloud infrastructure layer consists of cloud resources, modeled such that the physicality is uniformly abstracted regardless of the nature of service—IaaS or PaaS. Oracle offers technologies to support both physical and virtual environments. In each of these cases, the cloud comprises multiple subclouds, called *zones*. Each zone consists of a pool of physical servers, representing a logical entity such as a datacenter location, a department, or a certain level of availability. In terms of implementation, zones may be either of the following:

■ An Oracle VM Zone, representing a bunch of servers with the Oracle VM hypervisor installed

■ A PaaS Infrastructure Zone, which can comprise multiple physical hosts (with Oracle Enterprise Manager agent installed) or a preexisting Oracle VM Zone that is used by higher-order services like PaaS

When a service is exposed to the end consumer, the physical resources within the zone are all concealed from a user-interaction perspective. The end user simply selects the zone to deploy the service onto.

■ Zones encapsulate physical resources, including attached storage and network resources.

■ Zones can serve as a boundary for chargeback and metering, because Oracle Enterprise Manager allows assignment of charge plans at the zone level.

■ Zones can be exposed either directly as an Oracle VM Zone directly
   or as a PaaS Infrastructure Zone.

■ Members of a zone are selected by cloud administrators.

■ Within a zone, there are groupings of homogeneous resources,
   called pools.

An Oracle VM Zone is made up of virtual server and storage pools. A
virtual server pool can contain a maximum of 32 Oracle VM Servers. There
must be at least one virtual server in the server pool. One of the servers acts
as a master server for the server pool.

All virtual servers in a server pool should have CPUs in the same CPU
family, but the configuration of the CPUs can differ, such as the number of
cores. If the CPUs are not in the same CPU family, some operations, such as
live migration, may fail. Other hardware components on the host computer
may also differ, such as the amount of RAM, the number and size of disk
drives, and so on. All the servers in a pool should share a common file
system (either a NAS export or a mounted LUN).

A storage pool can consist of external storage elements such as storage
servers, exported file systems, and LUNs. An external storage element is
created on dedicated storage hardware, such as a server configured for NAS
offering NFS shares. The server on which the storage element is present
must be accessible by the Oracle VM Servers through a Fiber Channel or
Ethernet network.

Similarly, a PaaS Infrastructure Zone may comprise database or middleware
pools, representing hosts with homogeneous software installations, such as
a particular database or a middleware version, so that the placement within
the pool can be done transparently and the same QoS can be guaranteed
independent of the placement.

To summarize, resource pools

■ Are typically homogeneous

■ Are defined against a single zone

   ■ Underlying physical resource shared across resource pools

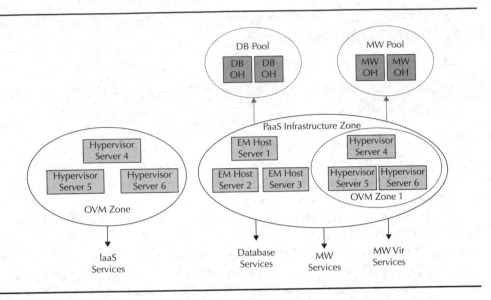

FIGURE 2-6. *Cloud resource model*

- Have membership criteria set by integrators

  - Based on software requirements for a particular service (for example, 10.3.5.0 Middleware homes or a bunch of 10.2.0.4 RAC clusters)

- Can have certain limits imposed by the underlying technology (for example, number of schemas supported within a database)

The organization of zones and pools is depicted in Figure 2-6.

Cloud Infrastructure Planning

Now that the cloud resource models have been defined, cloud administrators can use the concepts to plan their transition strategy. Cloud can be delivered in the form of discrete services, such as OS infrastructure (IaaS), and runtime platforms (PaaS), such as databases (DBaaS) or middleware (MWaaS). In addition, tailored services can be offered for testing (TaaS) or delivering packaged software as services (SaaS). Server virtualization is suited to deliver

IaaS, but it may fall short in delivering PaaS. Whether to choose server virtualization or build the cloud directly on physical servers depends on several factors:

- **Type of service**   **The type of service offered** (IaaS, DBaaS, or PaaS) may determine the underlying infrastructure required.

- **Isolation**   Do the tenants need to be isolated, so that they can be patched and upgraded independently? VMs offer the maximum degree of isolation because everything from the guest operating system and up is isolated to a tenant.

- **Nature of the application**   Owing to performance reasons, especially related to I/O, certain workloads, such as production databases, are best run on physical hosts. Similarly, some applications may be more conducive to nonclustered pools.

- **Skill set of the administrator**   The skill set of the person that plans and delivers the cloud, such as a database administrator (DBA) or a system administrator (sysadmin) may determine the technology they are most comfortable working with

- **Manageability**   VMs offer isolation, but may also result in sprawl. Administrators often may find it difficult to maintain thousands of VMs from a compliance perspective. Other models, such as a RAC-based DBaaS, offer better consolidation and could be easier to manage.

The good news is that Oracle Enterprise Manager supports different deployment models for each of these use cases. It offers a variety of architectural choices to the cloud provider to support all the aforementioned service types, in both virtual and physical environments. Figure 2-7 depicts some of the choices an administrator has available. You can deploy multitier applications on virtualized servers or deploy databases and applications on pre-created platforms, whether physical or virtual. Even within the realm of virtualization, Oracle offers choices! You can choose virtualization based on Oracle VM Server for x86, Oracle VM Server for SPARC, or Solaris Containers

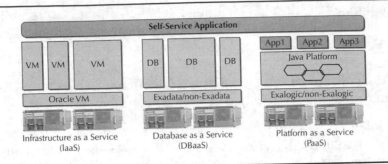

FIGURE 2-7. *Various architectural choices mapped to cloud services*

(though this book covers only Oracle VM Server for x86, which is supported by Oracle Enterprise Manager Cloud Control 12*c*).

Oracle Enterprise Manager 12*c* comes with a Service Catalog that is rich with service templates for these different technologies. Using Oracle Enterprise Manager 12*c*, a cloud provider can create one or more of these services and characterize them based on size (total CPU, memory, etc.), QoS, version, and other attributes that are inherently part of the Oracle Enterprise Manager's discovery and collection process.

So, what actions does the administrator need to perform to set up the cloud? As previously discussed, administrators are in the business of cloud enablement, for which Oracle Enterprise Manager 12*c* ships with out-of-the-box roles such as cloud administrator and self-service administrator. Oracle Enterprise Manager also provides out-of-the-box automation for these roles. The cloud administrator can set up the cloud infrastructure, such as servers, storage, and database resource pools, and group them into zones. The self-service administrator then defines access controls, quotas, retirement policies, and the charge plans for the service and releases the service in the self-service catalog. Figure 2-8 shows the various activities an administrator performs for setting up a cloud.

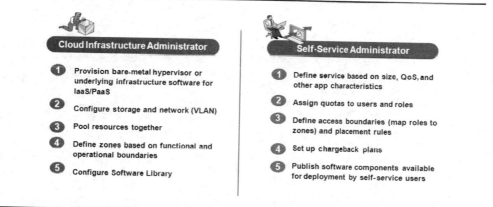

FIGURE 2-8. *Oracle Enterprise Manager–enabled cloud setup activities*

Summary

In this chapter, you were introduced to cloud computing concepts and the various reasons why planning is an important and unavoidable aspect of building a cloud. You learned about

- Automated discovery of IT assets

- The IaaS and PaaS cloud service delivery models and how the different consolidation technologies from Oracle can serve them

- The cloud resource models and the concepts of zones and pools, which will be very important in subsequent chapters

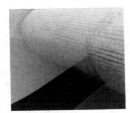

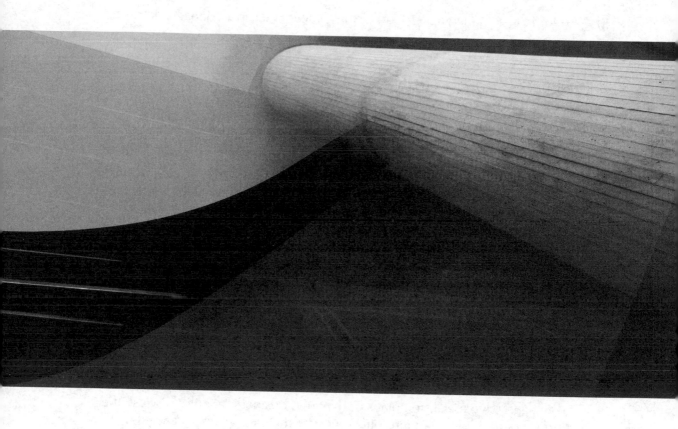

CHAPTER
3

Self-Service
Provisioning

Ten years ago, data centers were running databases, application servers, and applications in silos with no form of standardization or automation. The introduction of grid computing brought remarkable improvements in standardization and automation, but it also spawned a huge proliferation in the number of operating systems and databases running on commodity servers. Data centers now have hundreds to thousands of databases spanning test and production systems. Some of these databases have long lives, while others often last only for the duration of the project. While grid computing did drive standardization, it did not drive automation.

The grid computing model suffers from two challenges: IT organizations, traditionally, have been entrusted with provisioning these resources on behalf of the users who need them; and, a typical application-provisioning activity spans multiple teams that deal with hardware, storage, operating system, database, middleware, and finally the application. The hand-off between these teams is mostly managed either via e-mail communication or by some form of ticketing system. While such a system may work for small and medium-size companies, it poses severe challenges to companies who have aggressive expansion plans or dynamic business models, because the sign-off of multiple IT admins often become the gating factor in fulfilling the requests.

In this chapter, we analyze the challenges with running a typical datacenter, and how these can be overcome with adoption of a self service way of life. We study the various tools provided by Oracle like Oracle Enterprise Manager Cloud Control 12*c* and Oracle Virtual Assembly Builder that help enable self service provisioning of various software artifacts across both virtual and physical infrastructure. Finally, we look at the out of box self-service portal and APIs provided by Oracle Enterprise Manager 12*c*.

Benefits of Self-Service Provisioning

To understand the benefits of self-service provisioning, we first need to analyze the business and technical challenges faced by large companies in managing their datacenters. Some of the typical such challenges are

- Lack of agility in service rollouts
- Lack of secure and standardized practices

- Security and compliance issues

- Maintenance of quality of service while reducing downtime

- High manual labor costs

Most IT organizations have been looking for new and innovative technologies to help address these challenges. In such an environment, the emergence of cloud computing is more than coincidental. This idea has been conceived with the single aim of resolving a large number of IT woes. Let's see how.

Lack of agility is the first of these five challenges identified by most companies. Being agile allows IT organizations to respond to dynamic user demands in a timely fashion, which improves go-to-market speed and, thus, opens doors to new business opportunities. The cloud aims to achieve agility by enabling faster provisioning of IT resources and providing capacity on demand via automation of labor-intensive tasks.

The next two challenges are those of standardization, and security and compliance issues. The automation of datacenter tasks, a key cloud characteristic, forces IT organizations to standardize on a common set of tools and processes. The need for standardization is further enforced by restrictions imposed by security and regulatory compliance frameworks. For example, companies that process credit card payments or data have to comply with the Payment Card Industry Data Security Standard (PCI DSS) framework; similarly, every company in the health care industry has to follow the security and privacy rules set by the Health Insurance Portability and Accountability Act of 1996 (HIPAA). Thus, automation efforts can inherently enforce standardization and compliance and thus address the challenges faced by growing companies.

Self-service provisioning via the cloud computing model completely changes the paradigm to one where the consumers (end users) of IT services can provision resources without being intermediated by IT admins. This is a very powerful concept, as it tries to enable and empower the end users to provision and monitor their own resources, thus freeing up IT personnel to focus on more critical tasks, such as maintaining QoS and ensuring uptime, all with small, focused teams. This addresses the last two challenges of maintaining QoS while lowering downtime and high manual labor costs.

In a typical self-service offering, a lead administrator performs the design-time activity of creating or customizing procedures that automate deployment as per best practices or company standards, and the procedures are executed on demand by the end user. To make self-service provisioning simple and appealing, it is often presented by a unified interface or console that lists all available deployment options. These different deployment options can be exercised by providing some basic inputs, such as deployment scale and size.

The goals of a self-service application are to accomplish the following:

- Provide a simplified console for rapid and on-demand deployment of resources

- Expose standard procedures to a wide variety of users—from developers to application administrators

- Enforce controls on resource consumption through retirement, quota, and chargeback policies

- Cut down the resource requisition and deployment window for important projects

- Permit senior administrators and IT personnel to focus on more important and strategic tasks

These goals are focused completely on addressing the five issues identified in the beginning of this section.

In the next section, you will learn about the various provisioning tools provided by Oracle Enterprise Manager 12*c* for end-to-end provisioning and patching of the complete application stack, and how these tools can serve as the building blocks of the self-service provisioning capabilities, all the while adhering to compliance and security regulations.

Oracle Self-Service Provisioning Tools

Oracle Enterprise Manager 12*c* aims to provide capabilities to manage both the complete Oracle stack and non-Oracle products via its large and ever-expanding Oracle Partner Network and its flexible and extensible architecture. Specifically, in the case of provisioning, Oracle Enterprise

Manager provides the capability to automate software deployment of physical and virtual infrastructure, operating systems, databases, middleware, and packaged and custom applications. In fact, Oracle Enterprise Manager can automate not only the deployment of these resources but also the maintenance of these deployments. This makes critical datacenter operations easy, efficient, and scalable. Figure 3-1 illustrates the software deployment life cycle.

When setting up an Oracle Self Service Portal, the infrastructure used to create the cloud environment will dictate the tools required to achieve rapid provisioning. The infrastructure used will depend on the cloud delivery model:

■ **Infrastructure as a Service (IaaS)**   For provisioning of virtual machines with or without preconfigured software

■ **Database as a Service (DBaaS)**   For rapid provisioning of databases

■ **Middleware as a Service (MWaaS)**   For provisioning of a middleware container to deploy Java Platform, Enterprise Edition (Java EE) applications

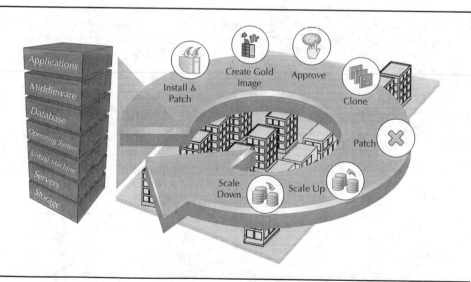

FIGURE 3-1.   *Software deployment life cycle*

Figure 3-2 illustrates the different phases of the Self Service Portal setup and the tools required during each of these phases. The next section explains the different phases involved, after which the Oracle Enterprise Manager 12*c* provisioning framework is described in depth.

Self-Service Provisioning Setup Phases

The primary role that is active during the self-service provisioning setup is the self-service administrator (SSA). Typically, an organization would have numerous SSAs, each serving a different application team and each adopting one or more cloud models. For example, a database SSA (DBaaS admin, or DBA) will publish Service Templates for database configurations that are suitable for their custom application deployments, and an infrastructure SSA (IaaS admin, or sysadmin) will publish Virtual Assemblies with preconfigured

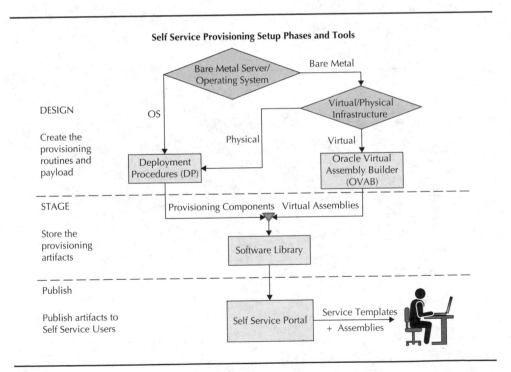

FIGURE 3-2. *Self-service provisioning setup phases and tools*

software that can be used to rapidly set up their Oracle Fusion Applications environment. An SSA has to go through three key phases, described next, to successfully set up a Self Service Portal.

Phase 1: Design

In this phase, the SSA has to create or configure provisioning routines and the appropriate packages for deployment. Which tools to use is decided on the basis of the selected cloud model and the infrastructure platform—virtual vs. physical. For virtual environments, the SSA can leverage Oracle Virtual Assembly Builder (OVAB) to create Virtual Assemblies. For physical environments, the SSA can use established Deployment Procedures. (Both of these tools will be covered in subsequent sections.) There are also prerequisites for the use of the different provisioning routines, such as:

- Deployment of Virtual Assemblies requires that the relevant cloud infrastructure administrator pre-provision the hypervisor on a bare-metal server.

- For physical environments that support DBaaS, the database administrator has to preinstall and properly configure software such as Database Oracle Home, Clusterware (CRS), and Automatic Storage Management (ASM).

Phase 2: Stage

As part of the design phase, numerous provisioning artifacts are created that will participate in the self-service provisioning process. For example:

- **Virtual environment** Oracle VM Templates and Oracle Virtual Assemblies for Oracle Enterprise Linux or Oracle Red Hat Linux, Oracle WebLogic Servers, Oracle RAC, Oracle Fusion Applications, custom Java EE applications, and so forth

- **Physical environment** Templates, scripts (SQL, PL/SQL, WLST, JMX, and so forth), and Deployment Procedures for different Oracle Database and Oracle WebLogic Server configurations

The Oracle Enterprise Manager 12*c* Software Library (or just Software Library) is used to stage all of these provisioning artifacts. The Software

Library is a centralized repository that stores certified software images and scripts that assist in the deployment of these images. This repository is like any other media library and provides advanced features like role-based access and fine-grained privileges. More details on the Software Library will be covered in later sections.

Phase 3: Publish

In this last phase of the setup process, the SSA publishes the Deployment Procedures, Virtual Assemblies, and Oracle VM Templates to the Self Service Portal's service catalog. In the service catalog, the Deployment Procedures (part of the orchestration logic) for Oracle Database and WebLogic Server provisioning are exposed to the self-service users as Service Templates. Service Templates reference the Deployment Procedures to use for actual provisioning, but also store additional metadata like name, description, applicable zones, and applicable user roles. Meanwhile, the Virtual Assemblies and Oracle VM Templates (they are the payload, not the orchestration logic) are published as is to the service catalog. These contain the software, configuration, relationships, helper scripts, and so forth required to deploy them successfully.

Now that you are familiar with the self-service provisioning setup phases, the following sections present an overview of the different tools that.

Oracle Enterprise Manager 12*c* Provisioning Framework

As mentioned in the discussion of the design phase, Oracle Enterprise Manager 12*c* offers lifecycle management solutions in the form of Deployment Procedures (DPs). Deployment Procedures are out-of-the-box best practices that are composed of collections of steps that are orchestrated by Oracle Enterprise Manager 12*c*. In fact, Deployment Procedures are the primary orchestration mechanism provided by Oracle Enterprise Manager 12*c*. These Procedures are used for both physical and virtual deployments and can be customized to suit your needs. Oracle ships a set of best practice Deployment Procedures for provisioning and patching of numerous Oracle Products.

The following table lists just a few of these out-of-the-box Deployment Procedures:

Category	Details
Bare Metal Provisioning	Provisioning Linux operating system on bare-metal machines
Server Virtualization	Provisioning Oracle VM Server 3.0 on bare-metal machines
Provisioning	Creating Guest VMs using Virtual Assemblies, Oracle VM Templates, or via cloning other Guest VMs
Database Provisioning	Create Database on existing Oracle Home
	Clone Single Instance and Real Application Clusters Database
	Upgrade Database (version 10.2.0.4 and above)
	Real Application Clusters Scale out and Scale back
Database Patching	Patching of the Database, and Clusterware and ASM layers on Engineered and non-Engineered systems
Middleware Provisioning	Provision Middleware Home or Oracle WebLogic Domain (clone or from release media)
	Scale up Middleware domain add a managed server on same server
	Scale out Middleware domain (i.e., to add a managed server on new server)
Middleware Patching	Patching for Oracle WebLogic Software
Java Application Provisioning	Deploy Custom Java EE Applications on Oracle Fusion Middleware
Packaged Application Provisioning	E-Business Suite Cloning and Provisioning

NOTE
Deployment Procedures provided by Oracle Enterprise Manager 12c allow provisioning of artifacts from the operating system tier to the application tier, thus covering the complete stack. For information on the latest set of out-of-the-box Deployment Procedures, refer to the product documentation on OTN (http://docs.oracle.com/cd/E24628_01/index.htm).

The Deployment Procedures offered by Oracle Enterprise Manager 12*c* have been created with consideration for all the best practices in the industry in mind. The steps embedded within a Deployment Procedure ensure that they meet most provisioning and patching requirements. While these Procedures can be used with the default settings, they can also be customized to include additional steps and to disable unwanted steps.

The Deployment Procedures subsystem is one piece of Oracle Enterprise Manager 12*c*'s provisioning framework and depends on two other key subsystems: the Software Library and the Job System. The following sections provide an in-depth look at these two subsystems and how they interact with Deployment Procedures.

Software Library

The Oracle Enterprise Manager Software Library, shown in Figure 3-3, is a centralized repository that stores certified software images (for example, Oracle Database, Oracle VM Templates, Virtual Assemblies, operating system, Oracle RAC, and third-party software) and scripts that assist in the deployment of these images.

The contents of the Software Library are referred to as Software Library entities. The two main entity types are Components and Directives. There are some specialized categories as well, like Virtualization and Bare Metal Provisioning, but these contain subtypes that serve the same purpose as components and directives.

Components

Components are entities that represent software clones, archives, patches, release media, applications, and other forms of data. These different categories are represented by component subtypes. Examples of these are

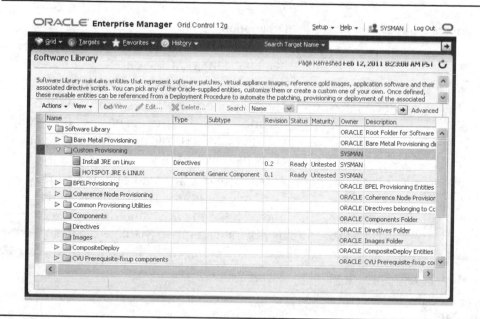

FIGURE 3-3. *Software Library console*

database clones, provisioning profiles, application archives, and generic components.

Directives

Directives are entities that represent a set of instructions to be performed. These are constructs used to associate scripts with the software component. These scripts contain directions on how to interpret and process the contents of a particular component. Thus, together, components and directives can allow for any kind of automation to be achieved.

In order to use the Software Library, the administrator first needs to configure a storage location. A prerequisite for selection of a storage location is that it should be accessible from all Oracle Management Service (OMS) instances. This storage location is used to store the payload associated with components and directives. As shown in Table 3-1, there are three supported storage options.

Storage Option	Description
OMS Shared File System	These are shared locations (using protocols like NFS, DBFS, ACFS, OCFS2, and so on) that are accessible by all OMS instances.
OMS Agent File System	These locations are accessed by all OMS instances by using the agents installed along with the OMS. This is primarily useful for cross-platform installs.
Referenced Locations	These locations are read-only in nature. Currently supported mechanisms are HTTP- and NFS-based URLs, and directories on any of the Enterprise Manager agents.

TABLE 3-1. *Software Library Storage Options*

TIP
OMS Shared File System is the recommended storage option for a multiple OMS deployment of Oracle Enterprise Manager 12c. This option provides significantly better performance over OMS Agent File System.

Following are some of the features provided by the Software Library:

- **Creation of new components and directives**   Users are free to create components of any subtype or directives for any kind of script. For components that do not fit in any of the registered subtypes, a special subtype called *Generic Component* is available for use. For scripts in the directives, Perl and OS-specific shell interpreters are made available by default. For other languages, interpreters need to be made available by the user on the destination targets.

- **Customization of Oracle-provided entities**   By default, Oracle-provided entities are read only (cannot be modified by end users). Users can perform a *Create Like* operation (copy and edit) on Oracle-provided entities and then customize them to their liking.

- **Automatic versioning**   All changes made to an entity are versioned. Version numbers are incremented automatically. Any version of these entities can be used by Deployment Procedures.

- **Maturity levels for entities**   The lifecycle status of Software Library entities can be tracked using the maturity levels. The three maturity levels supported are Untested, Beta, and Production. These levels are in line with Information Technology Infrastructure Library (ITIL) recommendations and thus provide a strong relationship with industry standards.

- **Export and import of entities**   A collection of entities can be selected and exported or imported at will. These entities are exported as Provisioning Archive (PAR) files.

The Software Library is the backbone of the Oracle Enterprise Manager 12c provisioning framework and is used by every Deployment Procedure either to store the components required for the provisioning action or to stage scripts required to process the component payload.

Job System

The Job System is the next important subsystem of Oracle Enterprise Manager 12c's provisioning framework. A job scheduling tool is an integral part of any data center. A job scheduler is typically entrusted with either execution of micro-tasks that belong to a larger process, like stopping a database as part of the patching process, or for execution of monolithic tasks, like database backup. To meet these needs, Oracle Enterprise Manager 12c provides Oracle Enterprise Manager 12c Job System, a job scheduler that is powerful, simple to use, and, best of all, free.

The Job System provides a large collection of *job types*, which are template definitions of commonly performed tasks like OS command (execute an operating system command on a server), SQL script (execute a SQL script on a database), and execute Recovery Manager (RMAN) script for database backup. Besides scheduling jobs against these predefined job types, the Job System supports the following features:

- A user-friendly console for defining, scheduling, and tracking the progress of jobs

- Privilege delegation mechanisms like sudo and PowerBroker pbrun

■ Notifications via e-mail and SNMP traps

■ Fine-grained access control

■ Lifecycle operations like submit, suspend, resume, stop, and retry

■ A Job Library to store custom job definitions, and much more

These features enable a datacenter administrator to automate many of the menial, monolithic tasks. In addition to supporting monolithic tasks, the Job System integrates with the Deployment Procedures framework to provide a library of common tasks that can be performed as part of a larger process. This integration is discussed in the next section.

Deployment Procedures

The final subsystem of this provisioning framework is that of Deployment Procedures. Deployment Procedures are the primary orchestration mechanism provided by Oracle Enterprise Manager 12*c*. These Procedures are used for both physical and virtual deployments, and can be customized to suit your needs. Some of the out-of-the-box Procedures provided by Oracle were described earlier in this chapter. This section takes a step back and explores some of the benefits of these Procedures, how they integrate with the Software Library and the Job System, and why they are such a critical part of this provisioning framework.

Deployment Procedures are designed to be extensible, reusable, and hot-pluggable in nature and, thus, can easily be customized and extended per customer needs:

■ **Extensible** The objective of Deployment Procedures is to provide as many best practice methods, out-of-the-box, as possible. But there are always some deployment steps that are specific to customer environments. Thus, Oracle Enterprise Manager 12*c* allows users to either copy and edit Procedures provided out-of-the-box Procedure or create entirely new Procedures.

■ **Reusable** As mentioned in prior sections, Deployment Procedures seamlessly integrate with the Software Library, and the Software Library entities can be shared between multiple Deployment Procedures.

■ **Hot-pluggable**   Deployment Procedures and Software Library entities can be easily exported and imported between different environments. Hence, a Procedure developed in the test environment can easily be promoted to production without any outage.

These attributes are possible due to the unique way in which Deployment Procedures are *modeled,* which refers to the arrangement of different artifacts that comprise a Deployment Procedure, also called the *Procedure definition.* As shown in Figure 3-4, the Deployment Procedure model comprises various phases and steps that run serially or in parallel to perform operations.

The artifacts that make up the Deployment Procedure definition are described next.

Name	Upgrade Oracle Database
Description	This procedure upgrades the selected Single Instance Oracle Databases to the destination version specified.
Type	Upgrade Oracle Database
Last Modified By	Oracle
Procedure Utilities Staging Path	%emd_root%/EMStage
envVarEditInput	
Profile (Privilege Delegation Settings)	
Last Updated	Feb 12, 2011 9:19:36 AM PST
Note	

Expand All | Collapse All

Name	Type	Description
▽ Upgrade Oracle Database		This procedure upgrades the selected Single Instance Oracle Databases to the destination version specified.
Initialize Deployment Procedure	Computational	Initializes the necessary data required for database upgrade.
Break point for Initialize DP step	Manual	Verify if values are initialized properly.
▽ For each Host	Parallel	For each Host
▽ Execute System Checks	Rolling	Executes System level prerequisite checks
Execute System Prerequisite checks	Procedure Step	Executes System level prerequisite checks
Break point for System Prerequisite step	Manual	Verify if values are prerequisites checks are executed.
▽ For each host	Parallel	For each host
▽ Deploy Oracle Database Software	Rolling	Deploys the Database Software on the list of hosts selected

FIGURE 3-4.   *Deployment Procedure definition*

Phases

A *phase* is a looping construct that performs different operations on a collection of targets. A phase can contain numerous steps or more phases. There are two supported types of phases:

- **Rolling phase** All steps are run serially or sequentially across targets.

- **Parallel phase** All steps are run in parallel across targets.

For example, suppose you are running a command across two servers, server A and server B. In a rolling phase, the command will be executed first on server A and then, upon completion, on server B. In a parallel phase, the command will be executed on both servers A and B at the same time.

The parallel phase is heavily used in mass deployment scenarios, where the same set of actions need to be repeated on multiple destination servers. A typical example is single instance database provisioning. The rolling phase, on the other hand, is usually used in scenarios where there is a dependency between the destination servers. A typical example is patching of nodes in a RAC configuration, where all operations are first performed on the first node, then on the second node, and so on.

Steps

A step is an abstraction of a unit of work. For example, starting the database is a step. It either could be part of a phase or could be independent. The different types of steps, as shown in Figure 3-5, are Manual, Computational, Procedure, Job, Directive, Component, and Host Command.

A Manual step, as shown in Figure 3-6, is a task that requires user interaction and cannot be automated. Typically, this type of step displays the instructions that need to be performed by the user. After the operation has been performed, you can proceed to the next step by clicking Confirm or you can exit by stopping the execution. Examples of a Manual step include logging into a system and updating the kernel parameter, rebooting a system, or providing special privileges to the user.

A Computational step is a task whose operations are performed within Oracle Enterprise Manager and do not require any user intervention. This step gathers additional information for running a Procedure and cannot be manually inserted by the user. Examples of a Computational step include

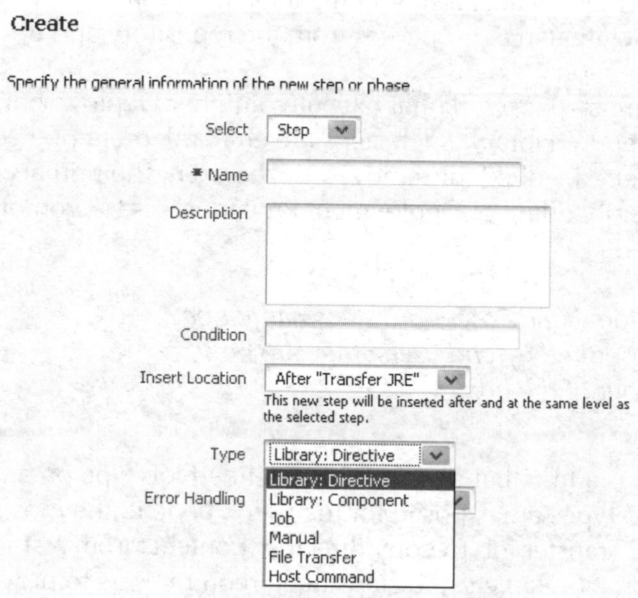

Create

Specify the general information of the new step or phase.

Select [Step ▼]

* Name [ ]

Description [ ]

Condition [ ]

Insert Location [After "Transfer JRE" ▼]
This new step will be inserted after and at the same level as the selected step.

Type [Library: Directive ▼]

Library: Directive
Library: Component
Job
Manual
File Transfer
Host Command

Error Handling

FIGURE 3-5. *Different types of steps*

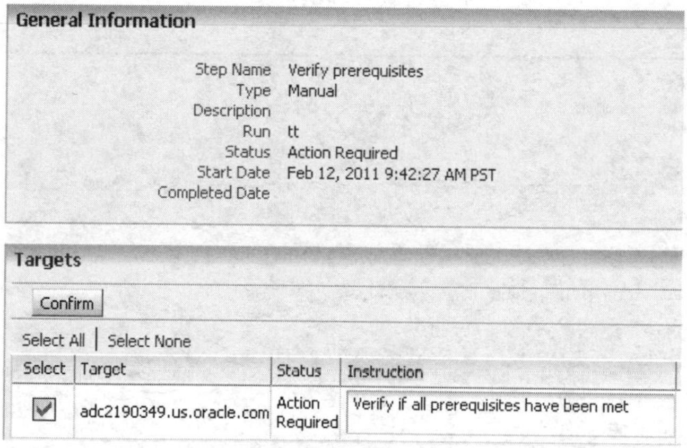

General Information

Step Name Verify prerequisites
Type Manual
Description
Run tt
Status Action Required
Start Date Feb 12, 2011 9:42:27 AM PST
Completed Date

Targets

[Confirm]

Select All | Select None

Select	Target	Status	Instruction
☑	adc2190349.us.oracle.com	Action Required	Verify if all prerequisites have been met

FIGURE 3-6. *Example of a Manual step, which requires clicking Confirm to proceed with the execution of the next step*

running an SQL query against a schema to gather more data for other steps to run, or retrieving target properties from the repository and updating the runtime information.

A Procedure step is a task that executes another Deployment Procedure from the Procedure Library. Such steps are embedded out of the box and cannot be inserted, edited, or removed by the user. The primary motivation behind such embedding of Deployment Procedures is to promote reuse.

NOTE
Computational and Procedure steps cannot be inserted or edited by end users; they are only available out of the box.

A Job step is a task that executes a predefined job type on a target. Numerous job types are exposed for the user's benefit, the most popular being the File Transfer job to copy directory contents from a single source to multiple destination targets. Job steps often require users to provide inputs for the job type parameters.

A Directive step is a task that deploys a directive from the Software Library alone. This is useful when users want to store their custom scripts in the Software Library and reuse them in a Deployment Procedure.

A Component step, as shown in Figure 3-7, is a task that deploys a Software Library component and the associated directive. The Deployment Procedure

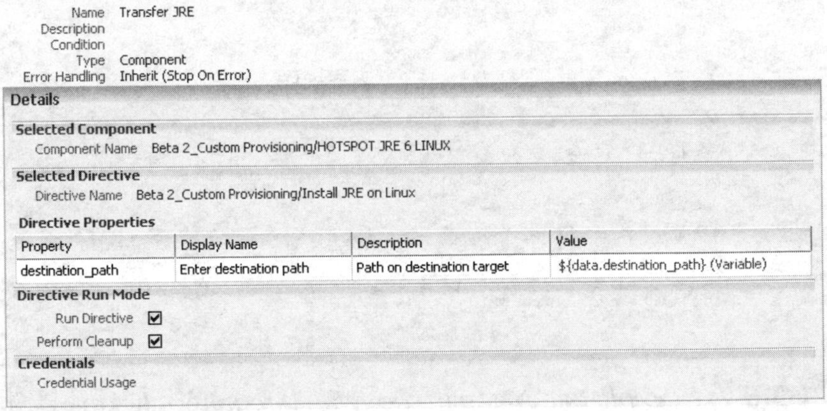

Name	Transfer JRE
Description	
Condition	
Type	Component
Error Handling	Inherit (Stop On Error)

Details

Selected Component
Component Name   Beta 2_Custom Provisioning/HOTSPOT JRE 6 LINUX

Selected Directive
Directive Name   Beta 2_Custom Provisioning/Install JRE on Linux

Directive Properties

Property	Display Name	Description	Value
destination_path	Enter destination path	Path on destination target	${data.destination_path} (Variable)

Directive Run Mode
Run Directive ☑
Perform Cleanup ☑

Credentials
Credential Usage

FIGURE 3-7. *Component step*

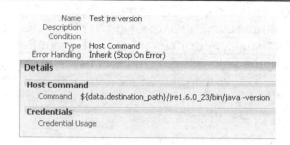

FIGURE 3-8. *Host Command step*

executes the directive with respect to the component. Components used for the Component step, typically, have at least one directive associated with them. This association is done by selecting both the component and directive while inserting the step.

A Host Command step, as shown in Figure 3-8, is a task that encapsulates simple host commands. This step allows the user to enter a command line or a script (multiple commands) to be executed on the target host. The user can either choose Perl or the default agent shell for running scripts, or specify a path to another interpreter that is available on the target system.

Now that you are familiar with the various pieces of the provisioning framework and the various artifacts that comprise a Procedure, you are ready to explore the possibilities for customizing Deployment Procedures.

Deployment Procedure Customization

Deployment Procedures support two types of customization: editing out-of-the-box Procedures, and creating new Procedures from scratch. Using a combination of these two types of customization supports automation of any provisioning and patching activity for both Oracle and non-Oracle products, and thus provides a single tool for the complete enterprise.

Editing Out-of-the-Box Procedures

The first type of customization enables you to clone an out-of-the-box Procedure and then make edits to incorporate the required changes. This function is called *Create Like* in Oracle Enterprise Manager 12*c* and allows you to make the following edits:

- Add new phases and steps
- Enable or disable phases and steps
- Change Procedure privileges
- Change error-handling modes
- Change e-mail settings
- Change credential usages assigned to steps

Making edits to customize the out-of-the-box Procedures enables you to adapt them to any environment.

Creating New Procedures

The second type of customization is the ability to create new Procedures from scratch. These Procedures are called User-Defined Deployment Procedures (UDDPs). UDDPs allow users to perform the same edits listed for the first type of customization, while also supporting the addition of new target lists and automatic generation of launch-time wizards. An example of an UDDP is shown in Figure 3-9.

NOTE
All three subsystems, Software Library, Job System, and Deployment Procedures, in the provisioning framework are enhanced with regular frequency. Refer to the product documentation on OTN for the latest information and list of new enhancements (http://docs.oracle.com/cd/E24628_01/index.htm).

Name	Install JRE on Linux 32
Description	Install JRE 6 on Linux 32
Type	User Defined
Last Modified By	ORACLE
Procedure Utilities Staging Path	%emd_root%/EMStage
envVarEditInput	

Profile (Privilege Delegation Settings)	
Last Updated	Feb 12, 2011 11:27:02 AM PST
Note	

Expand All | Collapse All

Name	Type	Description
▽ Install JRE on Linux 32		Install JRE 6 on Linux 32
▽ Default Phase	Rolling	This is the default phase for the user-defined procedure.
Transfer JRE	Component	
Test jre version	Host Command	

FIGURE 3-9. *Sample User-Defined Deployment Procedure*

Oracle Virtual Assembly Builder

Deploying applications in the cloud is a huge challenge. Typically, various components of the application are deployed individually and then manually wired together. Some vendors even allow you to deploy a bunch of VMs together, but you still have the hard and painful job of connecting the dots. The problem gets even worse if you start to think about other deployment constraints, such as which components should and should not be co-located, what the network topology of the application should be (i.e. Database and Middleware should be in different network segments), which components can scale out, and how should the scale out happen. Oracle Virtual Assembly Builder (OVAB) and Oracle Enterprise Manager 12c address this challenge.

Oracle Virtual Assembly Builder Studio, shown in Figure 3-10, is designed to help organizations create and configure entire multitier application topologies and provision them onto virtualized resources, which is an integral part of IaaS and PaaS. OVAB Studio enables IT organizations to take multitier enterprise applications—for example, a web server, an application server, and a database—and package them into self-contained, single-purpose virtual machines called software appliances. Going further, Oracle Virtual Assembly Builder structures the process of combining these

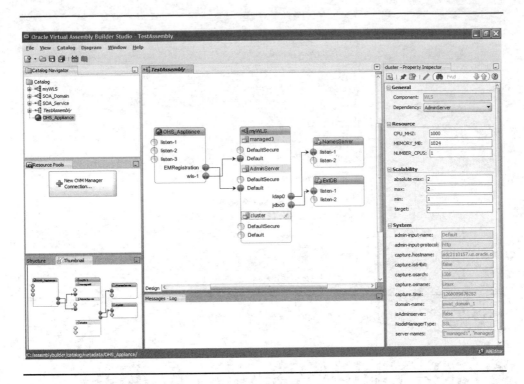

FIGURE 3-10. *Oracle Virtual Assembly Builder Studio*

appliances into cohesive, reusable units known as *Virtual Assemblies*.
It makes the necessary connections between these appliances and then
deploys the entire Virtual Assembly—which comprises the complete
multitier application—as a single unit. When that Virtual Assembly is
deployed, the components are configured automatically.

The key benefits of Oracle Virtual Assembly Builder are

- **Ultra-fast deployment**   Drive single-step, template-based deployment
  of multitier applications to virtualized environments

- **Operational efficiency and agility**   Leverage "fluid" virtualized
  hardware by dynamically scaling up or scaling down underlying
  software infrastructure and applications

- **Application-aware physical to virtual**   Capture the configuration of
  each software component from an existing application environment
  and package them into a collection of customized software appliances

Virtual Appliance

A virtual appliance (*appliance*) represents a single software component and its local execution environment. Depending on your choice of deployment technology, the component's local environment may be a single operating system instance or, using Oracle JRockit Virtual Edition, a Java Virtual Machine instance without a conventional operating system.

NOTE
Oracle JRockit Virtual Edition is a high-performance JVM specifically designed to run in a virtual environment without the overhead of a general-purpose operating system.

Virtual Assembly

The real challenge in deploying full-fledged applications is in the late binding configuration of individual component tiers. A Virtual Assembly (*Assembly*) is a collection of interrelated software appliances that are automatically configured to work together upon deployment. Assemblies are deployed onto a pool of hardware resources with minimal user input.

While an Assembly is simply a collection of appliances with defined interconnects, it must provide a set of capabilities, including the following, in order to be useful in a production environment:

- Allow for the composition of appliances and external systems

- Externalize configuration in the form of metadata that can easily be customized

- Optionally define the start order of appliances to reflect interdependencies

- Provide a management domain that integrates into existing management infrastructure, allowing for metadata definition, deployment, oversight, and diagnostics

In addition to being composed of appliances, Assemblies can also contain references to external systems. This is necessary to represent infrastructure such as databases, servers, or security providers that cannot or should not be included in an Assembly.

Life Cycle of an Assembly

Just like any other software concept, Assemblies have a life cycle of their own. Assembly creation and deployment comprises a four-step process, outlined in Figure 3-11.

Introspect

In the introspection phase, you

- Capture configuration metadata for individual software components

  or

- Collectively capture metadata for multiple distributed components

Target components may reside locally or remotely on multiple distributed systems, which may be physical or virtual.

Configure

In the configuration phase, you

- Visually drag and drop components to create complex Assemblies using appliances maintained in a navigable catalog

- Establish relationships and connections between appliances by using a wiring tool that automatically checks for protocol compatibility

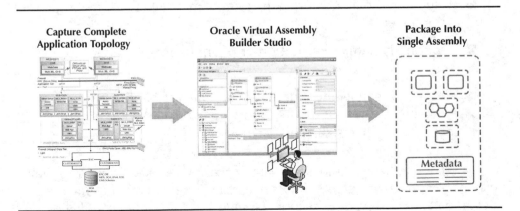

FIGURE 3-11. *Life cycle of an Assembly*

■ Create connections from appliances to external resources (such as database, security provider, messaging, and so on) that are not included within the Assembly

The configuration of an Assembly is stored in the form of industry-standard Open Virtualization Format (OVF) metadata.

Prepare
In the preparation phase, you

■ Create bootable virtual machine disk images with customized operating system distributions (for example, Oracle Enterprise Linux) and configurable metadata allowing for deploy-time customization of the software component

■ Optimize appliances containing Java applications by incorporating Oracle JRockit Virtual Edition

Deploy
In the deployment phase, you

■ Register multiple instances of Oracle Enterprise Manager 12c using their web service APIs

■ Publish all appliance disk images and entire Assemblies to the Software Library, where they are further published to the Self Service Portal service catalog

■ In Oracle Enterprise Manager, create customized deployment plans for Assemblies that override base configuration properties for appliances within the Assembly, and provide values for late-binding parameters

■ In Oracle Enterprise Manager, create policies to scale different appliance instances from an Assembly after initial deployment, based on usage statistics or time of the day (for example, add another RAC node to the Siebel Assembly based on high CPU usage, or shut down a server from a WebLogic cluster on weekends due to a low number of users)

Now that you have studied your options for software provisioning on both physical and virtual infrastructures, it's time to bring it all together by tying it to the out-of-the-box Self Service Portal made available for infrastructure, database, and middleware in Oracle Enterprise Manager 12*c*.

Oracle Enterprise Manager Self Service Portal

As stated earlier, self-service provisioning aims to enable and empower the end users to solve their own IT problems, thus freeing up IT personnel from performing the most commonly requested tasks. A self-service application or portal is an important aspect of this new paradigm. The self-service portal should hide the complexity involved in performing the provisioning tasks, while providing a simple interface to the user. In many ways, it is a pretty wrapper that abstracts and hides complex and involved processes.

Oracle Enterprise Manager 12*c* provides a rich and powerful Cloud Self Service Portal, as shown in Figure 3-12. This single portal supports three different cloud models:

- **IaaS**   For provisioning of virtualized servers with or without preconfigured software

- **DBaaS**   For rapid provisioning of databases

- **MWaaS**   For provisioning of a middleware container to deploy Java EE applications

The cloud users are able to log in to the Self Service Portal and identify the services (virtual machine, database, middleware container) they need, reserve some resources (compute power, storage, memory, and so forth), provision the services with minimal inputs, and specify for how long they will need them. They can also define policies to scale up or scale back their systems based on certain metrics or schedules. For example, a cloud user can select a two-node RAC database image and provision it to hosts with two CPUs and 4GB of RAM, and then specify a policy to extend the node whenever the utilization goes above 80 percent. Or, for example, a user can shut down some virtual machines over the weekend because they are not utilized to full capacity. More details about the Self Service Portal application provided by Oracle Enterprise Manager 12*c* will be provided in later chapters.

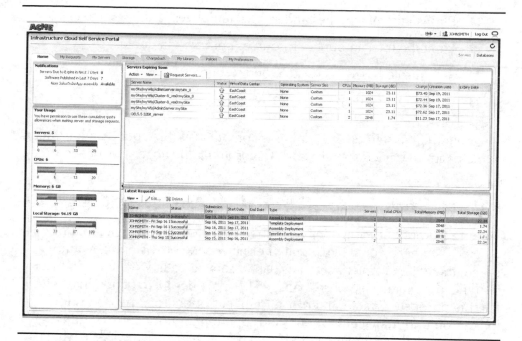

FIGURE 3-12. *Oracle Enterprise Manager 12c Self Service Portal*

The look and feel of Oracle Enterprise Manager's out-of-the-box Self Service Portal can be customized in a limited fashion. Providers can incorporate their own branded logos in the portal so that Oracle Enterprise Manager's role as the backbone of the provisioning process is entirely concealed from the corporate end user.

Oracle Enterprise Manager also provides administrative consoles that allow self-service administrators to configure the cloud resources and monitor and manage them on an ongoing basis. In terms of setup, the cloud administrators

- Provision prerequisite software (Oracle VM Server 3.0 or Database Oracle Homes, clusterware, and ASM)

- Create zones for Oracle VMs, databases, and middleware

- Create Virtual Assemblies and Database Oracle VM Templates and store them in the Software Library

- Publish the Assemblies and service templates to the service catalog
- Limit the total amount of resources per user via quotas
- Set up role-based access to cloud resources
- Create charge plans

Similarly, the self-service administrator will visit the cloud administration home pages to track resource usage trends and add capacity as needed.

Web Services–Based APIs and CLI

Despite the out-of-the-box Self Service Portal, there are many scenarios where customers would like to call the self-service provisioning features from either different interfaces or as part of some greater workflow. To meet such needs, Oracle Enterprise Manager 12*c* provides the required interfaces for this purpose. Oracle Enterprise Manager offers two interfaces for execution and management of cloud functionality: a command-line interface, called *EMCLI*, and a RESTful web service management API, which can be accessed from different programming languages. This management API allows users to request services like provisioning of Assemblies and databases, and track other aspects like usage tracking, querying chargeback information, and control state of your virtual servers and databases. Using this management API, internal groups, partners, or customers can develop client applications that can eitherintegrate with other third-party systems like ticketing, change management, runbook automation, and other target workflows. This management API can also be used to build your own Self Service Portal if you so desire.

NOTE
Refer to the Cloud Administration Guide, *available at http://docs.oracle.com/cd/E24628_01/index.htm, for more details on the supported cloud APIs and for examples.*

Summary

The notion of self-service provisioning is revolutionary and looks to be the future for end users' interaction with IT. With IT departments struggling with budget cuts and resource squeezes, while being forced to be more dynamic and function more as a service provider, it is not hard to imagine why IT departments would like to empower end users to serve their own needs and solve their own problems. Now that you have an overview of the self-service provisioning tools and the out-of-the-box Self Service Portal provided by Oracle Enterprise Manager 12c, subsequent chapters will dive into the details of this portal and address specific service types: IaaS, DBaaS, and MWaaS.

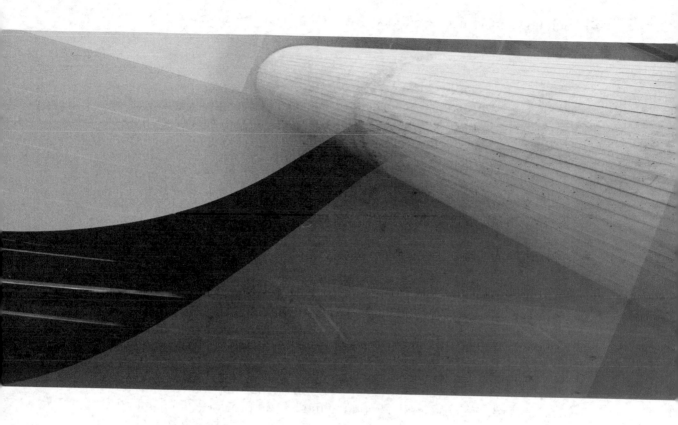

CHAPTER
4

Infrastructure
as a Service

nfrastructure as a Service (IaaS) was the first cloud service model made popular by Amazon when it started offering the service on a commercial basis in the form of early Amazon Web Services (AWS). In the IaaS model, the end user has complete access to and control over the infrastructure components, such as the operating system and the storage. What IaaS really is, then, is a transformation of server, storage, and network assets into a well-defined portfolio of services that other users can subscribe to and consume.

Just as an e-commerce website, hosted on certain IT infrastructure, provides a service to subscribers over the Internet, the IT infrastructure itself can be viewed as a service too. Instead of owning your own infrastructure, you can subscribe to an IaaS cloud. The cloud provider is responsible for maintaining and managing the data center (power, cooling, real estate, hardware assets, and so forth) and providing a self-service interface for you to request and interact with the hardware resources. As a cloud consumer, you can run any applications you want and deliver any services you like without worrying about managing the underlying infrastructure. The cloud provider can host several consumers like you on the same shared infrastructure. This shared services/cloud computing model can provide significant cost savings to consumers by offloading maintenance tasks to specialized providers that can manage them at a much lower cost due to efficiencies of scale.

For large enterprises, it may make sense to provide IaaS as an internally managed private cloud. One reason is that public cloud services may pose significantly greater risk, as the supplier is not under direct control of the consumer. For a cloud consumer, the potential cost savings of public clouds must be significant enough to offset the potential risks and legal complexities. Hosting noncritical, low-risk services on public clouds may help mitigate some of these risks.

Providing private cloud services to lines of business (LOBs) within the same organization makes a lot of business sense. The gains of consolidation and offloading are achievable without the legal and contractual risks of public clouds. The use of central IT to provide common services, such as infrastructure, database, and middleware, including security and integration, to sister organizations is a mature and well-understood IT business model. Cloud computing builds upon this model and formalizes the interactions between various organizations to increase agility, accountability, and reduced costs through optimal use of a self-service interface to IT resources.

In this chapter, we will discuss how Oracle Enterprise Manager 12*c* enables complete lifecycle management for an Infrastructure as a Service cloud. We will start by looking at server virtualization technologies as building blocks for the cloud and then delve into storage and network setup. We will explore different ways of packaging cloud services and configuring the self service application for use by cloud self service users. Lastly, we will talk about how cloud administrators can use Oracle Enterprise Manager for keeping the Infrastructure as a Service cloud operational.

Role of Server Virtualization in Cloud Computing

Server virtualization technologies help organizations create administrative and resource boundaries between applications. The system administrator uses a software application to divide one physical server into multiple isolated virtual environments. The virtual environments are often called virtual private servers or virtual machines (VMs), but they are also known as guests, instances, containers, or emulations. Server virtualization masks, or virtualizes, from server users the physical server resources, including the number and identity of individual physical servers, processors, and, in some cases, operating systems. This approach provides improved resource utilization and application security through application isolation, and also can be a vehicle for rapid application provisioning and reduced software maintenance by delivering preinstalled, preconfigured VM images of enterprise software.

Cloud computing enables the IT organization to administer resources for users on demand. Enabling the IaaS model, however, requires administrators to put automation in place to rapidly provision server, storage, and network resources. Server and storage virtualization technologies lend themselves very well to this kind of automation and thus are used extensively for enabling IaaS clouds. Virtual machines can be provisioned quickly and easily upon user request and with the right amount of compute, storage, and network resources. Users can also alter the configuration of these machines to add or remove virtual resources.

IaaS solutions using server virtualization can help companies to consolidate applications onto fewer physical systems to achieve better resource utilization, reduce the number of unique operating system images to manage, improve security, lower licensing costs, and reduce the time to install and configure software, thereby speeding time to market or project realization.

Oracle Server Virtualization Technologies

Because no two environments have exactly the same needs, Oracle's full range of server virtualization technologies provides varying degrees of isolation, resource granularity, and flexibility, and the technologies can be used separately or together to tackle specific deployment challenges. For example, companies can take advantage of Oracle VM Server for x86, Oracle VM Server for SPARC, and Oracle Solaris Containers to create cloud environments that can run a wide range of operating systems and take advantage of the latest platform advancements without changing applications, thereby protecting investments. In environments needing bare-metal performance and availability, dynamic system domains can be used to divide a single system into multiple electrically isolated partitions for the ultimate in workload isolation. When rapid software deployment is a key concern, organizations can use the preinstalled and preconfigured software images available as Oracle VM Templates or Oracle Virtual Assemblies to shorten time to market, eliminate installation and configuration costs, and reduce ongoing maintenance and operational costs. Figure 4-1 shows various server virtualization technologies available from Oracle, which are discussed next in turn.

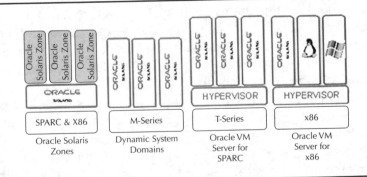

FIGURE 4-1. *Oracle's server virtualization portfolio*

Oracle VM Server for SPARC

Oracle VM Server for SPARC is a Type 1 hypervisor, which implies that the hypervisor runs directly on the hardware. In comparison, a Type 2 hypervisor runs on top of a host operating system. For example, Oracle VM VirtualBox is a Type 2 hypervisor that can run on top of Windows or Linux operating systems. Oracle VM Server for SPARC is a thin hypervisor that performs hardware virtualization on SPARC T-Series servers. As a result, Oracle VM Server for SPARC provides a technology for running multiple logical domains (or guests) on one system. Each domain runs its own operating system, such as Oracle Solaris, and is independent from the other logical domains.

Oracle VM Server for SPARC performs the subdividing or partitioning of a system on logical boundaries, such as a thread in a core in a CPU, and it divides the I/O resources through I/O services or by assigning I/O devices. Therefore, it is possible to have more logical domains than physical devices, which leads to sharing of devices between logical domains. This sharing can happen with the network interfaces, the boot disks, or the storage HBAs. To manage these items, you can create specific I/O domains. You can also create the domains in a redundant, highly available setup.

Another thing to keep in mind is that when a single physical device is shared among separate domains, the domains can influence the throughput of the underlying single physical device. Therefore, techniques such as using the network virtualization features in Oracle Solaris 11 can help define the networking quality of service (QoS) attributes for a specific domain.

The benefits of Oracle VM Server for SPARC include the following:

- No additional software is needed.

- No additional licenses are needed.

- The hypervisor adds no overhead.

- Oracle VM Server for SPARC is fully supported by Oracle Solaris.

- Physical-to-virtual migration/conversion tools are available.

- Fine-grained subdivision of multi-CPU and multicore systems (up to 128 logical domains per physical system) is possible.

- Cold, warm, and hot (live) migration is possible.

■ Oracle VM Server for SPARC is accepted as a licensing-limit/boundary by Oracle, which means Oracle software running inside a logical domain on a Oracle VM server for SPARC may only be licensed for the CPUs configured for that domain and not for all the CPUs on the physical server.

■ Oracle VM Server for SPARC provides support for and is supported by Oracle Solaris Cluster.

Oracle Enterprise Manager Ops Center provides management for Oracle VM Server for SPARC virtualized environments. As a cloud administrator, you can provision and configure logical domains and operating systems such as Oracle Solaris 11 using automated workflows. You can monitor and manage the hardware, including firmware, and guest operating systems to ensure a solid SPARC-based infrastructure foundation for your cloud.

This book does not cover Oracle Enterprise Manager Ops Center. You can refer to the following OTN Oracle Enterprise Manager Ops Center web page for more information: www.oracle.com/technetwork/oem/ops-center/index.html.

Oracle VM Server for x86

Oracle VM Server for x86 is a scalable x86 server virtualization solution that has been tested to handle mission-critical enterprise workloads. Oracle VM Server for x86 has support for up to 160 physical CPUs and 2TB of memory. For virtual machines, Oracle VM Server for x86 can support up to 128 virtual CPUs and 1TB memory per guest VM. Oracle VM Server for x86 supports industry-standard x86 operating systems and servers from Oracle and other leading vendors, and it supports a broad range of network and storage devices, making it easy to set up an IaaS cloud on Oracle and non-Oracle hardware.

Oracle VM Server for x86 has been designed from the ground up for excellent scalability, manageability, and ease of use. The latest Oracle VM Server for x86 delivers significant enhancements to make it faster and easier to roll out operating systems, enterprise applications, and middleware across your entire data center—not just the Oracle software environment—while reducing costs and making your data center or cloud environment highly available and secure.

Oracle VM Server for x86 is the only x86 server virtualization solution fully certified by Oracle. Oracle products such as Oracle Database, Oracle Fusion Middleware, and Oracle Applications are officially certified when running in Oracle VM–based environments. Oracle VM Server for x86 consists of Oracle VM Server and Oracle VM Manager. Figure 4-2 shows the various components.

Oracle VM Server

Oracle VM Server (for x86) software installs directly on server hardware with x86 Intel or AMD processors and does not require a host operating system. An Oracle VM Server is composed of a hypervisor and a privileged management domain (Domain0, or Dom0) that allow multiple domains or VMs (such as Linux, Solaris, Windows, and so forth) to run on one physical machine.

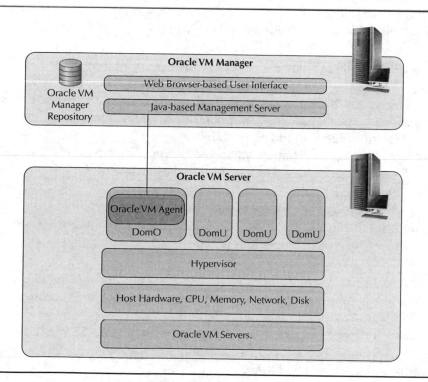

FIGURE 4-2. *Oracle VM Server for x86 components*

The hypervisor runs directly on the hardware, serving as the abstraction layer for all hardware operations from the guest OS, such as CPU, I/O, and disk requests. By separating the guest VMs from the hardware, the hypervisor is able to run multiple operating systems securely and independently. The Dom0 privileged management domain running on the hypervisor has direct hardware access and guest management responsibilities.

Hardware support (such as support for the network and storage devices) is provided by the device drivers installed in Dom0. Dom0 has unique privileges for access to the hypervisor that are not allocated to any other guest domains, which are known as User Domains (DomU). These privileges allow Dom0 to manage all aspects of guest domains, such as starting, stopping, I/O requests, and so forth. Users can perform all the management functions from the easy-to-use Oracle VM Manager 3 interface, and there's no need to log in to Dom0 to perform guest management or device configuration. Dom0 of Oracle VM Server is specially built to handle enterprise-class workload requirements. It leverages Oracle Linux with the 64-bit Oracle Unbreakable Enterprise Kernel (UEK), but has been customized and minimized for tight security and scalability in a virtualized environment.

Oracle Cluster File System 2   Oracle Cluster File System 2 (OCFS2) is a free, open-source, general-purpose, extent-based clustered file system that Oracle developed and contributed to the Linux community. OCFS2 provides an enterprise-class alternative to proprietary cluster file systems and provides both high performance and high availability.

OCFS2 is incorporated into Oracle VM Server software as the underlying cluster file system. The file system is used to cluster several Oracle VM servers into server pools. It is also used as a storage repository among Oracle VM servers to store VM files. In addition, advanced features, including thin provisioning and instant cloning, in OCFS2 enable significantly faster and more efficient VM provisioning and cloning.

Oracle VM Agent   The Oracle VM server (Dom0) runs a process called Oracle VM Agent, which receives and processes management requests and provides event notifications and configuration data to the management framework. It processes requests by interacting with the Oracle VM hypervisor, Oracle VM Storage Connect plug-in, Distributed Lock Manager (DLM), and the HA framework provided by OCFS2.

Oracle VM Agent also serves as a proxy agent for Oracle Enterprise Manager for managing the Oracle VM servers. Hence, installing a separate Oracle Enterprise Manager Agent on an Oracle VM server is not required.

Guest Virtual Machines   Oracle VM supports Linux, Windows, and Solaris guest VMs. Guest VMs can be in one of the following modes:

- **Paravirtualized mode (PVM)**   In this mode, the kernel of the guest operating system is modified to distinguish that it is running on a hypervisor instead of on the bare-metal hardware. As a result, I/O actions and system clock timers in particular are handled more efficiently, as compared with nonparavirtualized systems where I/O hardware and timers have to be emulated in the operating system. Oracle VM supports PV kernels for Oracle Linux and Red Hat Enterprise Linux, offering better performance and scalability.

- **Hardware virtualized mode (HVM) or fully virtualized mode**   When support for hardware virtualization (Intel VT-x or AMD-V) is available in the host server hardware, the guest operating system may run unmodified and depend on the hardware features to ensure proper operation in a virtualized environment. However, HVM can introduce additional overhead since it relies on binary translation and device emulation. But it brings the benefits of compatibility: largely, any "unmodified" operating system image such as Linux, Solaris, or Windows that is not virtualization-aware can run as an HVM guest without any changes, making it easy to consolidate existing physical server images, leaving them essentially untouched. With the recent development in Intel and AMD processors, in some scenarios, hardware-assisted virtualization will also provide performance benefits.

- **Hardware virtualized mode using paravirtualized drivers (PVHVM)**   This mode is identical to HVM but with additional paravirtualized I/O drivers installed in the guest operating system to improve VM performance. This allows the operating system to essentially run unmodified, but uses PV drivers that have been modified specifically to execute I/O commands efficiently in a virtualized environment to minimize overhead. Oracle provides PV drivers for Microsoft Windows. PV drivers are provided as part of the operating system for Oracle Linux and Oracle Solaris.

Oracle VM Manager

Oracle VM Manager provides an easy-to-use centralized management environment for configuring and operating Oracle VM servers and guest VMs. The browser-based interface supports the primitives required for managing storage, network, and clustering in the Oracle VM environment. Oracle Enterprise Manager connects to the Oracle VM Manager API to expose the virtualization management capabilities of Oracle VM Manager in the Oracle Enterprise Manager console. Oracle Enterprise Manager then builds upon these basic capabilities to provide a complete IaaS cloud management solution.

As shown in Figure 4-3, managing Oracle VM environments using Oracle Enterprise Manager requires that an existing Oracle VM Manager be registered with Oracle Enterprise Manager Agent.

TIP
For best performance and reduced network latency, installing Oracle Enterprise Manager Agent on the same machine as the Oracle VM Manager it is managing is recommended.

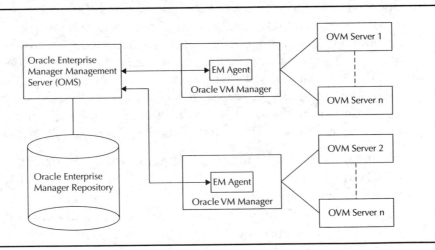

FIGURE 4-3. *Oracle Enterprise Manager architecture for Oracle VM Management*

Setting Up the Cloud Infrastructure

Depending on the number of cloud users and the sizing of workloads to be provisioned in the cloud, the right amount of server, storage, and network resources need to be provisioned. Furthermore, as discussed in Chapter 2, these infrastructure resources need to be grouped into server pools and cloud zones to provide high availability, ease of management, and mapping to business functions. Oracle Enterprise Manager provides automated workflows for setting up the cloud infrastructure.

Provisioning Oracle VM Servers

Your cloud project may involve buying new hardware or repurposing existing hardware for the cloud. Oracle VM Server for x86 software installs directly on server hardware with x86 Intel or AMD processors and does not require a host operating system. Administrators can bring new hardware into the cloud in one of the following ways:

- Bare-metal provisioning of Oracle VM servers
- Discover existing Oracle VM servers

Bare-Metal Provisioning

Oracle Enterprise Manager uses the standard Preboot Execution Environment (PXE) booting process for provisioning Oracle VM software on either bare-metal hardware or live servers with existing operating systems on them. It provides GUI-based workflows for easily creating standard Oracle VM software gold images and initiating automated, unattended installs of the images on hardware.

The provisioning process consists of the following two high-level tasks to be performed by administrators:

1. *Set up the provisioning environment.* Administrators are required to set up and configure a boot server, a DHCP server, a stage server, and an RPM repository. During the PXE provisioning process, the boot server is used to fetch the Oracle VM kernel files; the DHCP server provides the IP address and hostname; and the RPM repository provides the Oracle VM server software packages. The stage server is used to store the standard Oracle VM gold image configuration that needs to be provisioned.

2. *Initiate the PXE process.* Administrators launch the bare-metal provisioning wizard in Oracle Enterprise Manager to initiate the PXE boot process on the desired hardware by specifying the MAC addresses or subnet for the hardware machines. In the case of re-imaging existing servers that are already managed operating system host targets in Oracle Enterprise Manager, the wizard allows the administrators to pick these targets from a drop-down list. Once the wizard is submitted, any machines that are powered on the network with matching MAC address or subnet information are automatically configured with Oracle VM server software.

Upon completing the Oracle VM installation, Oracle Enterprise Manager also registers the new Oracle VM servers in the management framework, so they show up as newly available cloud resources in the Oracle Enterprise Manager console.

NOTE
For detailed instructions on using Oracle Enterprise Manager for bare-metal provisioning, refer to Chapter 23 of the Oracle Enterprise Manager Lifecycle Management Administrator's Guide, *available at http://docs.oracle.com/cd/ E24628_01/index.htm.*

Discovering Servers

Administrators can bring new hardware with preinstalled Oracle VM server software into the cloud by going through the discovery process in Oracle Enterprise Manager. It is important that the Oracle VM servers be configured properly for the discovery process to work correctly. Refer to the *Oracle VM Server Installation Guide*, available at http://docs.oracle.com/cd/E15458_01/ nav/portal_booklist.htm, to correctly install and configure the Oracle VM server software on x86 hardware.

Cloud administrators go through a quick wizard to provide the IP address or hostname information and Oracle VM Agent credentials for the Oracle VM servers to be discovered. Once the servers are discovered, they show up as managed targets in the Oracle Enterprise Manager console. The newly discovered Oracle VM server contains some basic information about itself, and about any immediate connectivity to the network and storage, but it is considered to be in an unconfigured state. After the storage and networking has been configured, the Oracle VM virtual servers are ready to be used in the cloud.

Network Configuration

One of the main tenets of cloud computing is resource pooling and sharing of common infrastructure among multiple cloud consumers. The network is one such shared resource. Without proper network isolation, cloud consumers can intentionally or unintentionally end up consuming a large part of the network, intrusively see data on the network that does not belong to them, or invoke attacks by intruding into others' networks. As part of the cloud infrastructure setup, it is important for cloud administrators to put in place a proper network design that includes resource control and security.

Segmented networks are often created to isolate network traffic for various applications owned by different cloud consumers. This can be done physically or logically. In physical network isolation, network interface cards (NICs) are dedicated to a specific application or group of applications, and thus physical segmentation is provided between networks. Logical network isolation uses software such as virtual LANs (VLANs), network interface virtualization (vNICs), or multiple logical listening endpoints to partition physical network resources. Traffic for multiple applications share the same physical interfaces, but each application sees only the network traffic and resources assigned to it, and cannot see traffic or resources assigned to other applications.

Oracle Enterprise Manager provides flexible network configuration options to support both physical and logical network segmentation when using Oracle VM as a foundation for IaaS. Before you define the logical networks in Oracle Enterprise Manager, you have to review the physical network configuration that you intend to use for the cloud, such as VLAN and subnet usage. You also take into account the number of network ports, or NICs, available to your Oracle VM Servers. The minimum recommended number of ports required on a single Oracle VM Server is two, although one port would suffice for test or demonstration purposes. Oracle VM supports both 1- and 10-gigabit NICs.

Creating a new logical network in Oracle Enterprise Manager requires you to consider two aspects:

- **Network elements** The network elements include network ports, bonds, and, optionally, VLAN segments if VLANs are used in the cloud environment. A logical network in Oracle VM is built on top of these physical connections. Each physical connection is called a network port. Other names for this physical connection include network interface card, NIC, or network interface.

- **Network functions** Creating various networks for different usage allows the administrator to control which traffic goes on which network. Oracle VM supports functions such as "Management network," "Cluster-Heartbeat network," and so on. This minimizes the impact of one type of network traffic on another. For example, Cluster-Heartbeat network might need to be a very low-latency network with dedicated traffic, to guarantee that the Oracle VM server pool failover functions properly.

You define a name or alias for each logical network that you create in Oracle Enterprise Manager.

Networking for Multitenancy

Different network elements provide different levels of physical and logical network isolation for cloud consumers.

Physical Network Isolation Separate physical NICs on Oracle VM servers can be used to carry traffic for logically grouped applications. In this case, vNICs of guest VMs owned by different cloud consumers map to different Oracle VM server physical NICs, thus ensuring isolation of traffic for applications owned by different tenants. Network traffic is still carried across the same set of enterprise switches and routers, so network convergence still exists.

NOTE
To have a completely isolated network, a siloed network with separate networks and routes needs to be in place. A completely isolated network is not recommended, as it does not promote optimal sharing of cloud network resources and adds significant management overhead.

The first step in configuring your Oracle VM environment is to discover your Oracle VM Servers. When you discover the first Oracle VM Server, the management network is created automatically and takes its name from the subnet to which the Oracle VM Server is connected. Each additional Oracle VM Server discovered from Oracle VM Manager either adds an entry into the existing management network or creates a new management network if the server is connected to a subnet where no Oracle VM Server was previously discovered. One NIC designated for the "Management" function is automatically added to the default management network.

Oracle VM supports bonding of physical NICs on Oracle VM servers. *Network bonding* refers to the combination of network interfaces on one host for redundancy and/or increased throughput. Redundancy is the key factor: you want to protect your virtualized environment from loss of service due to failure of a single physical link. This network bonding is the same as the Linux network bonding. Using network bonding in Oracle VM may require some switch configuration. In Oracle VM, there are three modes of network bonding:

- **Active-passive**   One NIC is active while another NIC is asleep. If the active NIC goes down, another NIC becomes active.

- **Link aggregation**   Aggregated NICs act as one NIC, which results in a higher throughput.

- **Load-balanced**   The network traffic is equally balanced over the NICs of the machine.

Logical Network Isolation Using Network Bridges/vNICs   Adding additional physical NICs to the Oracle VM server forevery application or group of applications belonging to a tenant is not always possible and usually isn't necessary. In Oracle VM, a physical NIC can be mapped to multiple vNICs via a network bridge to create network stacks that are kernel isolated and kernel dedicated. Thus, a physical network interface can be presented as several vNICs and shared between one or more VMs. However, each vNIC is assigned a unique IP address and MAC address; thus, from a Layer 2 perspective, each vNIC is distinct. All network packets generated by the VMs are sent to the bridge configured for the VMs' network. The bridge acts as a Layer 2 switch and directs packets to other VMs running on the Oracle VM Server, or to the port or bond if the packets' destination is outside of the Oracle VM Server.

When a logical network is created with the "virtual machine" function, a network bridge is automatically created in each Oracle VM server participating in this network.

Oracle Linux and Oracle Solaris, which can be used as guest operating systems on Oracle VM, come with paravirtualized I/O drivers for improved network throughput of vNICs. Oracle VM Windows PV Drivers, signed by Microsoft for the Windows Logo Program, are available to improve Windows guest I/O throughput. The management domain (Dom0) of the Oracle VM server has direct access to the physical devices. It exports a subset of the devices in the systems to guest domains (DomU). A virtual device driver (also known as a front-end driver) appears to the guest operating system as a real device. The network configuration is the same way and will look like a regular host with a MAC address, IP address, and so forth. It can receive I/O requests from its kernel, but since it does not have direct access to the hardware, it must pass those requests to the back-end driver running in Dom0. The back-end driver, in turn, receiving the I/O requests, validates them for safety and isolation. It then proxies them to the real device. When the I/O operation completes, the back-end driver notifies the front-end driver that the operation was successful and is ready to continue. The front-end driver then reports the I/O completion to the guest OS kernel.

Logical Network Isolation Using VLANs   A VLAN, as specified by the IEEE 802.1Q standard, is a method for segregating network traffic within a bridged LAN infrastructure. VLANs allow two logically separated networks to use the same physical medium, while not allowing them to intercommunicate without a Layer 3 device (router). This VLAN configuration is done at the physical switch and defines mapping between VLANs and ports. This configuration also allows QoS to be implemented at the switch layer.

Oracle VM supports multiple VLANs on the same network port or bond. Each VLAN is essentially an independent logical network operating with other VLANs over the same physical connection. This means that VMs deployed on different networks, connected through the same Oracle VM Server port (or bond), can have traffic directed to different VLANs. This feature is implemented using VLAN groups.

Configuring VLANs involves creating one or more VLAN groups, each of which can house multiple VLANs. Each VLAN is assigned a distinct VLAN identification. The VLAN ID is used by an attached VLAN switch to segregate traffic among the different VLANs operating on the same link. When a VLAN is configured, it functions exactly like a separate physical connection.

Oracle Enterprise Manager provides GUI wizards to create logical "networks" in the cloud, specify the network roles, and, optionally, configure them to use VLANs.

Network Roles
A network can serve one or more of the following roles:

- **Server Management**   This role is used to manage the physical Oracle VM Servers in a server pool, for example, to update the Oracle VM Agent on the different Oracle VM Servers. In Oracle VM, the management network interface and the public interface (that is, the default route) are expected to be the same on each Oracle VM Server. Other types of network usage are allowed on the same interface, for example, through the use of VLANs and/or network bridges.

- **Live Migrate**   This role is used to migrate VMs from one Oracle VM Server to another in a server pool, without changing the status of the VM.

- **Cluster Heartbeat**   This role is used to verify if the Oracle VM Servers in a clustered server pool are up and running. The cluster heartbeat role has a network component, where a TCP/IP communication channel is created with each Oracle VM Server. Each Oracle VM Server sends regular keep-alive packets, which are used to determine if each Oracle VM Server is alive. It is recommended to separate the cluster heartbeat role from networks with high load, such as storage and live migration networks. If bandwidth drops too low, connectivity within the cluster might be interrupted and the cluster heartbeat might not be detected, which could lead to automatic rebooting of VMs and Oracle VM Servers.

- **Virtual Machine**   This role is used for the network traffic between the different VMs in a server pool. The Virtual Machine role can be either standard inter-server (routable through standard switches) or intra-server (without a route to an external physical network and dedicated to the selected Oracle VM Server). Note that having multiple networks with the Virtual Machine role in one Oracle VM Manager is not only possible, but very likely.

- **Storage**   This role is used for all storage transport in a server pool. It is used by the Oracle VM Servers to connect to Ethernet-based storage repositories and server pool file systems. As with the Virtual Machine role, it is possible to have multiple networks with the Storage role.

To be able to provision guest VMs on Oracle VM servers, there must be at least one network with the Virtual Machine role configured for those Oracle VM servers. Figure 4-4 shows the various steps involved in setting up networking for the cloud using Oracle Enterprise Manager Cloud Control 12*c*.

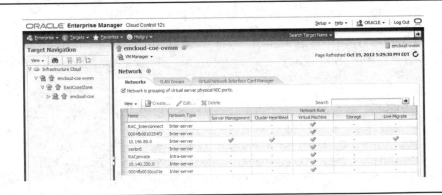

FIGURE 4-4.   *Cloud network setup in Oracle Enterprise Manager Cloud Control 12*c

Storage Configuration

Oracle Enterprise Manager can be used to configure a wide variety of storage types for Oracle VM–based cloud environments. Once the cloud storage is set up, subsequent VM deployments by cloud users will result in creation of either virtual disks (disk image files on a file system) or raw physical disks (LUNs accessed directly by the VM) on the fly. This automated provisioning and availability of storage for application deployments results in faster time to market, which is one of the key benefits of the cloud.

Oracle VM Storage Connect

Oracle VM Storage Connect is a partner program and a framework that provides a storage discovery and provisioning API. It enables customers to provision and manage partner storage platforms through Oracle Enterprise Manager, simplifying virtual infrastructure management and delivering faster VM configuration and control. Public and private cloud infrastructures using virtualized compute and storage services can benefit from accelerated provisioning and simpler, integrated management. An Oracle VM Storage Connect plug-in is written by the storage vendor to leverage the unique capabilities of that vendor's storage array and take advantage of the advanced features already built into its products. Oracle has partnered with several storage vendors to make available these plug-ins to customers.

In addition, Oracle VM Storage Connect provides a layer of abstraction, so virtualization administrators do not need to know the specific behavior of each storage array they control and are, therefore, able to perform many operations as a natural part of the resource provisioning process. This opens up a variety of opportunities and enables the IT organization to become more agile by reducing dependencies, shortening the provisioning cycle, and empowering the virtualization administrator to complete the storage provisioning process in the most efficient way.

Oracle supports two types of Oracle VM Storage Connect plug-ins, one for file systems and another for storage arrays. The Oracle VM Storage Connect framework is able to present the capabilities of these two different types of storage facilities in a similar way, and a user would need to have only basic knowledge of storage to be able to manage either of them. Depending on the storage sizing for the various services supported in the cloud and the number of service deployment requests expected from the cloud users, appropriate amount of storage needs to be set up for the cloud. Oracle VM allows the use of different storage types.

Using Local Storage   Local storage consists of hard disks installed locally in your Oracle VM Server. In a default installation, Oracle VM Server uses only the first disk (/dev/sda), leaving other disks available for storage. As long as no partition and data are present, the device will be detected as a raw disk. The choice is yours to use the local disks either to provision logical storage volumes as disks for VMs or to install a storage repository. If you place a storage repository on the local disk, an OCFS2 file system is installed.

Local storage is fairly easy to set up because no special hardware for the disk subsystem is required. Since the virtualization overhead in this setup is limited, and disk access is internal within one physical server, local storage offers reasonably high performance. However, the downsides are quickly revealed when you think about configurations with multiple Oracle VM Servers. Local storage by definition remains local and cannot be shared between different servers. Therefore, even if you set up a pool of multiple servers and use the advantages of clustering, VMs using local storage can never benefit from high availability: they cannot be migrated from one server to another.

Using Shared Network Attached Storage (NAS)   Network Attached Storage—typically NFS—is a commonly used file-based storage system. NFS storage can be discovered via the server IP or hostname and typically presents storage to all the servers in a server pool to allow them to share the same resources. This, along with clustering, helps to enable high availability of your environment: VMs can be easily migrated between host servers for the purpose of load balancing or protecting important VMs from going offline due to hardware failure.

NFS storage is exposed to Oracle VM Servers in the form of shares on the NFS server that are mounted onto the Oracle VM Server's file system. Since mounting an NFS share can be done on any server in the network segment to which NFS is exposed, it is possible to share NFS storage not only between servers of the same pool but also across different server pools.

In terms of performance, NFS is slower for virtual disk I/O compared to a logical volume or a raw disk. This is due mostly to its file-based nature. For better disk performance, you should consider using block-based storage, which is supported in Oracle VM in the form of Internet Small Computer System Interface (iSCSI) or Fibre Channel SANs.

Using iSCSI Storage Attached Network (SAN)   With Internet SCSI, or iSCSI, you can connect storage entities to client machines, making the disks behave as if they are locally attached disks. iSCSI enables this connectivity by transferring SCSI commands over existing IP networks between what is called an initiator (the client) and a target (the storage provider). To establish a link with iSCSI SANs, all Oracle VM Servers can use configured network interfaces as iSCSI initiators. The administrators need to do the following tasks to configure iSCSI storage for the cloud:

■ Configure the disk volumes (iSCSI LUNs) offered by the storage servers

■ Discover the iSCSI storage through Oracle Enterprise Manager

■ Set up access groups, which are groups of iSCSI initiators, through Oracle Enterprise Manager to determine which LUNs are available to which Oracle VM Servers

Performance-wise, an iSCSI SAN is better than file-based storage (such as NFS) and is often comparable to direct local disk access. Because iSCSI storage is attached from a remote server, it is perfectly suited for a clustered server pool configuration where high availability of storage and the possibility to live migrate VMs are important factors.

Using Fibre Channel Storage Attached Network (SAN)   Functionally, a Fibre Channel SAN is similar to an iSCSI SAN. Fibre Channel (FC) is actually older technology and uses dedicated hardware instead: special controllers on the SAN hardware, host bus adapters (HBAs) on the client machines, and special Fibre Channel cables and switches to interconnect the components. Like iSCSI, the Fibre Channel Protocol (FCP) is used to transfer SCSI commands between initiators and targets and establishes a connectivity that is almost identical to direct disk access. The same concepts previously described that apply to the iSCSI SAN apply equally to the Fibre Channel SAN. Both generic and vendor-specific Storage Connect plug-ins are available to discover FC storage arrays.

Registering Storage in the Cloud
Figure 4-5 shows Oracle Enterprise Manager console for setting up storage in the cloud.

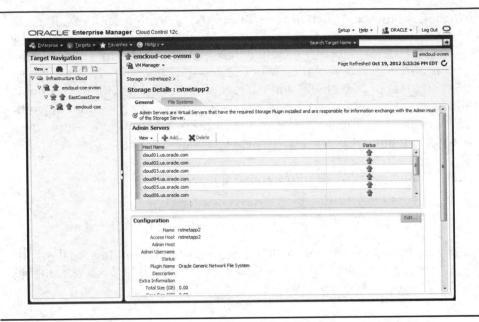

FIGURE 4-5. *Cloud storage setup in Oracle Enterprise Manager*

A storage file server (in case of NAS) or a storage array (in case of iSCSI or FC SAN) needs to be registered as a logical "Storage" entity in the Oracle Enterprise Manager console. Before registering the storage with Oracle Enterprise Manager, an external storage element is created on storage hardware: a server configured for NAS offering NFS shares, generic iSCSI targets and LUNs, or SAN devices from your preferred storage vendors. You have to make sure that the server or disk subsystem offering the storage is reachable by the Oracle VM Servers in the cloud environment through a Fiber Channel or Ethernet network. When using a vendor-specific Storage Connect Plug-in, make sure that the plug-in software is installed on all the Oracle VM servers that need to use that storage in the cloud.

After you have registered the storage server with Oracle Enterprise Manager, you can assign the storage resources to the Oracle VM server pools by creating a storage repository. A storage repository is a logical storage space on top of physical storage hardware, made available to one or more Oracle VM Servers in the same server pool or across various server pools. It defines where Oracle VM resources may reside. Resources include

VMs, templates for VM creation, VM assemblies, ISO images, shared virtual disks, and so on.

After you have created the storage repository, you can propagate it to one or more Oracle VM servers. When the storage repository is prepared and created, it still must be made available for use by your Oracle VM servers before it can be used. Typically you "present" the storage repository to all the Oracle VM servers in the server pool.

Creating Server Pools and Zones

As discussed in Chapter 2, the cloud consists of one or more zones, and zones in turn consist of pools of resources. In an IaaS cloud, these pools of resources correspond to pools of Oracle VM servers with properly configured network and storage.

Oracle VM server pools provide a boundary for live migration, which means any guest VMs running application workloads can be moved around from one physical Oracle VM server to another without disruption in application availability. Hence, it may be helpful to think of the server pool as if it were one big server with an aggregate amount of CPU, memory, storage, and network bandwidth. As such, planning for deploying VMs into a pool is much like planning for a server consolidation. It involves deciding how much aggregate capacity is needed to support normal and peak workloads as well as which types of workloads are appropriate to share the pool or server. Workload profiles should be considered in addition to how predictable or unpredictable the workloads may be.

Oracle VM server pools can contain up to 32 physical servers. In some cases, it is better to have relatively fewer but larger servers in a pool. In other cases, a greater number of relatively small servers or blades could be a better fit. Both deployments may provide the same aggregate CPU, memory, storage, and bandwidth, but the implications of the deployment in a pool can be different.

Oracle VM server pools can also be HA enabled, which means that if any physical servers in the pool fail, the guest VMs are automatically restarted on other servers in the pool. Although this functionality is very useful to ensure that the application workloads don't suffer long downtimes, it has important implications on workload performance. You should plan for enough excess capacity in aggregate across the pool to support running all guest VMs at appropriate service levels even when one or more servers in the pool are out of service.

Server Pool Capacity Planning
Administrators should allocate adequate resources when creating server pools. The pool capacity should account for both load balancing of workloads and fault tolerance.

- When performing maintenance on servers in the pool, live migration allows administrators to migrate guest VMs to other servers in the pool without interrupting service. To take advantage of this capability, there should be enough excess capacity in aggregate across the pool so that a server can be taken offline without inappropriately impacting service levels.

- There should be sufficient capacity to support hosting additional guest VMs on relatively fewer physical machines in the event that one or more of the servers fail and their VMs end up being restarted on the remaining, healthy servers, if only temporarily.

One or more zones can be carved within a cloud. A zone consists of one or more server pools that, in turn, contain server, storage, and network resources. As discussed in Chapter 2, the concept of a zone can be used for functional, geographical, or departmental segregation of cloud resources. Oracle Enterprise Manager provides a simple wizard to create a zone.

A zone that is marked for self-service use can also be exposed to cloud users through the Self Service Portal. This allows greater control for cloud administrators because they can restrict self-service deployments to only consume certain resources in the cloud.

Charge plans can be associated with zones to meter and charge for resources consumed in a zone.

Packaging and Publishing Cloud Services

The primary reason for cloud users to access the cloud is to consume services. In an IaaS cloud, this means requesting and relinquishing infrastructure resources in a self-service fashion. In its simplest form, this could be requests for machines with preconfigured storage and network or direct requests for storage resources. A more sophisticated version of the same is a request for a set of machines with a preinstalled and preconfigured application environment. As a cloud provider, the service design is aimed at determining what to offer users through a service catalog. At its most basic, a service catalog is a listing of services from which a user can choose, thus initiating the cloud service provisioning process.

When designing a service catalog, it is helpful to identify your cloud users to determine their needs. Potential consumers of services to consider while designing critical service offerings include:

- The development team of software engineers and testers

- R&D groups (for example, those engaged in scientific research)

- The application team in charge of building and maintaining internal applications

The challenge of service design is that there is a natural tension between users, who want the ability to completely customize their offerings, and the IT group, which has to maintain tight controls on the services in the environment. The role of the service catalog is to bridge that gap. The service catalog enables IT to define the areas of configuration and choice that users can select, according to their role. Users then feel some measure of customizability of their cloud services.

Oracle Enterprise Manager allows self-service administrators to publish standard software configurations in the form of Oracle VM Templates and Oracle Virtual Assemblies. These software components allow IT to standardize the deployments in the cloud, while giving enough flexibility to the cloud users to customize the service deployment as per their requirements. In addition, Oracle Enterprise Manager allows administrators to set governance policies and access controls to dictate what, when, and how much cloud users consume. The following attributes can be set by an administrator when publishing services in the Enterprise Manager Self Service Portal:

- Resource configurations, including CPU, memory, and storage sizes

- Operating system configurations

- Applications offered

- Networking options—simple network configuration to multitenancy support
- Quotas and access control
- Metering and charge associated with each component, if desired

Oracle VM Templates

An Oracle VM Template is a VM that contains Oracle or other software and is prebuilt, preinstalled, preconfigured, and ready to use. Templates can contain a complete Oracle software solution, such as Siebel CRM or Oracle Database, including the operating system (Oracle Enterprise Linux) and even your internally developed software or third-party software. Templates eliminate application installation and configuration costs, reduce ongoing maintenance costs, and help organizations achieve faster time to market and lower cost of operations.

Oracle provides out-of-the-box templates for various Oracle products, which can be downloaded from the Oracle Software Delivery Cloud (https://edelivery.oracle.com/oraclevm). The following is a list of several Oracle VM Templates, broken down by category:

Virtualization and Management

- Oracle VM Manager
- Oracle VM Template Builder Oracle VM Server
- Sun Ray Software
- Oracle Secure Global Desktop
- Oracle Enterprise Manager Cloud Control

Applications

- E-Business Suite
- E-Business Suite Sparse Middle Tier
- JD Edwards EnterpriseOne and JD Edwards EnterpriseOne Tools

- PeopleSoft ELM
- PeopleSoft FSCM
- PeopleSoft CRM
- PeopleSoft Portal Solutions
- PeopleSoft HCM
- Siebel CRM SIA

Middleware

- Oracle WebLogic Server
- Oracle Business Intelligence Enterprise Edition
- Oracle Application Server WebCenter
- Oracle Identity Management
- Oracle Fusion Middleware Service Oriented Architecture (SOA)

Database & Real Application Clusters (RAC)

- Oracle RAC
- Oracle Database
- MySQL Enterprise Edition

Operating Systems

- Oracle Linux
- Oracle Solaris

Oracle VM Templates can also be built by customers, by third parties such as independent software vendors (ISVs), and by solution providers. For building custom templates, Oracle provides a secure, minimized Oracle Linux OS that is freely redistributable and backed by enterprise-class support. Oracle Linux JeOS (Just Enough OS) includes a prepackaged, small-footprint Oracle Linux image for x86 and x86-64, along with a script to customize the OS image. With Oracle Linux JeOS, anyone can put their applications on top of a small-footprint, enterprise-class operating system and build a full-stack virtual machine or Oracle VM Template. The resulting Oracle VM Template is freely redistributable, without trial license requirements.

Oracle VM Template Builder

Oracle VM Template Builder is an open-source, graphical utility that makes it easy to use Oracle Linux JeOS–based scripts for developing prepackaged virtual machines for Oracle VM. Oracle VM Template Builder uses JeOS to facilitate building an operating system instance with only the absolute minimum packages needed for an Oracle VM Template, helping to reduce the disk footprint by up to 2GB or more per guest VM, and to improve security and reliability. Figure 4-6 shows the Oracle VM Template Builder console.

Oracle VM Template Builder is distributed as software packages via the Oracle Unbreakable Linux Network (ULN) and Oracle's public yum repository, but it's also distributed as an Oracle VM Template that you can download from the Oracle Software Delivery Cloud. For more information, refer to the *Oracle VM Template Builder Installation and User's Guide.*

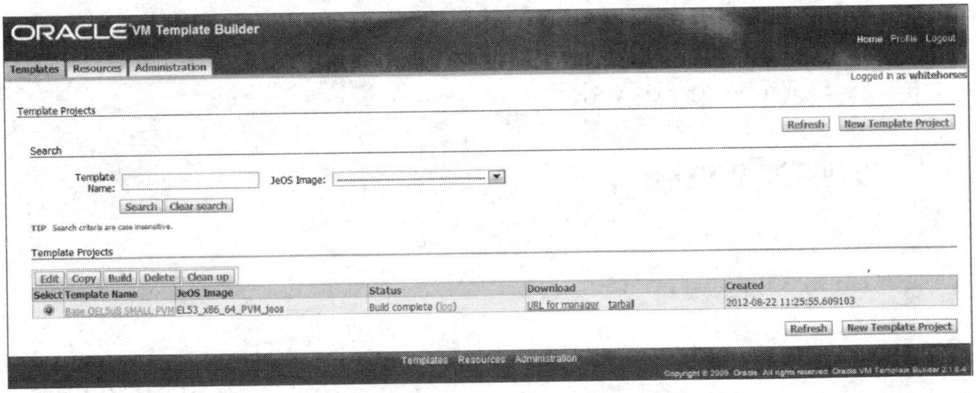

FIGURE 4-6. *Oracle VM Template Builder*

Oracle Virtual Assemblies

Multitier enterprise applications are increasingly being deployed in virtualized server environments to realize the benefits of consolidation and flexibility. However, administrators still follow the same time-consuming practices for installing, configuring, and deploying all software (operating system, database, middleware, applications, and so on) in virtual machines that have traditionally been prescribed for physical environments. The introduction of Oracle Virtual Assemblies brings in a new approach.

An Oracle VM Template packages a single VM that contains the operating system and one or more software components. A Virtual Assembly, on the other hand, is a packaging of a multitier application stack, which results in multiple wired VMs when deployed. In that sense, Oracle Virtual Assemblies extend the concept of Oracle VM Templates. Consider a typical enterprise application: An application stack consisting of a front-end HTTP server, middle-tier application server, and a database back end can be packed as a Virtual Assembly. All the software components can be preinstalled, and the base configuration can be done during the creation of the Assembly. This allows the designer of the Assembly to standardize the application configuration, increase compliance to IT best practices, and reduce security risks.

Additionally, the Assembly designer can choose to leave some of the application parameters unconfigured, allowing the user to specify them during deployment time. This "late binding" of parameters provides immense flexibility by allowing the users to customize the deployment as per their requirements.

Oracle provides out-of-the-box assemblies for some Oracle products such as Oracle Database and Oracle RAC. Customers, partners, and cloud providers can customize these out-of-the-box assemblies or they can package their own applications using Oracle Virtual Assembly Builder (OVAB).

Oracle Virtual Assembly Builder

Oracle Virtual Assembly Builder Studio is a graphical tool intended for use by application administrators to quickly create and configure entire multitier application topologies and test them for deployment in an Oracle VM virtualized environment. Figure 4-7 shows a screenshot of OVAB Studio.

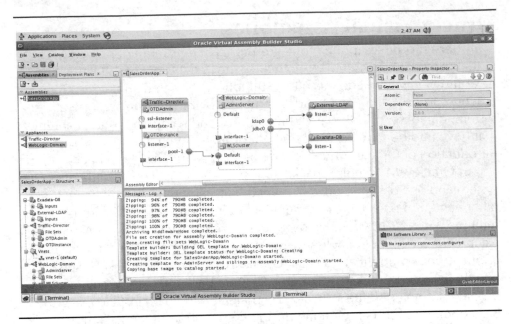

FIGURE 4-7. *Oracle Virtual Assembly Builder Studio*

The process of building assemblies using Oracle Virtual Assembly Builder consists of four steps: introspection, assembly, packaging, and testing.

Introspection   Assemblies can be built in either of the following ways:

- By capturing the configuration of an existing reference application environment and packaging all its components into a collection of customized software appliances

- By starting with pre-created, general-purpose software appliances representing the various components in an application topology

OVAB automates the former process of capturing the configurations of existing software components and packaging them into self-contained software appliances. This reduces the otherwise manual effort required to install and configure all the software into multiple VMs. Furthermore, incorporating additional metadata into each software appliance provides intelligence about starting up and configuring late-binding parameters for those components upon VM startup. This allows appliances to be treated like standardized building blocks that can be connected to each other to form assemblies, thus reducing time and eliminating errors associated with making multiple components work with each other.

The introspection process allows configuration metadata to be captured for individual software components or collectively for multiple distributed components. Target components may reside locally or remotely on multiple distributed systems that may be either physical or virtual. The introspection process can be scripted using the command-line interface.

Assembly   OVAB studio provides a visual drag-and-drop interface for creating complex assemblies using appliances maintained in a navigation catalog. Designers can establish relationships and connections between appliances using a wiring tool that automatically checks for protocol compatibility. They can create connections from appliances to external resources (for example, database, security provider, messaging, and so forth) that aren't going to be included within the assembly.

Packaging   Packaging refers to making the appliances ready for deployment in virtualized environments. It entails creation of bootable VM disk images with configurable metadata that allow for deploy-time customization of the software component contained in the appliance. For deployment in Oracle VM environments, assembly packaging introduces a customized operating system distribution (for example, Linux) into the appliance. Appliances containing Java applications can be further optimized by optionally packaging Oracle JRockit Virtual Edition, a high-performance JVM designed to run in a virtual environment without a general-purpose operating system. The packaging process can be scripted using the command-line interface.

Test Deployment   Once the assembly is packaged, it is ready to be tested. OVAB allows deployments to be tested in Oracle VM environments. Integration of OVAB Studio with Oracle Enterprise Manager allows assemblies to be uploaded into Oracle Enterprise Manager Software Library directly from within OVAB Studio. OVAB users can use an Oracle Enterprise Manager account to create a connection, and then upload the assemblies there. Once they are available in the Software Library, they can be versioned, tested by administrators, certified, and published into the service catalog for consumption by the cloud self-service users.

Figure 4-8 shows a connection from OVAB Studio to Oracle Enterprise Manager Software Library.

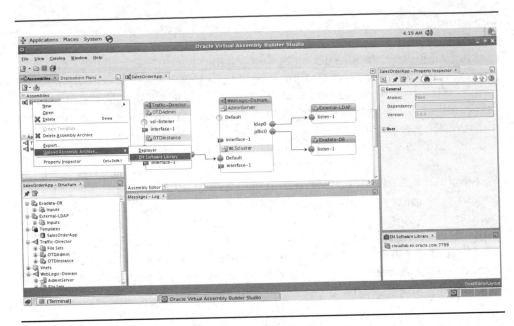

FIGURE 4-8. *Integration of OVAB with Oracle Enterprise Manager*

Setting Up the Self-Service Application

Oracle Enterprise Manager Self Service Portal provides quick access to cloud resources. Cloud users can deploy cloud services that are published in the form of Oracle VM Templates and Oracle Virtual Assemblies, administer requested resources, and get metering and chargeback information. But before consumers can use the portal, cloud administrators need to set the access control and governance policies for users.

Machine Sizes

An IaaS cloud allows users to request machines. Oracle Enterprise Manager allows administrators to control the sizes of machines the users can request. Administrators can define standard buckets of resources—for example, "Very Small" machine size can mean a machine with one CPU, 2GB memory, and 100GB local storage. Standard sizes makes it easier for cloud

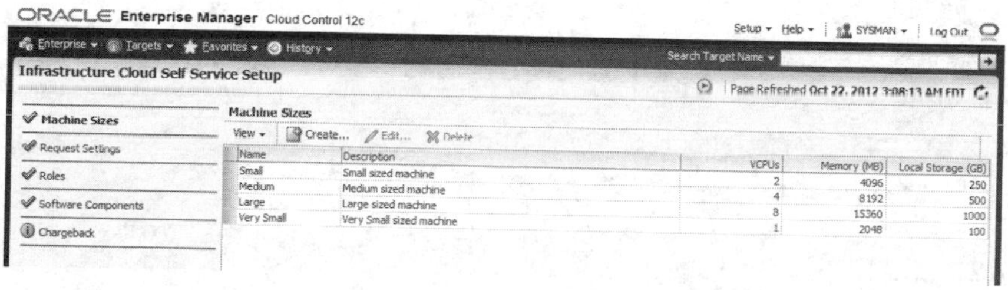

FIGURE 4-9. *Infrastructure Cloud Self Service Setup, Machine Sizes page*

administers to administer the deployments, plan for capacity, and optimize the overall use of cloud infrastructure resources. Figure 4-9 shows out-of-the-box machine size definitions in Oracle Enterprise Manager.

Request Settings

Traditionally, one of the problems IT faces is the tracking and retirement of machines provided to the users. Rarely do users willingly or unwillingly give back IT resources. With the proper implementation of the cloud, IT has more control. Administrators can not only track the allocated resources, but also set policies to reclaim them at set intervals.

Oracle Enterprise Manager provides this control. Administrators can dictate how far in advance users can request resources thorough the Self Service Portal and, once provisioned, for how long users can keep the resources. Figure 4-10 shows these settings in Oracle Enterprise Manager.

Access Control and Quotas

Cloud computing empowers the consumers as well. It lets cloud users request resources on demand without requiring IT to gate every request. Once the cloud administrator sets the rules, all cloud users play by those rules. Administrators can map certain roles of self-service users to certain zones within the cloud. This ensures that deployments by users with those roles land up on physical servers within those zones. This can be done for ease of managing user deployments or for allocating portions of the cloud for dedicated use by certain users or departments.

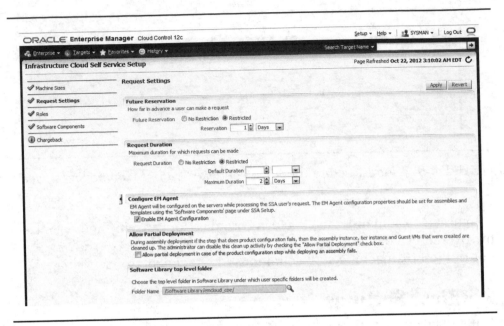

FIGURE 4-10. *Infrastructure Cloud Self Service Setup, Request Settings page*

Administrators can also constrain the users by defining fixed quotas for how much resources they can consume. For example, in your environment, you might want developers to not get more than five machines, or for testers to never consume more than 100GB of storage. Oracle Enterprise Manager allows aggregate quotas to be defined for roles of users based on cloud infrastructure resources such as CPU, memory, storage, and so forth. Administrators can also restrict deployments by certain users to certain networks through the use of network profiles.

Network profiles define a pool of static IP addresses within a subnet. Self-service users can be granted access to certain profiles, which restricts their deployments to use only allocated IP addresses within certain networks. Figure 4-11 shows the quota and access control for the Application Developer role.

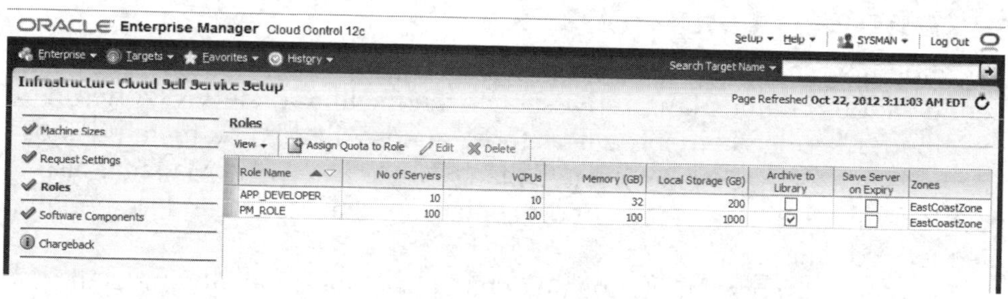

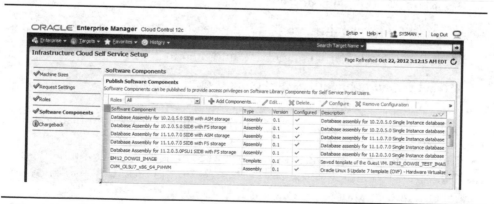

FIGURE 4-11. *Infrastructure Cloud Self Service Setup, Roles page*

Publishing Software Components

As you saw earlier, Oracle VM Templates and Oracle Virtual Assemblies are the primary mechanisms for publishing cloud services in Oracle Enterprise Manager. Administrators can store these components in Oracle Enterprise Manager Software Library and publish them to the Self Service Portal as required. It is also possible to publish different software components to different user roles, thus allowing cloud administrators to cater to the particular needs of different users. Figure 4-12 shows the Oracle VM Templates and Oracle Virtual Assemblies published in the self service catalog.

FIGURE 4-12. *Infrastructure Cloud Self Service Setup, Software Components page*

Setting Up Chargeback

Based on how the cloud users need to be charged, cloud administrators can define various charge plans and associate them with Oracle VM zones in the cloud. User deployments within those zones will then be metered and charged according to the associated plan. Oracle Enterprise Manager also enables administrators to set up cost centers for chargeback and to report on the metered data.

Chapter 7 discusses metering and chargeback functionality in detail.

Self Service Application

Oracle Enterprise Manager provides both API- and GUI-based access to its self-service application. The out-of-the-box GUI-based Self Service Portal can be used by organizations looking to roll out self-service functionality quickly. Organizations that are looking to build their own, custom self-service portal or wanting to integrate with existing systems can use the APIs.

The GUI-based access is essentially in the form of a configurable Self Service Portal that can be deployed as part of the Oracle Enterprise Manager installation. The Self Service Portal allows the cloud users to

- Upload Oracle VM Templates and Oracle Virtual Assemblies

- Request and retire VM deployments

- Request additional storage for VMs

- Monitor availability and performance of the requested VMs

- View metering and chargeback information

- Set e-mail notifications and other user preferences

Figure 4-13 provides a snapshot of the Home page of the Infrastructure Cloud Self Service Portal within Oracle Enterprise Manager.

Oracle Enterprise Manager provides a RESTful cloud API, which can be used to provision and de-provision resources in the cloud. It also allows management operations such as starting/stopping VMs and editing the configuration of VMs. The cloud resource model exposed by the API is shown in Figure 4-14. For detailed explanation of the resource model, refer to the *Oracle Enterprise Manager Cloud Control Administrator's Guide*.

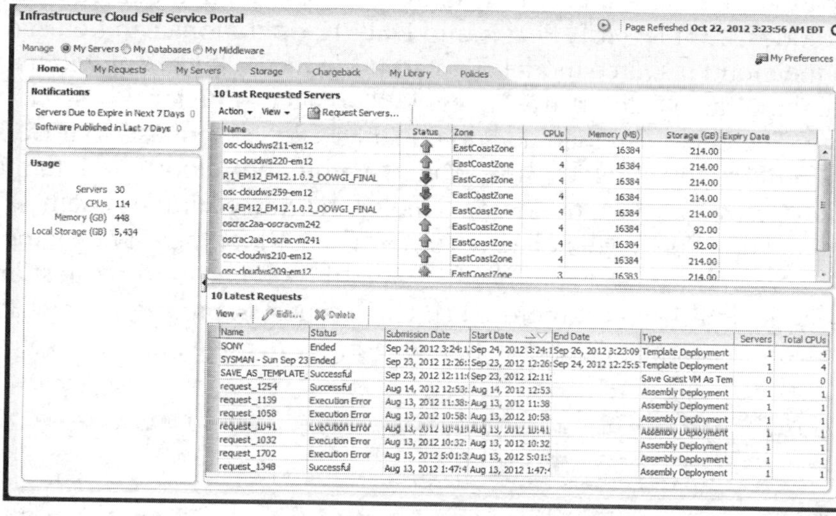

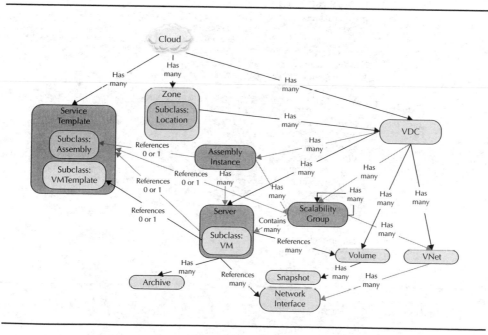

FIGURE 4-13.   *Oracle Enterprise Manager Self Service Portal for IaaS*

FIGURE 4-14.   *Oracle Enterprise Manager cloud API resource model*

Because the cloud API is RESTful, there is no state maintained across client requests. HTTP GET, POST, and DELETE operations can be used to access the cloud resource model. To start using the API, a client will have to provide the Oracle Enterprise Manager URL to access the top-level "cloud" resource. The client can then do additional HTTP GET requests to traverse the cloud hierarchy to retrieve the "zones" within the "cloud" and, further, the resources within a "zone." For example, an Oracle Virtual Assembly is represented as a service template resource. The URI for the service template can be retrieved from a "zone," which can then be used to request an assembly deployment. A sample HTTP GET request to provision a guest VM using a service template is shown below along with the expected response:

```
Example Request:
POST the following payload to /em/cloud/zone/2
        POST /em/cloud/zone/2
        POST /em/cloud/vdc/2?assembly_instances
        Host: cloudcompany.com
        Authorization: Basic xxxxxxxxxx
        Content-Type: application/oracle.com.cloud.common.
        AssemblyInstance+json
        Accept: application/oracle.com.cloud.common.
        AssemblyInstance+json
            {
                    "based_on" : "/em/cloud/ /servicetemplate/oracle:
                    defaultService:em:
                      provisioning:1:cmp:Virtualization:Assembly:
                      AAB9E4657CE9D9C5E040E80A9F546A81:0.1",
                    "deployment_plan" : "<?xml version=\"1.0\" encoding=\"UTF-8\"
                    standalone=\"yes\"?>
                    <ns2:ConfigurationData xmlns:ns2=\
                    "http://www.oracle.com/sysman/vt/
                     RequestConfigData\">
                    <AssemblyDeployment assemblyInstanceName=\
                    "MY ASSEMBLY DEPLOYMENT TEST\">
                    <SourceBinary type=\"TYPE_SWLIB\"name=\
                    "oracle:defaultService:em:
                     provisioning:1:cmp:
                     Virtualization:Assembly:
                     AAB9E4657CE9D9C5E040E80A9F546A81:0.1\"/>
                     <DeploymentTarget type=\"oracle_vm_zone\"name=\
                    "5F8E8D0DC97891BF465FBE49A20233DB\"/>
                    <AcceptedAllEULAs>false</AcceptedAllEULAs>
                    <InstallEMAgent>true</InstallEMAgent>
                    ...
                    </AssemblyDeployment>
                    </ns2:ConfigurationData>"
                    }
```

Example Response

```
HTTP/1.1 200 OK
   Content-Type: application/oracle.com.cloud.common.
   AssemblyInstance+json
   Content-Location: /em/cloud/assembly/byrequest/55
   Content-Length: nnn
   {
     "uri" : "/em/cloud/assembly/byrequest/55",
     "name" : "MY ASSEMBLY DEPLOYMENT TEST",
     "created" : "08/31/2011 8:45:04AM",
     "resource_state" : {
       "state" : "CREATING",
       "messages" : [
         { "text" : "The Assembly Instance request
           with ID '55' is being processed, and has Job Id
           '3SDI929SKDKL92SD9'"}
       ]
     }
   }
```

The preceding HTTP POST request is to request a deployment of an assembly with resource ID "AAB9E4657CE9D9C5E040E80A9F546A81:0.1." This response returns an assembly instance with URI /em/cloud/assembly/byrequest/55.

Monitoring Cloud Resources

Successful buildup of the cloud infrastructure and delivery of cloud services are only two stages of a successful cloud deployment. A large part of a successful cloud deployment is the management of cloud resources and capacity. It is important to ensure that the cloud security, availability, and performance requirements are met. The cloud infrastructure must have adequate capacity to meet the requirements of the cloud users, but it also must be monitored to ensure that it is optimally utilized.

Tracking Self-Service Requests

Oracle Enterprise Manager provides a Requests Dashboard to track the IaaS requests submitted by the self-service users. Administrators can view the status of requests and drill down into specific requests to view and monitor the provisioned resources. In case of failed requests, administrators can track the Oracle Enterprise Manager's back-end job and determine the root cause of the failure. Figure 4-15 shows self-service requests made in the cloud.

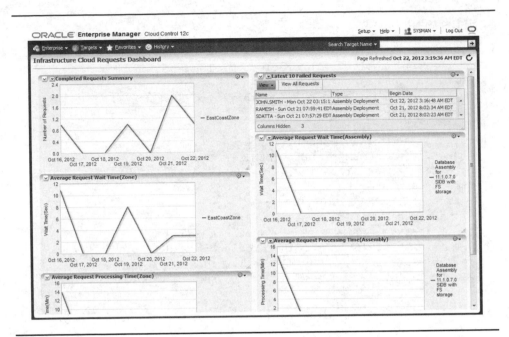

FIGURE 4-15. *Infrastructure Cloud Requests Dashboard*

Chapter 8 covers the monitoring and management of the cloud in more detail.

Summary

Oracle Enterprise Manager provides a complete end-to-end solution for managing the life cycle of an Infrastructure as a Service cloud. It provides automated workflows for setting up the server, storage, and network for the cloud, delivering cloud services, and managing and metering cloud resources.

Oracle VM Templates and Oracle Virtual Assemblies provide powerful mechanisms for packaging enterprise-class applications. Together, Oracle Virtual Assembly Builder (OVAB) and Oracle Enterprise Manager provide a complete solution for packaging, testing, and delivering cloud services.

The cloud self-service functionality can be consumed by deploying the Self Service Portal for a quick rollout or by using the cloud API. Oracle Enterprise Manager provides a comprehensive solution for not just building IaaS clouds, but also ensuring highly available, reliable, and secure cloud operations.

CHAPTER
5

Platform as a Service

latform as a Service (PaaS) is a model for deploying cloud computing services that provides a complete application development and deployment environment via the cloud. In the classic deployment model of cloud computing, the PaaS layer is drawn above the IaaS layer and offers a higher level of abstraction than IaaS. Unlike IaaS, which delivers bare-bones compute resources such as operating systems, storage, and networking, PaaS, as shown in Figure 5-1, delivers a complete runtime environment composed of all services necessary to deploy and run an enterprise-class application, including services such as application hosting, persistence store, application integration, and APIs that enable programmatic access to additional computing services that might be required by an application. Identity services are an example of APIs available within a PaaS environment.

PaaS assumes that the operating system environment may or may not be set up; therefore, in some cases, the operating system deployment is a part of the PaaS deployment, while in other cases the platform is deployed on top of a pre-provisioned operating system. In general, a PaaS environment may be language specific (for example, a PaaS for J2EE applications), but it can also offer multilanguage runtimes.

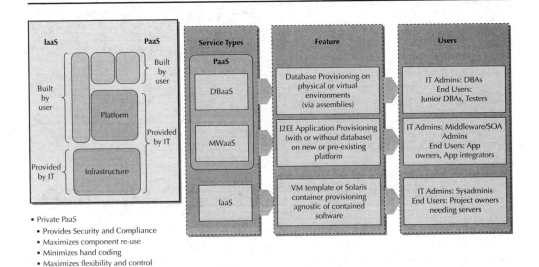

FIGURE 5-1. *Increasing enterprise value with PaaS*

An application developer is a typical user of a PaaS cloud. In this model, a developer can request the cloud for an application runtime and, in a few clicks (or API calls), deploy an application binary to the runtime. The developer does not have to worry about installing or configuring hardware, storage, networking, application servers, or any other middleware components. The platform takes care of furnishing all the resources necessary for deploying an application.

Once deployed, the application is ready for use. More importantly, the computing resources underlying the application are *elastic*—they can be scaled dynamically to accommodate variations in application load. From a cost standpoint, the developer is responsible for only the resources consumed while the application is serving load.

The most proficient PaaS environments also have built-in application monitoring and diagnostics. Any application deployed to these environments is automatically instrumented, and metrics concerning its health and performance are made available to the developer. This facilitates self-service management for the application, wherein the developer shares the burden of managing the application with the cloud administrator.

In a public PaaS scenario, the developer is almost exclusively responsible for the upkeep of the application. The cloud provider guarantees only that the platform will operate within specific service-level agreements (SLAs). The developer must optimize the application to perform within the PaaS environment. In a private PaaS scenario, however, the cloud administrator shares responsibility with the developer, given that both of them belong to the same enterprise and have a common goal—delivering systems that enable efficient business. Between the two, there is a lot more control over the behavior of the application. As such, it is conventionally held that private PaaS is better suited to production or mission-critical enterprise applications, whereas public PaaS is more suitable for development and testing.

PaaS facilitates the deployment of applications without requiring the developer to deal with the complexity of the underlying hardware and software components, thereby achieving cheaper and faster time to delivery.

PaaS offerings may also include facilities for application design, development, testing, deployment, and hosting, as well as application development services such as team collaboration, web service integration and marshalling, database integration, security, scalability, storage, persistence, state management, application versioning, application instrumentation, and developer community facilitation. In terms of Oracle

PaaS Market

In addition to Oracle, Salesforce.com (Force.com), Microsoft (Azure), and Amazon (Elastic Beanstalk and RDS), Google App Engine and startups such as CloudBees offer PaaS services. While Azure provides a .NET platform and Force.com provides both a Ruby on Rails platform and a Java platform, most others provide standard Java platforms. According to several industry analysts, by 2015, full PaaS suites will be available, delivering a combination of services in a single, integrated offering.

products, these could be further subcategorized into Database as a Service (DBaaS), Middleware as a Service (MWaaS) or Java as a Service (JaaS), Identity Management as a Service, Integration as a Service, Bigdata as a Service, and so forth.

PaaS can be hosted either in the public domain (commonly known as *public PaaS*) or within an enterprise's own intranet (commonly known as *private PaaS*). Oracle offers both flavors of PaaS as part of its product portfolio.

Oracle Enterprise Manager 12*c* offers a single management tool for creating, monitoring, and managing a private or public PaaS environment. Henceforth, this chapter refers to this solution as Middleware as a Service (MWaaS). Database as a Service is covered in detail in Chapter 6.

In this chapter, we will study the different deployment models supported by MWaaS. Followed by the three key roles that are required to setup and manage MWaaS and their responsibilities.

Middleware Cloud Deployment Models

Oracle Enterprise Manager 12*c* comes with an out-of-the-box solution for provisioning a complete application runtime on demand. This application runtime can be deployed in two distinct patterns: via Oracle Virtual Assemblies (*Assemblies* for short) on an Oracle VM ecosystem or via advanced automation in a physical cloud environment. These patterns are referred to as cloud deployment models and can be described as follows:

- **Java as a Service (JaaS)**   Java Runtime is offered as a service independent of the platform. The user simply defines data sources and deploys applications; no knowledge of the underlying infrastructure is required. This is primarily targeted toward developers who want to develop and deploy simple applications without any platform considerations.

- **Software Assembly as a Service**   The complete application environment is deployed via Oracle Virtual Assemblies as multiple Oracle VM guest images. This model is best suited for applications that require fine-grained control over application and platform configuration.

Each deployment model has its pros and cons, so it is important to select a deployment model that best satisfies the requirements of the organization. Some interesting considerations are

- **Platform dependence**   While Oracle Virtual Assemblies can only be deployed on Oracle VM Server for x86, JaaS, due to its abstract resource model, can support both physical and virtual platforms.

- **Initial setup**   When deployed to physical platforms, JaaS requires the operating system and required middleware software to be preinstalled, while Assemblies contain the operating system image and any other software required to set up the service.

- **Control over application and platform**   JaaS is best suited for simple applications that do not require access to a lot of application and platform settings. The developer can make do with a limited set of knobs to tweak the platform infrastructure. Assemblies, on the other hand, provide complete access to the underlying platform and allow for fine-grained access to both application and platform configuration.

- **Environment suitability**   Since JaaS supports simpler applications, it is more suitable for development, prototyping, and testing types of environments. Assemblies are a better fit for complex applications and thus better suited for production types of environments.

■ **Ease of management**   Since JaaS provides a Java Runtime, the user is not required to know or maintain any of the underlying infrastructure. In an Assembly deployment, the user is responsible for all activities, such as patching, backup, performance tuning, and so forth and, thus, becomes the administrator of that guest virtual image.

It is expected that most enterprises will adopt a combination of delivery models to suit their consumers' needs. For example, some simple applications, like wikis or internal blogs, may be deployed via the JaaS model, but more complex applications like Oracle Applications may require significant tweaking of the platform and, thus, would need deployment of a software assembly. Oracle Enterprise Manager's MWaaS offering enables enterprises to implement and manage multiple such deployment models using a single console.

Oracle Virtual Assembly Builder

Oracle Virtual Assembly Builder (OVAB) is a key building block of Oracle's PaaS offerings. It enables construction of reusable application runtimes that can be provisioned on the fly in a cloud environment. OVAB was covered in detail in Chapter 3, so this section provides just a quick recap as it relates to PaaS.

Provisioning complete multitier application environments can be a complicated and time-consuming process for administrators. Deploying applications on virtualized resources involves the additional complexity of configuring the operating system and all of the software multiple times in all of the virtual machines. OVAB offers a graphical tool, OVAB Studio, for creation and configuration of multitier application runtimes, grouping them into atomic units called Assemblies. It can then provision these runtimes onto the virtualized resources. In the context of PaaS, you can think of each Assembly as a "platform" that is provisioned when a developer requests resources for application deployment. When an Assembly is deployed (or instantiated), it results in multiple, connected software appliances, each representing one tier of the multitier runtime. OVAB takes care of the networking between each tier as well configuration of the components hosted within that tier. For example, you might create an OVAB Assembly composed of Oracle HTTP Server, Oracle WebLogic Server, and Oracle Database to create the classic three-tiered deployment environment for web applications. The resulting instantiation will have three virtual machines, the first containing the web tier, the second containing the application server tier, and the third containing the database.

Using this approach, application administrators can standardize the deployment environment to enterprise specifications, making their deployments relatively pain free and error free.

NOTE
Oracle Enterprise Manager 12c ships a wide collection of out-of-the-box Software Assemblies via its Self Update feature. Download and try these Assemblies to kick-start your journey to a PaaS cloud.

Middleware Cloud Life Cycle

Like any product in the market, the cloud has a life cycle of its own. Oracle Enterprise Manager 12c is designed to give users a unified and complete solution that works with the breadth and depth of the enterprise. Oracle Enterprise Manager offers a guided path through setup, use, and management of cloud services. Figure 5-2 outlines the complete cloud life cycle along with its various phases, which can be logically grouped together as follows:

- Plan and setup

- Build, test, and deploy

- Monitor and manage

- Meter, charge, and optimize

Plan and Setup

The plan phase guides you through the process of deciding whether to build new data centers or transform your existing data centers into a cloud environment. As discussed in Chapter 2, before setting up a cloud, you need to collect the infrastructure requirements, such as physical and virtual networks,

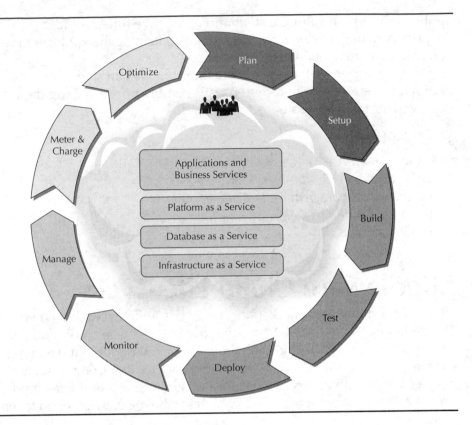

FIGURE 5-2. *Complete cloud life cycle*

storage arrays, and so on. Many of these requirements will depend on the type of application and the selected deployment model.

The *auto discovery* feature in Oracle Enterprise Manager helps you to discover and baseline all physical and virtual IT assets in an enterprise. Oracle Enterprise Manager's Consolidation Planner is a powerful tool that helps administrators plan the PaaS cloud architecture. It allows administrators to identify source and destination targets and applicable technical and functional constraints, such as where the application can reside. Administrators can generate consolidation advisories that may include plans to move from physical to virtual (P2V), physical to physical (P2P), or physical to an Exadata solution for your database platform.

The setup phase is all about putting the plan into action. Based on the choice of platform—virtual or physical—the setup phase offers capabilities such as bare-metal provisioning of the hypervisor, setting up of server and storage pools, and grouping them into zones based on functional or QoS characteristics. The setup phase also provides workflows for provisioning of WebLogic software, domain configuration, load balancer configuration, creation of admin and managed servers, and application of required patches.

Oracle Enterprise Manager comes with role-based access control, and integration with LDAP allows Oracle Enterprise Manager to inherit enterprise roles. Roles are also used to set resource limits, implemented with quotas that prevent rogue usage of a service while also preventing a few users from devouring the majority of the resources in the cloud.

Build, Test, and Deploy

Administrators can define standardized Service Templates for various WebLogic configurations, versions, and so on and publish them as services to the cloud service catalog.

In the build phase, Oracle Enterprise Manager uses Oracle Virtual Assembly Builder (OVAB) to help package application topologies as Assemblies for deployment on Oracle VM Server for x86, while it uses Deployment Procedures (DPs) for deployment on non-Oracle virtual machine and physical platforms.

After an Assembly or a service template has been built to support an application, it needs to be tested (test phase) before being published (deploy phase) to the service catalog. Oracle Enterprise Manager provides a testing portfolio that allows users to test both application changes and changes to the database. The testing solution provides the ability to capture a production load and replay it in a test environment, so that the results are predictable. The testing solution also leverages the diagnostic capabilities built into the technology layers and provides prescriptions for remediation. Tested Assemblies and service templates are then published to the service catalog. Once published, these services can be provisioned by the consumers via the out-of-the-box Self Service Portal.

Monitor and Manage

The operational aspects of the cloud are important and often overlooked. The MWaaS administrative home pages in Oracle Enterprise Manager allow cloud administrators to get a summary view of the requests as well as the general state of the service, such as zones, pools, servers, middleware containers, and so forth. In addition, Oracle Enterprise Manager provides the ability to collate targets into groups for better manageability. This Administration Group feature allows administrators to define monitoring settings, compliance standards, and cloud policies through templates. It also allows them to organize each target in multiple hierarchies, such as Line of Business and Lifecycle status. This allows the monitoring framework to scale to thousands of servers, databases, and middleware targets in the cloud.

Oracle Enterprise Manager comes with an in-built Incident Management system that can manage by exceptions. Administrators can review, suppress, escalate, and remediate the events as needed, and also integrate the system with ticketing systems. Oracle Enterprise Manager has the ability to define contractual SLAs that govern the contract between the application owner and the provider of the cloud. Administrators as well as users can also define management policies that automatically adjust the service resources to ensure that SLAs are met. Oracle Enterprise Manager's Configuration Management capabilities are optimized for cloud environments. Oracle Enterprise Manager can monitor vast numbers of configurations continuously, discover changes, measure drifts, pinpoint configuration errors, and offer insight into system topologies, all within a single console. Cloud management capabilities are also integrated with My Oracle Support. This integration delivers facilities such as Patch Advisories, Service Request Management, and Knowledge Management on premises and in context of the overall cloud.

Meter, Charge, and Optimize

With self-service provisioning becoming easier, there may be a tendency to overprovision. Lots of organizations are resorting to mechanisms such as metering and chargeback to control this consumption. The metering and chargeback features in Oracle Enterprise Manager support basic metrics like CPU, memory, and storage usage, and offer chargeback models based on fixed cost, usage-based cost, or configuration-based costs. Administrators can also extend the models to account for fixed costs, configurations, administrative expenses, people costs, energy utilization, or any combination of these. These capabilities enable enterprises to account for actual usage versus representative usage and also optionally integrate the usage data with billing systems.

Cloud management also entails an ongoing optimization of resources and processes to make sure that the service levels are persistent. Oracle Enterprise Manager provides administrators and application users with features that help them to rediscover assets, reevaluate performance, rebalance the cloud, and fine-tune the provisioning process. The tuning capabilities in the operating system, database, and middleware layers aid in continuous optimization and subsequent improvement.

Cloud Roles and Responsibilities

The cloud setup process spans multiple teams and multiple functions. All of the traditional administrators—storage, systems, network, security, and middleware—and the new set of administrators for the cloud services will have to work together to get the middleware cloud into place. In an effort to streamline the tasks to be undertaken, and to formalize the process followed by various teams, this new set of administrators can be grouped into the following three distinct roles that will coordinate and perform all actions required to set up the cloud infrastructure and to enable the service catalog and the Self Service Portal:

- Cloud infrastructure administrator
- Self-service administrator
- Cloud self-service user

The responsibilities of each of these roles are discussed in detail in the following subsections.

Cloud Infrastructure Administrator

The cloud infrastructure administrator (or simply cloud administrator) is in charge of putting together the overall cloud infrastructure, which includes both the physical and logical resources. The cloud administrator is responsible for

- Setting up the servers and storage using server and storage provisioning methods. The servers for MWaaS could be physical servers, hypervisors, or virtual machines, depending on operational needs.
- Setting up the network, physical and virtual IPs, VLANs/firewalls, and so forth.

■ Creating the self-service roles and users. The cloud administrator must ensure that appropriate self-service users can log in to the Self Service Portal. Also, specific privileges can be granted so that users are allowed to perform only certain operations. To achieve this, the cloud administrator defines roles that contain a select set of privileges to allow users to function as a self-service administrator or as a self-service user. These roles can also be imported from LDAP. Finally, the roles will be assigned to one or more users based on their function.

■ Setting up the Software Library. The Software Library can be co-located with the Management Server or set up remotely, depending on the location of the zones of the cloud.

■ Deploying Oracle Enterprise Manager agents and configuring credentials.

■ Setting up the PaaS Infrastructure Zones (discussed in Chapter 2).

■ Setting up the infrastructure to support various file transfer methods between the Software Library and the end servers that can be consumed by the procedures. This could involve using web servers for HTTP access, using the Oracle Enterprise Manager agent-to-agent transfer mechanism, or using NFS mounted copies (more popularly known as *thin provisioning*).

This role ensures the standardization of infrastructure to be procured so as to be used in the cloud across both physical and virtual environments. Since the tasks performed by this role span multiple tiers of the software stack, no one person can perform all these tasks and, hence, it is quite likely that multiple administrators—hardware, storage, network, security, and system—will wear this role's hat or that a cloud architect will coordinate these details with the aforementioned set of administrators.

Once all required infrastructure has been set up by the cloud administrator, the self-service administrator takes the process forward by defining various middleware pools, as discussed next.

Self-Service Administrator

The self-service administrator (alternatively known as the MWaaS administrator, or just service administrator) is responsible for setting up the service catalog and the Self Service Portal. MWaaS administrators can set up the Self Service Portal in a way that standardizes application deployments, complies with the datacenter best practices, and responds to the needs of the business users.

The MWaaS administrator is responsible for

- Setting up the middleware pools

- Creating quotas and assigning them to roles

- Configuring request settings

- Setting up the provisioning flows (Deployment Procedures) and publishing them to the service catalog as Service Templates

- Creating a chargeback plan and associating it with a zone

- Tracking request progress and managing the cloud resources on an ongoing basis

Each of these tasks is described in turn in the following subsections.

Setting Up the Middleware Pools

As mentioned, the setup of middleware pools is the responsibility of the MWaaS administrator. A pool is a logical grouping of servers with a homogeneous configuration. These servers could be using off-the-shelf hardware or could be part of a highly optimized engineered system such as the Oracle Exalogic Elastic Cloud appliance. (More details on Exalogic are provided toward the end of the chapter.) A cloud consumer (self-service user) must specify a zone (and indirectly a pool) when submitting a provisioning request via the Self Service Portal. As a prerequisite, the middleware (WebLogic) software needs to be installed on all servers that will belong to a pool.

The mandatory criteria for creating pools include

- Platform type (such as Linux 64-bit, Solaris, AIX, etc.)

- WebLogic software version (such as 10.3.1, 10.3.5, etc.)

Besides the mandatory criteria enforced by the product, administrators can use other, optional attributes to define homogeneous pools. Some of the many optional criteria for creating pools include

- SLAs (mission critical vs. noncritical)
- Security or regulatory compliance (PCI, HIPPA, etc.)
- Quality of service (such as Tier 1 vs. Tier 2 storage)

A sample pool administrative home page is shown in Figure 5-3. The homogeneity maintained between the members of a pool is required for ease of administration, to maintain operational consistency, and to guarantee provisioning success. Any cloud service has to provide the abstraction such that the quality of service becomes independent of placement. The homogeneity in terms of configuration guarantees that.

To protect the members of a pool from being abused due to over allocation of resources, Oracle Enterprise Manager 12*c* introduced the concept of *placement policy constraints* to the pool creation flow. Placement policy constraints can be used to set a maximum ceiling for any host in the zone and pool. These values are used during provisioning to filter out hosts that are overburdened. The constraints are partly defined at the PaaS Infrastructure

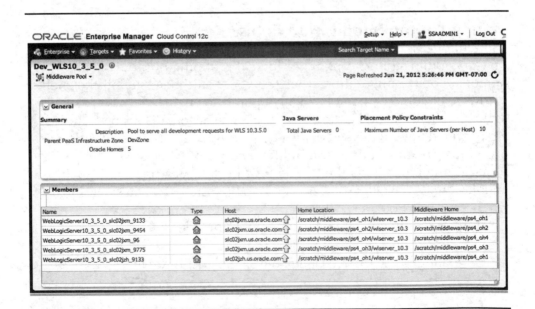

FIGURE 5-3. *Middleware pool member details*

Zone level and partly at the middleware pool level, but they apply to all the members of the pools. These constraints are taken into consideration when provisioning within a pool:

- **Maximum CPU Utilization**   Defined at the zone level; the average CPU utilization (expressed as a percentage) over the past 7 days (or fewer if the host metric collection duration is under 7 days)

- **Maximum Memory Allocation**   Defined at the zone level; the average memory utilization (expressed as a percentage) over the past 7 days (or fewer if the host metric collection duration is under 7 days)

- **Maximum Number of Java Servers (per host)**   Defined at the pool level; the number of Java servers that can be created on every host that is part of the middleware pool

Creating Quotas and Assigning Them to Roles

While the cloud gives the perception of infinite resources, such is not the case. MWaaS administrators may want to restrict the resources used by self-service users either to control the rate at which cloud resources are consumed or to restrict access based on budget allocation. Oracle Enterprise Manager 12c allows the MWaaS administrator to set quotas against self-service user roles, which in turn apply to the individual users. The supported quota attributes, as shown in Figure 5-4, are

- Number of application servers (or Java servers) that can be owned by the user at any point in time

- Total memory that can be assigned to a user for all the databases that the user owns

A user can be assigned multiple roles, and thus may inherit multiple quota limits. In such cases, the highest value assigned to a quota attribute is selected. For example, suppose the user is part of two roles that have different quota limits:

Role Name	Attribute	Value
DEV_USER_ROLE	Memory	10GB
	Java Server Count	5
TEST_USER_ROLE	Memory	15GB
	Java Server Count	3

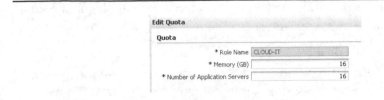

FIGURE 5-4. *Setting up a quota*

The effective quota limits for this user would be

Memory = MAX (10, 15) = 15GB
Java Server Count = MAX (5, 3) = 5

TIP
This is an effective way to boost the quota limits for a select set of users, but it requires proper planning because some users may unknowingly get access to more resources than the administrator desired.

Configuring Request Settings

While by default the self-service user can request resources for any duration of time, and can even schedule such a request for any time in the future, the MWaaS administrator does have the ability to override some of these request settings. The three options available to the MWaaS administrator are

■ **Future Reservation**   How far in advance a user can make a request. The default is set to No Restriction but can be limited to days, weeks, months, or years.

■ **Request Archive Retention**   Maximum duration after which an archived request will be automatically deleted by the system. The default is set to No Restriction but can be limited to days, weeks, months, or years.

■ **Request Duration**   Maximum duration for which requests can be made. The default is set to No Restriction but can be limited to days, weeks, months, or years.

A good example of a situation in which these settings might be used would be when rolling out a limited-time beta within an organization. They might be configured to allow, say, all developers to use a basic service template for a duration of 30 days, and allow them to request this database only a day in advance.

Setting Up Provisioning Flows and Publishing Them to Service Catalog as Service Templates

The self-service user selects a middleware Assembly on the Oracle VM platform (or a service template on a non-Oracle VM platform) for provisioning their desired application container configuration.

Middleware Assemblies   The MWaaS administrator can use Oracle Virtual Assembly Builder Studio to build middleware Assemblies.

Service Templates   For defining Service Templates, the administrator configures and saves the Middleware Provisioning Deployment Procedure. The Deployment Procedure allows users to run through an intuitive wizard that displays all inputs required to successfully execute the procedure. The following values need to be provided:

- Middleware profile

- Dummy destination host and its credentials ("dummy" because it will be replaced by the actual destination host during runtime)

- An existing Middleware home

- Domain name and WebLogic username and password

Once you have finalized the input values to the procedure, save the procedure for future use. To use a saved Deployment Procedure as a Service Template, launch the Service Template creation wizard from the Middleware Cloud setup page and select the saved Deployment Procedure.

The Service Template Wizard will let the MWaaS administrator set the following values:

- WebLogic username and password (these override the values set in the earlier Deployment Procedure)

- Ports range start and end values (the upper and lower bounds for choosing free ports)

- Memory usage per instance (memory, in gigabytes, for each additional instance)

- CPU usage per instance (CPU, in percentage, required for each additional instance)

A Service Template stores a reference to a saved Deployment Procedure along with some additional metadata. The metadata includes a meaningful name and description, a list of suitable zones and pools, and a list of roles that are allowed to execute the Service Template. A sample service catalog is shown in Table 5-1.

ID	Service Name	Description	Attributes	QoS Level	Service Contact
1	Small Java Service	Installs WebLogic 10.3.5	Heap = 4GB Cluster = 1 node	Gold	john.doe@acme.com
2	Medium Java Service	Installs WebLogic 10.3.5	Heap = 8GB Cluster = 1 node	Silver	jane.smith@acme.com
3	Large Java Service	Installs WebLogic 10.3.5	Heap = 12GB Cluster = 1 node	Gold	joe.smith@acme.com

TABLE 5-1. *Sample Middleware Service Catalog*

When a self-service user submits a request to provision a Service Template, the following steps are executed:

1. Initialization

2. User quota validation

3. Placement logic execution to find a suitable host

4. Domain creation

5. Deployment of Java application (optional)

Each step is described in turn next.

Step 1: Initialization   All values entered by the administrator, as part of the saved Deployment Procedure and service template, are aggregated and checked for data integrity.

Step 2: User Quota Validation   The user's current usage is evaluated against the quota limits set by the MWaaS administrator. The request fails if the resources required for the requested Java service template are above the quota limits.

Step 3: Placement Logic Execution to Find a Suitable Host   The purpose of the placement logic is to find a suitable host that can be used to create the domain and the Java server. In this step, to derive a list of suitable candidates, various computations are made, and therein lies the secret sauce. The placement logic considers

■ Average load (CPU and memory) over the last week on the hosts in the selected pool

■ Configuration, such as the current population (the number of Java instances) on each host

■ The placement policy constraint limits

Since all required data is regularly collected via performance and configuration metrics, the placement is handled automatically by Oracle Enterprise Manager. The first host that is selected by the placement logic is used for the Java server creation. At the time of writing, First-Match is the only algorithm used by the placement logic. There are plans to support other algorithms in the future, such as Best-Match, to find the host with the most available resources.

Step 4: Domain Creation   In this step, the actual WebLogic domain is created as per the configuration captured by the selected service template. Since a service template is just a wrapper, the actual creation of the domain is orchestrated by the Middleware Provisioning procedure.

Step 5: Deployment of Java Application   As part of the Java server creation, the user can optionally deploy a Java application that has been uploaded to the My Library tab in the Middleware Cloud Self Service Portal. This facility is provided for ease of use in cases where the user wants to deploy a single application to the WebLogic application server. But this may not be the most common scenario, as users may opt to deploy multiple applications to the same Java server. The portal allows users to create multiple data sources and deploy numerous applications as they see fit.

This completes the setup of Provisioning Flows.

Creating a Chargeback Plan and Associating It with a Zone

Since MWaaS is all about sharing a common infrastructure, it is important to meter the resources users consume and, optionally, charge them for their usage. Unlike siloed environments, where resources are dedicated, in a cloud environment, resources are shared, which makes it challenging to accurately measure resource usage across different users. Oracle Enterprise Manager's metering and chargeback features help to overcome this challenge. As part of the MWaaS setup, the administrator will associate a chargeback plan with the zone. This chargeback plan is applied to the middleware targets, once they are created as part of the service provisioning. The chargeback plan can be based on a flat rate or it can be usage based or configuration based. An example of a configuration-based chargeback plan is one that charges a higher rate for lower middleware versions, because lower versions incur more maintenance overhead. Metering and chargeback topics are covered extensively in Chapter 7.

Tracking Request Progress and Managing the Cloud Resources on an Ongoing Basis

The MWaaS administrator can track the progress or the status of any requests from the Requests Dashboard. Alternatively, the administrator can visit the zone or pool home page, as shown in Figure 5-5, to see the breakdown of all requests by zone or pool. Usually, considering the volume of requests in a cloud environment, there is no need for the administrator to track every request. The only exception to this rule would be tracking of failed requests. Besides request details, the administrator should also be able to view metering and chargeback information for other MWaaS users and roll them up using LDAP and/or group-based hierarchies.

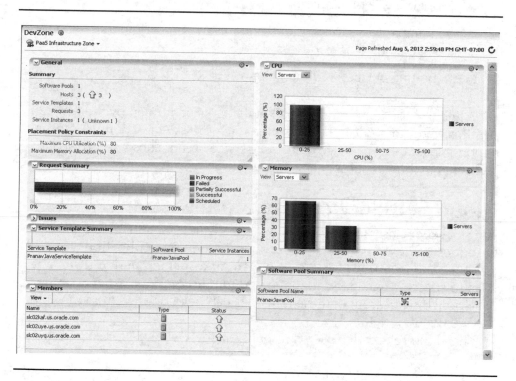

FIGURE 5-5.   *PaaS Infrastructure Zone administration console*

NOTE
For more information on Oracle Enterprise Manager 12c Cloud Management features, refer to the Oracle Enterprise Manager Cloud Administration Guide *in the documentation library available on OTN (http://docs.oracle.com/cd/E24628_01/index.htm).*

Other tasks performed by the MWaaS administrator on an ongoing basis are

- Patching Middleware Oracle homes
- Monitoring pool members
- Sending requests to the cloud administrator for additional memory, storage, and other resources
- Reporting outages and maintaining SLAs

While this list doesn't include all of the tasks performed by the MWaaS administrator, in a nutshell, the self-service or MWaaS administrator is responsible for the experience of the self-service user or consumer. This topic is covered in detail in subsequent chapters.

Cloud Self-Service User

The self-service user (or simply *user*) takes advantage of the cloud platform to request Java servers, create data sources, deploy applications, scale up/down the Java server, use the service for a specific period (from a few days to several years), and manage and monitor various aspects of the provisioned service. All of these functions can be performed from the Self Service Portal.

The cloud self-service user is responsible for

- Creating a middleware service
- Tracking requests
- Managing the application life cycle
- Scaling up/down the middleware service
- Uploading JEE components to Software Library

Creating a Middleware Service

To provision a middleware service with the desired configuration, the user chooses from a list of service templates by clicking on the Request Service button on the home page. Each service template requires the user to provide certain inputs as designated by the MWaaS administrator. Some mandatory inputs required for a database request are

- Service name

- PaaS Infrastructure Zone

- Schedule (start date and end date)

- (Optionally) Application name, component in the library, and deployment plan

The out-of-the-box Middleware Cloud Self Service Portal is shown in Figure 5-6.

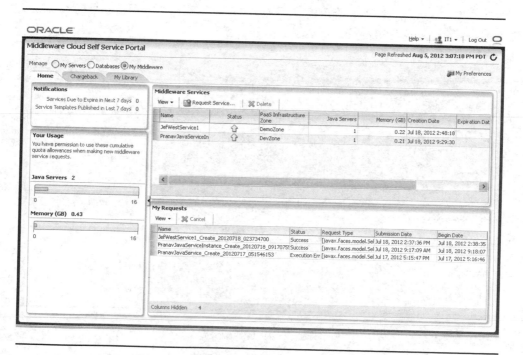

FIGURE 5-6.   *Middleware Cloud Self Service Portal*

Tracking Requests

The user can track the progress of a request by using the My Requests panel. A request will transition through various states, such as Scheduled, Running, Succeeded, Retired, and so forth.

Managing the Application Life Cycle

The Middleware Service home page, shown in Figure 5-7, displays detailed information about all components included in the service request:

- **Performance Summary** Shows the availability status of the service, the number of servers, and the performance metrics for the service. The metrics displayed are the metrics for the underlying WebLogic cluster associated with this service.

- **Resource Usage** Shows the CPU Usage and Heap Usage charts for all the servers in the cluster.

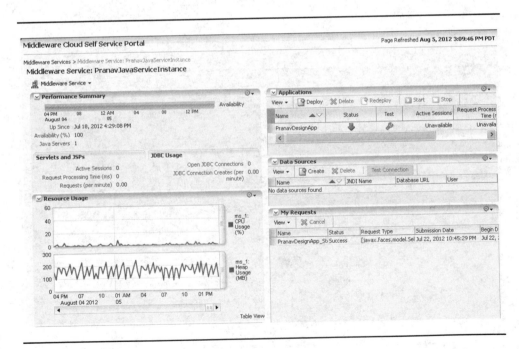

FIGURE 5-7.   *Middleware Service home page*

- **Applications**   Lists all the applications deployed to this service. This region supports the following actions:

    - **Deploy**   Deploy the application to the service.

    - **Delete**   Undeploy an application.

    - **Redeploy**   Redeploy an updated Java EE application component.

    - **Start/Stop**   Control the state of the application.

    - **Test**   Select an application and click the Test icon. A list of URLs is displayed in the Application URLs dialog box. Click the URL to navigate to the associated page.

        Clicking the application name displays the Application Home page, which provides additional monitoring details for the application. For each application, the name, status, and the key metrics such as Active Sessions, Request Processing Time, and Requests per Minute are displayed.

- **Data Sources**   Shows all the data sources that are available for this service. For each data source, the name, JNDI name, and the URL for the database are displayed. Users can create new data sources, edit or delete existing data sources, and test the connection to any specified data source.

- **My Requests**   Shows all the requests that have been submitted for this service. These include requests such as Deploy, Undeploy, Redeploy, Start, Stop, Create, Edit, and Delete data source.

Scaling Up/Down the Middleware Service

The Middleware Service home page, allows the self-service user to scale up or scale down their application environment by selecting the appropriate options from the Middleware Service menu:

- **Scale Up**   Users can scale up a service by adding one or more servers. The number of servers that can be added is limited by the set quota.

- **Scale Down**   Users can also scale down their service by specifying the number of servers to delete.

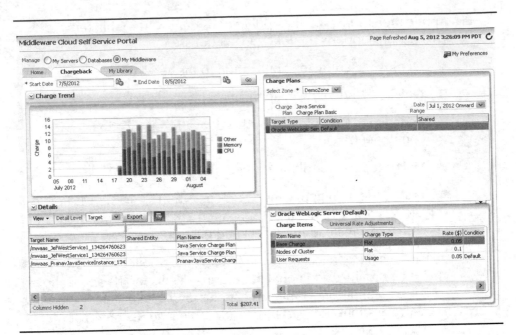

FIGURE 5-8. *Metering and chargeback details*

Thus, users have the option to start small and then scale their application infrastructure based on load and usage characteristics of the application.

In addition, users can click the Chargeback tab to view their own metering and chargeback information (shown in Figure 5-8), set personal preferences, monitor quota usage, and retire service instances if they are not required any more. They can also upload JEE components for their applications to the Software Library via the My Library tab. A JEE component can contain the application archive, a deployment plan, and pre/post deploy scripts.

Self-service users also have access to cloud APIs that can be used to operate and manage their middleware services.

Oracle Exalogic Elastic Cloud: Engineered System for Applications

As explained earlier, a middleware pool consists of a group of individual servers with a homogeneous configuration. These servers could be using off-the-shelf hardware or could be part of a highly optimized engineered system like Oracle Exalogic Elastic Cloud. This section explains what makes Exalogic so special.

Exalogic is hardware and software engineered together to provide extreme performance, reliability, and scalability for Oracle, Java, and other applications while delivering lower TCO, reduced risk, higher user productivity, and one-stop support. Exalogic dramatically improves performance of standard Linux, Solaris, and Java applications, without requiring code changes. It also reduces costs across the application life cycle, from initial setup to ongoing maintenance, as compared to conventional enterprise application platforms and private clouds assembled from disparate components sourced from multiple vendors.

The Exalogic system consists of two major elements:

■ **Exalogic X2-2**   A high-performance hardware system, assembled by Oracle, that integrates storage and compute resources using a high-performance I/O subsystem called Exabus, which is built on Oracle's Quad Data Rate (QDR) InfiniBand.

■ **Exalogic Elastic Cloud Software**   An essential package of Exalogic-specific software, device drivers, and firmware that is pre-integrated with Oracle Linux and Solaris, enabling Exalogic's advanced performance and Infrastructure as a Service (IaaS) capability, server and network virtualization, storage, and cloud management capabilities.

Exalogic X2-2 hardware is available in various configurations, as shown in Figure 5-9, and comes with upgrade kits for easy expansion.

Some of the key features of the Exalogic engineered system are captured in Table 5-2.

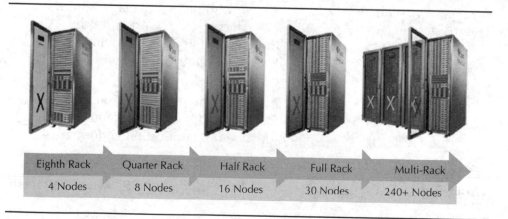

Eighth Rack	Quarter Rack	Half Rack	Full Rack	Multi-Rack
4 Nodes	8 Nodes	16 Nodes	30 Nodes	240+ Nodes

FIGURE 5-9.   *Standard Exalogic Elastic Cloud X2-2 hardware configurations*

Feature	Benefit
Fully integrated compute nodes, storage, and networking	Save yourself months of integration, benchmarking, and testing, and get a system fully optimized and certified for your applications.
Built-in linear scalability to hundreds of processors	Increase production deployments capacity with zero downtime and zero need for additional external switching capacity.
Superfast, low-latency, secure InfiniBand networking	Achieve maximum transaction throughput on critical applications, and eliminate concerns about running multiple applications on the same system.
Exabus high-performance communications backplane	Achieve seamless datacenter network connectivity with extremely high performance and security and dramatically lower management complexity.
Built-in, mission-critical virtualization with Oracle VM	Increase density and lower management costs by partitioning your system, so workloads are consolidated while you still maintain application isolation.
100% Oracle Linux and Oracle Solaris application compatibility	Get out-of-the-box support for thousands of Oracle and third-party applications.
Complete application-to-disk management with Oracle Enterprise Manager	Gain an applications-to-disk view of your system with proven management tools. Get users back to work faster by troubleshooting issues two times faster. Use cloud control capabilities to offer on-demand self-service.
Native leveraging of Oracle Exadata Database Machine	Achieve seamless integration with Oracle Exadata via Oracle InfiniBand technology, for superfast application performance.

TABLE 5-2. *Oracle Exalogic Elastic Cloud Features and Benefits* (continued)

Feature	Benefit
Rapid deployment with Oracle Virtual Assembly Builder	Deploy applications six times faster by provisioning application Assemblies that are preconfigured and optimized for your environment. Make your application deployment process reliable, predictable, and repeatable.
Load balancing with Oracle Traffic Director	Establish fast, reliable, secure, and scalable load balancing that doesn't require any additional hardware or software.

TABLE 5-2.   *Oracle Exalogic Elastic Cloud Features and Benefits*

Summary

Oracle Enterprise Manager Cloud Control 12*c* delivers capabilities spanning the entire middleware cloud life cycle. It lets the cloud and self-service administrators identify pooled resources, configure role-based access, and define the service catalog and the related chargeback plans. It allows cloud users to request middleware services and consume them on demand. It also allows users to scale up and down their platforms to adapt to changes in workload. Finally, it helps to understand the cost of the services delivered, and establishes accountability.

Thus, Oracle Enterprise Manager provides the most comprehensive solution for rolling out an Oracle-based Platform as a Service cloud for users in an enterprise. It offers the broadest and most complete set of capabilities to build, deploy, and manage the end-to-end life cycle of the cloud, all from a single console. The pre-integrated, unified solution ensures that enterprises can adopt the cloud quickly without having to invest in manual scripting or multiple point tools.

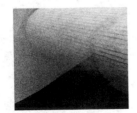

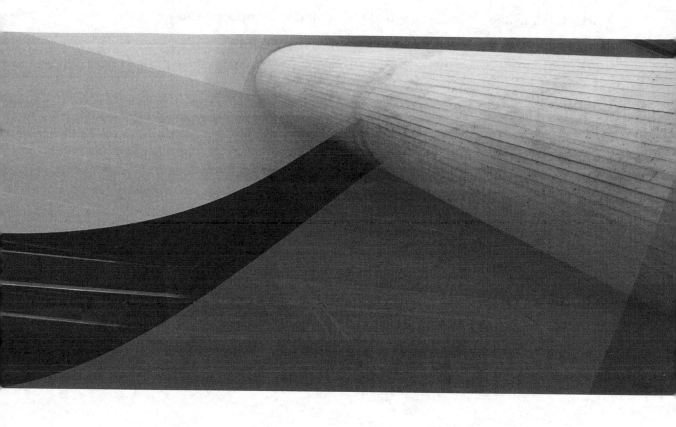

CHAPTER
6

Database as a Service

atabase as a Service (DBaaS) is a scalable relational or
nonrelational database service that allows users to quickly
provision databases and easily utilize the features of a database
without the burden of handling complex administrative tasks.
With this service, cloud users and database administrators can
provision and manage multiple database instances as needed. DBaaS is a
specialized form of Platform as a Service (PaaS) as it provides one of the key
platform components required to support business applications. The primary
business drivers for such a service in the enterprise are

- ■ **Enabling agility over the traditional IT delivery model** Traditional
  IT operations, as shown in Figure 6-1, are heavily administrator
  driven, and extremely customized for the application environments.
  These types of operations require specialized expertise, which
  makes them slow due to the necessary transitions between different
  administrative teams like hardware, storage, database, and so forth.
  It is not uncommon to hear stories where a database server takes
  weeks to provision for a project.

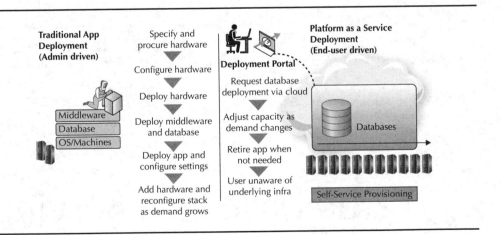

FIGURE 6-1. *Traditional IT operations vs. DBaaS*

- **Need for standardization and consolidation**   Most data centers have a mix of hardware, operating systems, database vendors, and database versions. Such diversity generally leads to high costs of deployment and operation and poor resource utilization.

- **Reduce the risk of cloud sprawl**   Due to IT's inability to deliver timely services, employees are increasingly reaching out to public cloud-based services for their needs. This is a huge risk, as public cloud services may not comply with IT policies for security and service level agreements (SLAs). Also, most employees will expense the cost incurred for these services, thus adding to corporate expenditure.

NOTE
Cloud sprawl *is a situation created by the ever-growing use of public cloud services and apps by individuals within a company, often without permission from the IT department.*

Oracle Enterprise Manager's Cloud Management provides a DBaaS or database cloud solution by automating the complete life cycle of a database and allowing users to request database services through the out-of-the-box Self Service Portal. With this solution, IT managers no longer have to perform mundane administrative tasks for provisioning databases. Some of the benefits provided by these capabilities are

- **Enabling faster deployment**   Building the database cloud infrastructure using the provided, standard building block components (servers, CPUs, storage, network, and so on), configurations, and tools enables a streamlined, automated, and simplified deployment process.

- **Increasing quality of service**   IT organizations are not only trying to drive down costs, they are also looking at solutions that will simultaneously improve quality of service in terms of performance, availability, and security. Cloud consumers inherently benefit from the high-availability characteristics built into the database cloud. Organizations can also enforce a unified identity and security infrastructure as part of standardized provisioning. Thus, instead of bolting on security policies, these policies and compliance regulations are part of the provisioning process.

- **Providing resource elasticity** The ability to grow and shrink the capacity of a database cloud, both in terms of storage size and compute power, allows applications the flexibility to meet the dynamic nature of business workloads.

- **Rapid and standardized provisioning** As mentioned, the database cloud can be rapidly provisioned via a self-service infrastructure, providing agility in application deployment. This reduces overall time in deploying production applications, deploying development platforms, or creating test-bed configurations.

Database Cloud Models

Oracle provides a complete stack and various options to implement DBaaS. These different options are referred to as database cloud models, as shown in Figure 6-2.

The following are the most popular Database Cloud Deployment Models:

- **Virtual server based** The database is deployed as a part of Oracle Virtual Assembly or an Oracle VM Template and several VMs share the same physical server or hypervisor. This offers the maximum level of isolation (at the OS level), but creates manageability problems owing to VM sprawl.

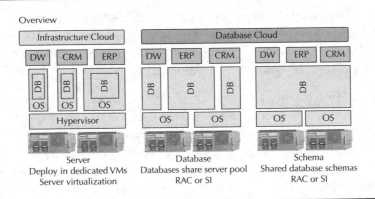

FIGURE 6-2. *Different Database Cloud Deployment Models*

- **Shared cluster** The database is deployed on an existing cluster. Typically, the Grid Infrastructure (Oracle Clusterware, Oracle ASM) and Oracle Database software is preinstalled. The cloud service entails the deployment of databases on top of that infrastructure.

- **Shared installation** The database is deployed as a single-instance database on an existing installation. The installation can be one of two types:

  - A regular installation on a host ready to house single-instance databases on demand. Each consumer creates a database instance running out of the shared installation.

  - A shared installation (read-only) mounted across multiple hosts that can house instances on demand.

- **Shared database** The database service is a schema deployment on an existing database. This is typically the case where a pool of developers shares the same database. It is assumed for purposes of metering and chargeback that each of the consumers of the database uses a different "database service" for access.

Each deployment model has its pros and cons, as outlined in Table 6-1, and hence it is important to select a deployment model that best satisfies the requirements of the organization. Some interesting considerations are

- **Consumer requirements** For example, an application test engineer may need to clone a production *clustered database* for performance or load testing, a DBA may need an *OS image* to verify patch application, or an application developer may require a small *schema* to build an application prototype.

- **Business and C*x*O needs** For example, a defined set of SLAs, and different levels of isolation for data protection, compliance, time-to-market period, ROI, and so forth would influence the selection of a deployment model.

- **Technical considerations** For example, available monitoring and management tools, reuse of existing infrastructure (such as physical servers), supported platforms, and so forth would influence the selection of a deployment model.

■ **Ease of management** As you move from the dedicated VMs model to the shared cluster model to the shared database model, the out-of-the-box business value provided increases and the complexity and management overhead for the user decreases. For example, in case of administering a database in a VM, the maintenance and administrative tasks performed by the DBA or user remain unchanged, as they must still patch, back up, tune, and secure their database environment. In the shared database model, the user is required to only maintain and manage their data, while the rest of the activities, like patching, backups, high availability (HA), disaster recovery (DR), and so on, are taken care of by the service provider.

It's expected that most enterprises will adopt a combination of delivery models to suit their consumers' needs. For example, some simple applications, like wikis or internal blogs, may be hosted using the shared database model since they may require just a schema, while other, more complex applications,

	Virtual Server as a Service (Shared Hypervisor)	**Database as a Service (Shared Cluster or Installation)**	**Schema as a Service (Shared Database)**
Implementation Effort	Easy (standardize on hypervisor)	Easy (standardize on OS)	Difficult (standardize on DB and OS)
Application Suitability	Some (deemed excessive in many cases)	All	Limited (homegrown; requires application validation)
Isolation	Excellent	Good	Least
Consolidation Density	Low (server and storage only)	High (server, storage, and OS)	Highest (server, storage, OS, and DB)
ROI	Low	High	Highest
Ease of Management	Involved (VM sprawl may pose additional challenges)	Very easy	Easy to involved (based on the required resource isolation)

TABLE 6-1. *Comparison of Different Database Cloud Deployment Models*

like Oracle Applications, may require significant tweaking of the database parameters and would need the shared cluster or shared installation model. Oracle Enterprise Manager's DBaaS offering enables enterprises to implement and manage multiple such delivery models using a single console.

NOTE
Very few scenarios should require spawning of a virtual image for just a single database; this, while easy to do, is unnecessary, provides limited performance, and significantly reduces consolidation density. On the other hand, the shared database model, while requiring more planning, provides the best consolidation achievable. The shared cluster/installation model provides a good compromise.

NOTE
The rest of the chapter follows the same structure as Chapter 5, barring the variations to account for differences in DBaaS and MWaaS. This is done on purpose to impress the idea that both MWaaS and DBaaS are built using the same concepts and design philosophy, while capturing the fine nuances of working with the two different software products. This similarity between MWaaS and DBaaS is evident in the cloud life cycle, and also in the three distinct roles involved in managing their life cycle. That said, the tasks performed by each of these roles vary.

Database Cloud Life Cycle

Like any product in the market, the cloud has a life cycle of its own. Oracle Enterprise Manager 12*c* is designed to give users a unified and complete solution that works with the breadth and depth of the enterprise.

Oracle Enterprise Manager offers a guided path through setup, use, and management of cloud services. Figure 6-3 outlines the complete cloud life cycle along with its various phases, which can be logically grouped together as follows:

- Plan and setup
- Build, test, and deploy
- Monitor and manage
- Meter, charge, and optimize

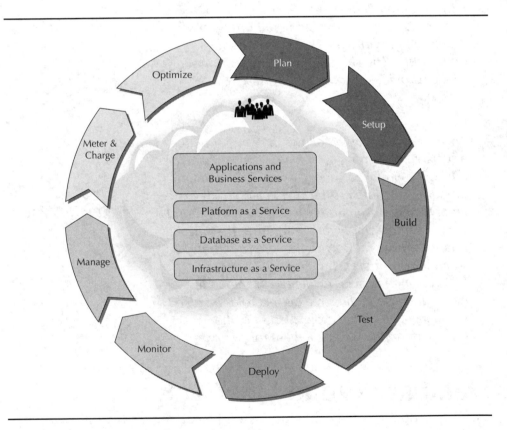

FIGURE 6-3.   *Complete cloud life cycle*

Plan and Setup

The plan phase guides you through the process of deciding whether to build new data centers or transform your existing data centers into a cloud environment. As discussed in Chapter 2, before setting up a cloud, you need to collect the infrastructure requirements, such as physical and virtual networks, storage arrays, RAC or non-RAC, and so on. Many of these requirements will depend on the type of application and the selected delivery model.

The *auto discovery* feature in Oracle Enterprise Manager helps you to discover and baseline all physical and virtual IT assets in an enterprise. Oracle Enterprise Manager's Consolidation Planner is a powerful tool that helps administrators plan the DBaaS architecture. It allows administrators to identify source and destination targets and applicable technical and functional constraints, such as where the application can reside. Administrators can generate consolidation advisories that may include plans to move from physical to virtual (P2V), physical to physical (P2P), or physical to an Exadata solution for your database platform.

The setup phase is all about putting the plan into action. Based on the choice of platform—virtual or physical—the setup phase offers capabilities such as bare-metal provisioning of the hypervisor, setting up of server, storage pools and grouping those into zones based on functional or QoS characteristics. The setup phase also provides workflows for provisioning of Oracle Clusterware, ASM, and the database software and for applying the required patches.

Enterprise Manager comes with role-driven access control, and integration with LDAP allows Oracle Enterprise Manager to inherit enterprise roles. Roles are also used to set resource limits, implemented with quotas that prevent rogue usage of a service while also preventing a few users from devouring the majority of the resources in the cloud.

Build, Test, and Deploy

Administrators can define standardized Service Templates for various database configurations, versions, options, and so on and publish them as services to the cloud service catalog.

In the build phase, Oracle Enterprise Manager uses Oracle Virtual Assembly Builder (OVAB) to help package database configurations as Assemblies for deployment on Oracle VM technology, while it uses

Deployment Procedures (DPs) for deployment on non-Oracle virtual machine platforms and physical platforms.

After an Assembly or a Service Template has been built to support an application, it needs to be tested (test phase) before being published (deploy phase) to the service catalog. Oracle Enterprise Manager provides a testing portfolio that allows users to test both application changes and changes to the database. The testing solution provides the ability to capture a production load and replay it in a test environment, so that the results are predictable. The testing solution also leverages the diagnostic capabilities built into the technology layers and provides prescriptions for remediation. Tested Assemblies and Service Templates are then published to the service catalog. Once published, these services can be provisioned by the consumers via the out-of-the-box Self Service Portal.

NOTE
Enterprise Manager 12c ships a wide collection of out-of-the-box Database Assemblies via its Self Update feature. Download and try these Assemblies to kick-start your journey to DBaaS cloud.

Monitor and Manage

The operational aspects of the cloud are important and often overlooked. The DBaaS administrative home pages in Oracle Enterprise Manager allow cloud administrators to get a summary view of the requests as well as the general state of the service, such as zones, pools, servers, databases, and so forth. In addition, Oracle Enterprise Manager provides the ability to collate targets into groups for better manageability. This Administration Group feature allows administrators to define monitoring settings, compliance standards, and cloud policies through templates. It also allows them to organize each target in multiple hierarchies, such as Line of Business and Lifecycle status. This allows the monitoring framework to scale to thousands of servers, databases, and middleware targets in the Cloud.

Oracle Enterprise Manager comes with an in-built Incident Management system that can manage by exceptions. Administrators can review, suppress, escalate, and remediate the events as needed, and also integrate the system with ticketing systems. Oracle Enterprise Manager has the ability to define contractual SLAs that govern the contract between the application owner and the provider of the cloud. Administrators as well as users can also define management policies that automatically adjust the service resources to ensure that SLAs are met. Oracle Enterprise Manager's Configuration Management capabilities are optimized for cloud environments. Oracle Enterprise Manager can monitor vast numbers of configurations continuously, discover changes, measure drifts, pinpoint configuration errors, and offer insight into system topologies, all within a single console. Cloud management capabilities are also integrated with My Oracle Support. This integration delivers facilities such as Patch Advisories, Service Request Management, and Knowledge Management on premises and in context of the overall cloud.

Meter, Charge, and Optimize

With self-service provisioning becoming easier, there may be a tendency to overprovision. Lots of organizations are resorting to mechanisms such as metering and chargeback to control the consumption. The metering and chargeback features in Oracle Enterprise Manager support basic metrics like CPU, memory, and storage usage, and offer chargeback models based on fixed cost, usage-based cost, or configuration-based costs. Administrators can also extend the models to account for fixed costs, configurations, administrative expenses, people costs, energy utilization, or any combination of these. These capabilities enable enterprises to not only account for actual usage versus representative usage and also optionally integrate the usage data with billing systems.

Cloud management also entails an ongoing optimization of resources and processes to make sure that the service levels are persistent. Oracle Enterprise Manager provides administrators and application users with features that help them to rediscover assets, reevaluate the performance, rebalance the cloud, and fine-tune the provisioning process. The tuning capabilities in the operating system, database, and middleware layers aid in continuous optimization and subsequent improvement.

Cloud Roles and Responsibilities

The cloud setup process spans multiple teams and multiple functions. All of the traditional administrators—storage, systems, network, security, and database—and the new set of administrators for the cloud services will have to work together to get the database cloud into place. In an effort to streamline the tasks to be undertaken, and to formalize the process followed by various teams, this new set of administrators can be grouped into the following three distinct roles that will coordinate and perform all actions required to set up the cloud infrastructure and to enable the service catalog and the Self Service Portal:

- Cloud infrastructure administrator
- Self-service administrator
- Cloud self-service user

The responsibilities of each of these roles are discussed in detail in the following subsections.

Cloud Infrastructure Administrator

The cloud infrastructure administrator (or simply cloud administrator) is in charge of putting together the overall cloud infrastructure, which includes both the physical and logical resources. As highlighted by the blue box in Figure 6-4, the cloud administrator is responsible for

- Setting up the servers and storage using server and storage provisioning methods. The servers for DBaaS could be physical servers, hypervisors, or virtual machines, depending on operational needs.

- Setting up the network, physical and virtual IPs, VLANs/firewalls, and so on.

- Creating the self-service roles and users. The cloud administrator must ensure that appropriate self-service users can log in to the Self Service Portal. Also, specific privileges can be granted so that users are allowed to perform only certain operations. To achieve this, the cloud administrator defines roles that contain a select set of privileges to allow users to function as a self-service administrator or as a self-service user. These roles can also be imported from LDAP. Finally, the roles will be assigned to one or more users based on their function.

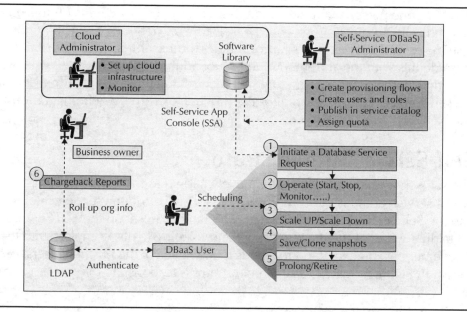

FIGURE 6-4. *Cloud infrastructure administrator responsibilities*

- Setting up the Software Library, which can be co-located with the Management Server or set up remotely, depending on the location of the database zones of the cloud.

- Deploying Oracle Enterprise Manager agents and configuring credentials.

- Setting up the PaaS Infrastructure Zones (discussed in Chapter 2).

- Setting up the infrastructure to support various file transfer methods between the Software Library and the end servers that can be consumed by the procedures. This could involve using web servers for HTTP access, using the Oracle Enterprise Manager agent-to-agent transfer mechanism, or using NFS mounted copies (more popularly known as *thin provisioning*).

This role ensures the standardization of infrastructure to be procured so as to be used in the cloud across both physical and virtual environments. Since the tasks performed by this role span multiple tiers of the software stack, no one person can perform all these tasks, and hence it is quite likely that multiple administrators—hardware, storage, network, security, and system—will wear this role's hat or that a cloud architect will coordinate these details with the aforementioned set of administrators.

Once all required infrastructure has been setup by the cloud administrator, the self-service administrator takes the process forward by defining various database pools, as discussed next.

Self-Service Administrator

The self-service administrator (alternatively known as the DBaaS administrator or just service administrator) is responsible for setting up the service catalog and the Self Service Portal. DBaaS administrators can set up the Self Service Portal in a way that standardizes application deployments, complies with the datacenter best practices and responds to the needs of the business users. As shown in Figure 6-5, the DBaaS administrator is responsible for

- Setting up the database pools
- Creating quotas and assigning them to roles

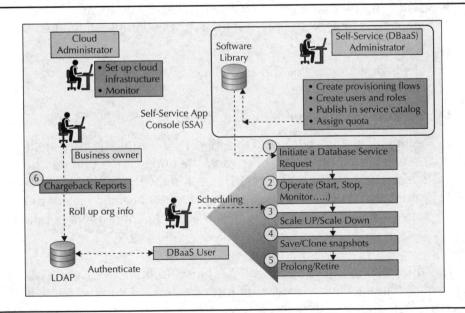

FIGURE 6-5. *Self-service administrator responsibilities*

- Configuring request settings

- Setting up the provisioning flows (Deployment Procedures) and publishing them to the service catalog as Service Templates

- Creating a chargeback plan and associating it with a zone

- Tracking request progress and managing the cloud resources on an ongoing basis

Each of these tasks is described in turn in the following subsections.

Setting Up the Database Pools

The setup of database pools is one of the key DBaaS concepts. A pool is a logical grouping of individual servers or clusters with a homogeneous configuration. These servers could be using off-the-shelf hardware or could be part of a highly optimized engineered system such as Oracle Exadata Database Machine. (More details on Exadata are provided toward the end of the chapter.) A database cloud consumer (self-service user) must specify a zone (and indirectly a pool) when submitting a provisioning request via the Self Service Portal. As a prerequisite, the database software needs to be installed on all servers or clusters that will belong to a pool. This includes the Oracle Clusterware and Oracle Automatic Storage Management (ASM) software (also known as Grid Infrastructure) and the listener.

The mandatory criteria for creating pools include

- Platform type (such as Linux 64-bit, Solaris, AIX, etc.)

- Database version (up to the fourth segment; 11.2.0.2, 10.2.0.5, etc.)

- Availability (single instance or RAC)

Besides the mandatory criteria enforced by the product, administrators can use other, optional attributes to define homogeneous zones. Some of the many optional criteria for creating zones include

- SLAs (mission critical vs. noncritical)

- Security or regulatory compliance (PCI, HIPPA, etc.)

- Infrastructure Tiers (Tier 1 vs. Tier 2 storage for the database)

The homogeneity maintained between the members of a pool is required for ease of administration, to maintain operational consistency, and to guarantee provisioning success. Any cloud service has to provide the abstraction such that the quality of service becomes independent of placement. The homogeneity in terms of certain configurations guarantees that. Figure 6-6 shows the setup screen for a database pool containing a two-node cluster.

An often asked question is, how can we protect the members of a zone or pool from being abused due to overallocation of resources? This is a common concern for a cloud environment, as numerous requests can be triggered by numerous users, and these requests will compete for resources on the servers in the zone. As the famous quote from William Forester Llyod says, "Any shared resource…will inevitably be destroyed by overuse." To support this requirement, Oracle introduced the concept of *placement policy constraints* to the zone and pool creation flow. Placement policy constraints can be used to set a maximum ceiling for any host in the zone and pool. The constraint values are used during database provisioning to

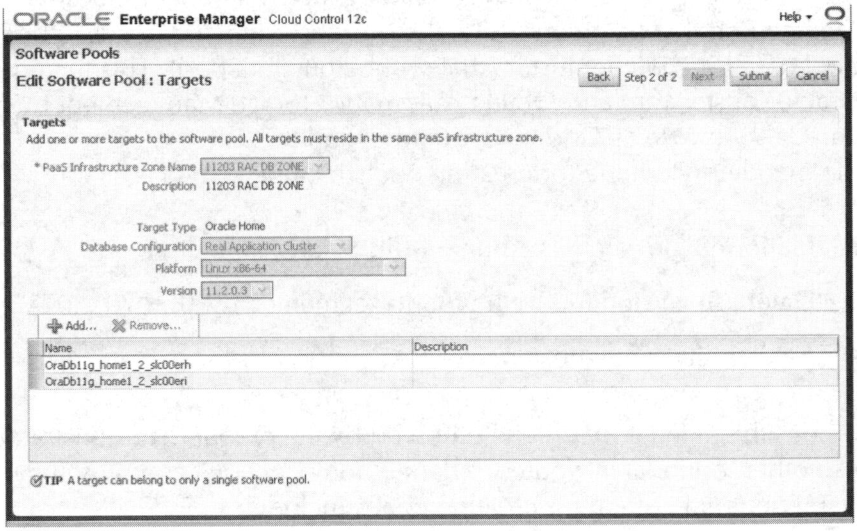

FIGURE 6-6. *Database pool composed of a two-node RAC cluster*

filter out hosts that are overburdened. The placement policy constraints supported are as follows:

- **Maximum CPU Utilization**   Defined at the zone level; the average CPU utilization (expressed as a percentage) over the past 7 days (or fewer if the host metric collection duration is under 7 days)

- **Maximum Memory Allocation**   Defined at the zone level; the average memory utilization (expressed as a percentage) over the past 7 days (or fewer if the host metric collection duration is under 7 days)

- **Maximum Number of Database Instances**   Defined at the pool level; the maximum number of database instances that can be running on each host in a zone

TIP
As an example of using placement policy constraints effectively, in a development environment, the CPU utilization limit might be set to 95%, while in a production environment, it might be set to 75%.

Creating Quotas and Assigning Them to Roles

While the cloud gives the perception of infinite resources, such is not the case. DBaaS administrators may want to restrict the resources used by self-service users either to control the rate at which cloud resources are consumed or to restrict access based on budget allocation. Oracle Enterprise Manager 12*c* allows the DBaaS administrator to set quotas against self-service user roles, which in turn apply to the individual users. The supported quota attributes, as shown in Figure 6-7, are

- Number of databases that can be owned by the user at any point in time

- Total allocated storage that can be assigned to a user for all the databases that the user owns

- Total allocated memory (SGA+ PGA) that can be assigned to a user for all the databases that the user owns

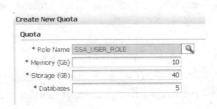

FIGURE 6-7. *Setting up a quota*

A user can be assigned multiple roles and, thus, may inherit multiple quota limits. In such cases, the highest value assigned to a quota attribute is selected. For example, suppose the user is part of two roles that have different quota limits:

Role Name	Attribute	Value
DEV_USER_ROLE	Memory	10GB
	Storage	20GB
	Database Count	5
TEST_USER_ROLE	Memory	15GB
	Storage	15GB
	Database Count	3

The effective quota limits for this user would be

Memory = MAX (10, 15) = 15GB
Storage = MAX (20, 15) = 20GB
Database Count = MAX (5, 3) = 5

TIP
This is an effective way to boost the quota limits for a select set of users, but it requires proper planning because some users may unknowingly get access to more resources than the administrator desired.

Configuring Request Settings

While by default the self-service user can request resources for any duration of time, and can even schedule such a request for any time in the future, the DBaaS administrator does have the ability to override some of these request settings. The three options available to the DBaaS administrator are

- **Future Reservation** How far in advance a user can make a request. The default is set to No Restriction but can be limited to days, weeks, months, or years.

- **Request Archive Retention** Maximum duration after which archived request will be automatically deleted by the system. The default is set to No Restriction but can be limited to days, weeks, months, or years.

- **Request Duration** Maximum duration for which requests can be made. The default is set to No Restriction, but can be limited to days, weeks, months, or years.

A good example of a situation in which these settings might be to use would be when rolling out a limited-time beta within an organization. They might be configured to allow, say, all developers to use a basic Service Template for a duration of 30 days, and allow them to request this database only a day in advance.

Setting Up Provisioning Flows and Publishing Them to Service Catalog as Service Templates

The self-service user selects a database Assembly on the Oracle VM platform or a Service Template on a non-Oracle VM platform for provisioning their desired database configuration. The DBaaS administrator can use Oracle Virtual Assembly Builder Studio to build database assemblies. For defining Service Templates, the administrator configures and saves the Create Database Procedure Deployment Procedure. The Deployment Procedure allows users to run through an intuitive wizard that displays all inputs required to successfully execute the procedure. Once the input values to the procedure have been finalized, the user can click the padlock icons accompanying the input values to lock them, and save the procedure for future use.

To use a saved Deployment Procedure as a Service Template, it is important to lock only the values as specified in Table 6-2.

Field	Description	Locked Y/N?
Version	Select from a list of supported database versions.	Y
Database Type	Select between different database configurations.	Y
Hosts (Oracle Home + Credential)	Select a single sample host, Oracle Home and credentials. For RAC database creation, select a cluster, the desired Oracle Home, credentials for the cluster, and a sample node. Note: These inputs will be overridden when the procedure is published as a Service Template.	N
Database Template	Select the Database Configuration Assistant (DBCA) database template location. The location can be the Software Library or Oracle Home. The template selected must be compatible with the selected Oracle Home version. If the Oracle Home option is selected, select the template from the Oracle Home. The default location is ORACLE_HOME/assistants/dbca/templates.	Y
Cluster Database Configuration Type [RAC Only]	Select the configuration type as Administrator Managed. There is no need to select the nodes, as suitable nodes will automatically be selected by the placement algorithm.	NA
Global Database Name	Enter a dummy value. This value will be auto-generated when this procedure is published as a Service Template.	N
SID	Enter a dummy value. This value will be auto-generated when this procedure is published as a Service Template.	N

TABLE 6-2.   *Deployment Procedure Variables and Their Locking Requirements (continued)*

Field	Description	Locked Y/N?
Passwords (SYS, SYSTEM, DBSNMP)	Specify all three passwords here. The SYS password is used and the SYSTEM and DBSNMP are displayed.	Y
Storage Type	Select the storage type, whether File System or ASM.	Y
Database File Location	Specify the location or disk group where data files, temporary files, redo logs, and control files will be stored.	N
Recovery File Location	To enable backup and restore for the self-service users, check the Use Fast Recovery Area and Enable Archiving check boxes. Use Fast Recovery Area will require the location/disk group and size for storing recovery-related files. This will allow the self-service user to schedule Oracle-recommended RMAN backups for the database.	Y
Memory Parameters	Specify this value according to the desired database size definition. For example, small = 1GB, medium = 2GB, large = 4GB, and so on.	Y
Database Sizing	Specify the Block Size and number of Processes. If a database template with data files is selected in the Database Template page, the Block Size cannot be edited.	Y
Host CPU Count	Specify this value according to desired database size definition. For example, small = 1 CPU, medium = 2 CPU, large = 4 CPU, and so on.	Y
Character Set	Select the required character set. The default character set is based on the locale and operating system.	Y

TABLE 6-2. *Deployment Procedure Variables and Their Locking Requirements* (continued)

Field	Description	Locked Y/N?
Database Connection Mode	Select the server mode. For shared server mode, specify the number of shared servers.	Y
Listener Configuration	As part of the prerequisites, a listener has to be configured per host or Oracle Home. Once configured, select the correct listener and lock the value.	Y
Custom Script	Optional. A custom SQL script, if provided, will be executed after the database creation with SYSDBA privileges.	Y
Schedule	This field will be ignored. The schedule is specified by the self-service user as part of the database request.	N/A
Review	Review all inputs provided to the Deployment Procedure. *Do not* click Submit; instead click Save and save the procedure with a meaningful name, and then click Cancel to exit the wizard.	N/A

TABLE 6-2. *Deployment Procedure Variables and Their Locking Requirements*

NOTE
If the variables are not locked exactly as specified in Table 6-2, errors will be displayed when registering a saved Deployment Procedure with a Service Template.

Once the procedure variables have been locked correctly and the procedure has been saved, the procedure can then be used to create a Service Template. A Service Template stores a reference to a saved Deployment

Procedure along with some additional metadata. The metadata includes a meaningful name and description, a list of suitable zones, and a list of roles that are allowed to execute the Service Template. A sample service catalog is shown in Table 6-3.

When a self-service user submits a request to provision a Service Template, the following steps are executed:

1. Initialization

2. User quota validation

3. Placement logic execution to find a suitable host or cluster nodes

4. Database creation

5. Assignment of target privileges

Each step is described in turn next.

ID	Service Name	Description	Features Enabled	QoS Level	Service Contact
1	High Performance Database 11.2.0.2	Installs Database 11.2.0.2 on a SPARC with high-speed NAS	Partitioning Instance caging	Gold	john.doe@acme.com
2	Highly Available Database 11.2.0.3	Installs Clustered Database 11.2.0.3	RAC	Silver	jane.smith@acme.com
3	E-Biz Database 10.2.0.5	Installs Database for E-Biz 12		Gold	joe.smith@acme.com

TABLE 6-3. *Sample Service Catalog*

Step 1: Initialization As part of the database request, the self-service user is required to provide a username and password for the master administrative account. This initialization step focuses mainly on the database master account validation. It checks the master account username to ensure that none of the default Oracle user names are used.

Here is the list of default Oracle usernames, which are case insensitive:

- ANONYMOUS
- APEX_030200
- APEX_PUBLIC_USER
- APPQOSSYS
- CTXSYS
- DBSNMP
- DIP
- EXFSYS
- FLOWS_FILES
- MDDATA
- MDSYS
- MGMT_VIEW
- OLAPSYS
- ORACLE_OCM
- ORDDATA
- ORDPLUGINS
- ORDSYS
- OUTLN
- OWBSYS
- OWBSYS_AUDIT
- SCOTT
- SI_INFORMTN_SCHEMA
- SPATIAL_CSW_ADMIN_USR
- SPATIAL_WFS_ADMIN_USR
- SYS
- SYSMAN
- SYSTEM
- USER
- WMSYS
- XDB
- XS$NULL

Step 2: User Quota Validation The user's current usage is evaluated against the quota limits set by the DBaaS administrator. The request fails if the resources required for the requested database Service Template are above the quota limits.

Step 3: Placement Logic Execution to Find a Suitable Host or Cluster Nodes The purpose of the placement logic is to find a suitable host or cluster nodes that can be used to create the database. In this step, to derive such a list of suitable candidates, various computations are made, and therein lies the secret sauce. The placement logic considers

- Average load (CPU and memory) over the last week on the hosts/nodes in the selected zone, pre-database creation

- Configuration, such as the current population (the number of database instances) on each host/node

- The placement policy constraint limits

- Estimated resource usage (memory) on selected host/node, post creation of database

All of the preceding data is already collected, and hence the placement is handled automatically by Oracle Enterprise Manager. The first host/node that is selected by the placement logic is used for database creation. At the time of writing, First-Match is the only algorithm used for database creation. There are plans to support other algorithms in the future, such as Best-Match, to find the host/node with the most available resources and other placement policy constraints such as disk and network I/O.

Step 4: Database Creation In this step, the actual database is created as per the configuration captured by the selected Service Template. Since a Service Template is just a wrapper, the actual provisioning of the database is orchestrated by the Create Database Procedure.

Step 5: Assignment of Target Privileges All provisioning and validation tasks, as previously described, are performed by a privileged user in Oracle Enterprise Manager. This privileged user comes configured out of the box, and the DBaaS or cloud administrator is not required to modify it in any way. Once all tasks related to the database request are complete, the self-service user (or requestor) is granted ownership of the provisioned database.

This completes the setup of Provisioning Flows.

Creating a Chargeback Plan and Associating It with a Zone

Since DBaaS is all about sharing a common infrastructure, it is important to meter the resources users consume and, optionally, charge them for their usage. Unlike siloed environments, where resources are dedicated, in a cloud environment, resources are shared, which makes it challenging to accurately measure resource usage across different users. Oracle Enterprise Manager's metering and chargeback features help to overcome this challenge. As part of the DBaaS setup, the administrator will associate a different chargeback plan to every database zone. This chargeback plan is applied to the database target once it is created as part of the service provisioning, based on the zone it belongs to. The chargeback plan can be based on a flat rate or it can be usage based or configuration based. An example of a configuration-based chargeback plan one that charges a higher rate for lower database versions, because lower database versions incur more maintenance overhead. Metering and chargeback topics are covered extensively in Chapter 7.

Tracking Request Progress and Managing the Cloud Resources on an Ongoing Basis

The DBaaS administrator can track the progress or the status of any requests from the Requests Dashboard. Alternatively, the administrator can also visit the zone home page, as shown in Figure 6-8, to see the breakdown of all requests on a zone. Usually, considering the volume of requests in a cloud environment, there is no need for the administrator to track the database requests. The only exception to this rule would be tracking of failed requests.

Besides request details, the administrator should also be able to view metering and chargeback information for other DBaaS users and roll the users up using LDAP and/or group-based hierarchies.

NOTE
For more information on Oracle Enterprise Manager 12c Cloud Management features, refer to the Oracle Enterprise Manager Cloud Administration Guide *in the documentation library available on OTN (http://docs.oracle.com/ cd/E24628_01/index.htm). This guide includes a section on troubleshooting failed DBaaS requests that describes well-known failure conditions and the steps to triage and fix them.*

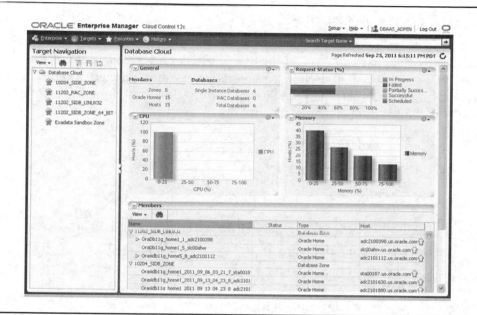

FIGURE 6-8.   *Cloud administration console*

Other tasks performed by the DBaaS administrator on an ongoing basis are

- Patching database Oracle homes

- Monitoring pool members

- Sending requests to the cloud administrator for additional memory, storage, and other resources

- Reporting outages and maintaining SLAs

While this list doesn't include all of the tasks performed by the DBaaS administrator, in a nutshell, the self-service or DBaaS administrator is responsible for the experience of the self-service user or consumer. This topic is covered in detail in subsequent chapters.

Cloud Self-Service User

The self-service user (or simply *user*) takes advantage of the cloud platform to request databases, deploy applications, use deployed applications for a specific period (from a few days to several years), and manage and monitor some aspects of the life cycle of the database. All of these functions can be performed from the Self Service Portal. As shown in Figure 6-9, the cloud self-service user is responsible for

- Creating a database service
- Tracking requests
- Monitoring and operating the database
- Backing up the database
- Retiring the database
- Viewing metering and chargeback information

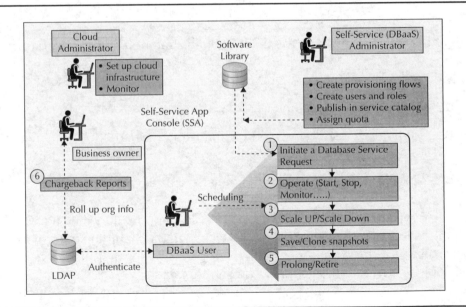

FIGURE 6-9. *Cloud self-service user responsibilities*

Creating a Database Service

To provision a database with the desired configuration, the user chooses from a list of Service Templates by clicking on the Request Database button on the home screen's My Databases panel of the Self Service Portal. Each Service Template requires the user to provide certain inputs as designated by the DBaaS administrator. Some mandatory inputs required for a database request are

- Request name
- Database zone
- Database master account username and password
- Schedule (start date and end date)

Once a request is submitted, it typically takes 5 to 10 minutes to complete. This timing is approximate and will depend on the amount of seed data included with the Database Configuration Assistant (DBCA) template.

Tracking Requests

The user can track the progress of a request by using the My Requests panel of the Database Cloud Self Service Portal, shown in Figure 6-10. A request will transition through various states, such as Scheduled, Running, Succeeded, Retired, and so forth.

Monitoring and Operating the Database

The Database home page, shown in Figure 6-11, displays monitoring details such as sessions, CPU, memory, disk I/O, and so forth and allows the user to perform limited operations on the database such as start, stop, back up, and restore. For advanced features, such as access to ADDM and ASH data, configuration management, custom reporting, and access to incidents, the user can ask the administrator for additional privileges since they are like any other Oracle Enterprise Manager user.

In addition, the users can view their own metering and chargeback information, set personal preferences, monitor quota usage, back up and restore databases, and retire databases if they are not required any more.

Self-service users also have access to cloud APIs that can be used to operate and manage their databases.

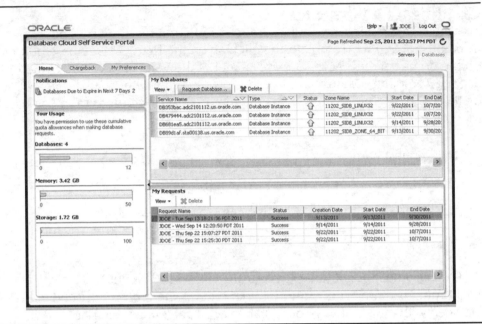

FIGURE 6-10. *Database Cloud Self Service Portal*

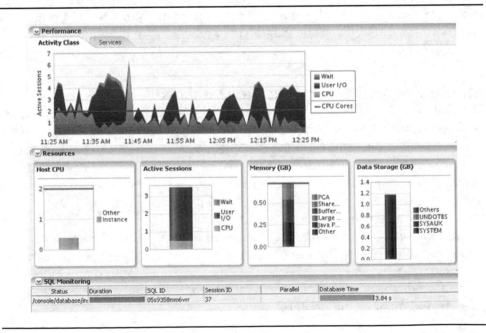

FIGURE 6-11. *Database home page*

Oracle Exadata: Engineered System for Databases

As explained earlier, a database pool can consist of a group of individual servers or clusters with a homogeneous configuration. These servers could be using off-the-shelf hardware or could be part of a highly optimized engineered system like Oracle Exadata Database Machine. This section explains what makes Exadata Database Machine so special.

Oracle Exadata is the only database machine that provides extreme performance for both data warehousing and OLTP applications, making it the ideal platform for consolidating on private clouds. As shown in Figure 6-12, it is a complete package of server, storage, networking, and software that is massively scalable, secure, and redundant. With Oracle Exadata, customers can reduce IT costs through consolidation, store up to ten times more data, improve performance of all applications, deliver a faster time to market by eliminating systems integration trial and error, and make better business decisions in real time.

At the heart of every Oracle Exadata Database Machine are Oracle Exadata Storage Servers, which combine smart storage software and industry-standard hardware to deliver the industry's highest database storage performance.

To overcome the limitations of conventional storage, Oracle Exadata Storage Servers use a massively parallel architecture to dramatically increase data bandwidth between the database server and storage. Innovative technologies such as Exadata Smart Scan, Exadata Smart Flash Cache, and Hybrid Columnar Compression, as outlined in Table 6-4, enable Exadata to deliver extreme performance for everything from data warehousing to online transaction processing to mixed workloads.

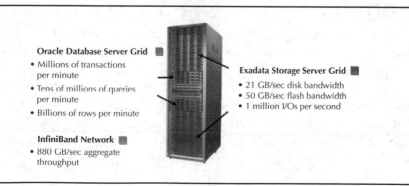

Oracle Database Server Grid ▪
- Millions of transactions per minute
- Tens of millions of queries per minute
- Billions of rows per minute

Exadata Storage Server Grid ▪
- 21 GB/sec disk bandwidth
- 50 GB/sec flash bandwidth
- 1 million I/Os per second

InfiniBand Network ▪
- 880 GB/sec aggregate throughput

FIGURE 6-12. *Oracle Exadata Database Machine*

Feature	Benefit
Oracle Database 11*g*	Deliver industry-leading security, high availability, and scalability with Oracle Database 11*g*, which has been significantly enhanced to take advantage of the Oracle Exadata Storage Servers.
Exadata Smart Scan	Improve query performance by offloading intensive query processing and data mining scoring to scalable intelligent storage servers.
Exadata Smart Flash Cache	Transparently cache "hot" data to fast solid-state storage, improving query response times and throughput.
Exadata Hybrid Columnar Compression	Reduce the size of data warehousing tables by 10 times and archive tables by 50 times to improve performance and lower storage costs for primary, standby, and backup databases.
InfiniBand Network	Connect multiple Exadata Database Machines using the InfiniBand fabric to form a larger single system image configuration. Each InfiniBand link provides 40 gigabits of bandwidth—many times higher than traditional storage or server networks.

TABLE 6-4. *Oracle Exadata Database Machine Features and Benefits*

Summary

Oracle Enterprise Manager Cloud Control 12*c* delivers capabilities spanning the entire database cloud life cycle. It lets the cloud and self-service administrators identify pooled resources, configure role-based access, and define the service catalog and the related chargeback plans. It allows cloud users to request database services and consume them on demand. It also allows users to scale up and down their platforms to adapt to changes in workload. Finally, it helps to understand the costs of the service delivered, and establishes accountability.

Thus, Oracle Enterprise Manager provides the most comprehensive solution for rolling out an Oracle-based Database as a Service cloud for users in an enterprise. It offers the broadest and most complete set of capabilities to build, deploy, and manage the end-to-end life cycle of the cloud, all from a single console. The pre-integrated, unified solution ensures that enterprises can adopt the cloud quickly without having to invest in manual scripting or multiple point tools.

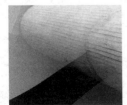

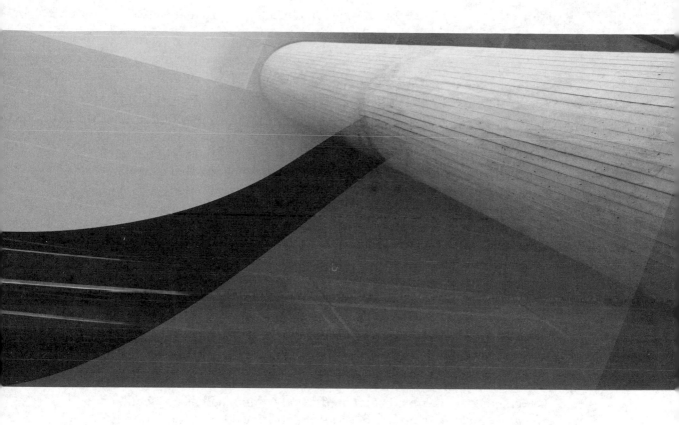

CHAPTER
7

Metering and
Chargeback

hargeback is a concept that has been widely employed in the past. Businesses such as public utilities and wireless phone companies have invested heavily in pay-for-use models for charging customers based on their usage and consumption of a service. As users become keenly aware of the amount of resources they are consuming and the costs associated with that usage, they become more efficient and more selective, thus lowering wastage and overall costs.

In enterprise computing, it was common for IT to centrally purchase large computers (such as mainframes) for use by all other departments, and the cost would be recovered with an internal cross-charge to "cost centers" based on how the mainframe resources were being used. As IT architectures shifted from shared mainframes toward a client-server model, with servers dedicated to each application, the concept of chargeback became less relevant because systems were purchased on a case-by-case basis to support specific application workloads, making it generally easy to determine the physical resources that each application was using and, therefore, to understand the costs incurred.

The emergence of virtualization and cloud computing has brought back the benefits of centralization and consolidation. With consolidation platforms such as Oracle Exadata and Oracle Exalogic, among others, there's renewed focus on chargeback. Similar to a mainframe, these technologies involve infrastructure being shared by a variety of workloads. As application workloads are abstracted from the physical infrastructure supporting them, it is not possible to build a chargeback model based on the allocation of physical resources in a dedicated fashion. Instead, it is necessary to meter the resources consumed by each application running on the shared infrastructure. *Metering* is the instrumentation of resources necessary for generating measurements for metric values, which can then be used for chargeback. Unless a resource is instrumented for metering, its usage cannot be included in the chargeback.

Today, organizations are looking to exploit the benefits of cloud computing, such as self-service provisioning and rapid elasticity. The shift toward user-driven provisioning means that cloud users can consume resources without first needing to seek approval or provide any business justification. Instead, they can rely on a budget for such usage. To ensure that cloud resources are correctly accounted for, it is necessary to have a mechanism for metering cloud resources and charging cloud users based on their consumption.

Without some form of consumption-based chargeback, users may be tempted to provision resources that they do not really need. This drives up the overall cost of IT as more servers, storage, and software licenses are required (a situation that has been coined "VM sprawl" in the virtualization world). Chargeback is used to help cloud users understand how their consumption of resources translates to a cost, which helps to keep them "disciplined." This benefits cloud users because it enables them to adjust their consumption in order to control their IT costs. It also benefits the IT organization because they can achieve higher resource utilization rates and recover the cost of providing services to the consumer. As IT strives to reduce costs across infrastructures, applications, and services, developing and implementing a chargeback strategy becomes an essential part of any cloud solution.

Whether to Use Chargeback or Showback

For IT to charge back business for their resource usage, they have to agree on the metrics on the basis of which to charge—and that's not always easy. Many times the infrastructure is funded on a project-by-project basis, which makes it hard to determine the fair share of the expense that should be allocated to a business unit. Business owners might complain that the cost allocation is not fair or that it doesn't provide enough details about the IT services that are provided. Moreover, IT budgets might be constantly changing, in which case it is hard to plan new service rollouts and pricing models around them. Due to these and other reasons, almost half of existing IT shops have stayed away from implementing any form of chargeback for IT costs.

Showback—a term more widely used in recent times—tries to address that. Although showback provides the same analysis of costs to IT and business units, it doesn't bill anyone for services. To implement chargeback, IT departments have to hand out formal bills to recover IT costs and integrate with finance and accounting systems. With showback, businesses are able to view at a granular level which resources their applications and services are consuming, and then choose whether or not that extra feature or function is worth the cost. Just as with chargeback, showback requires the instrumentation of resources for metering. Showback raises a level of awareness that IT services come at a cost and helps instill cost accountability and transparency.

To better understand the difference between chargeback and showback, consider as an example an IT organization in a retail company that realized its IT resources were not being consumed optimally. Users would make requests for new machines whenever new projects started, but would not relinquish them when the projects ended. IT was given an annual budget to provide services to various departments, but there was no accountability for who used how much, and the IT organization found it hard to reduce the wastage of resources.

The IT organization decided to implement a chargeback solution, wherein they would charge the respective departments for the resources they were consuming. But very soon after the implementation, the IT organization and the department heads reached a deadlock. The department heads complained that they were being allocated an unfair share of costs for shared resources such as the datacenter power and cooling, networking gear, and so forth. It also became very difficult to develop a consensus on which metrics to use for charging. Moreover, the finance and accounting departments needed to be involved to be able to charge back the IT bills to the respective cost centers.

To resolve this situation, the IT organization instead implemented showback. Every month the IT organization would generate a list of machines, sorted by each user. They also provided the percentage of total IT usage allocated to each department. Over the course of a few months, they saw the IT resource requests drop dramatically. Showback works on the premise that people want to do the right thing, given that they are provided the right level of information.

Oracle Enterprise Manager Features for Chargeback or Showback

Oracle Enterprise Manager 12*c* uses the rich monitoring and configuration data (metrics) that is collected for Oracle Enterprise Manager targets as the basis for a metering and chargeback solution. Oracle Enterprise Manager provides the administrator with

- Metering for Oracle Enterprise Manager targets

- Assignment of rates to metered resources

- Management of a cost center hierarchy

- Assignment of resources to cost centers

- Usage and charge reporting

- Security model with out-of-the-box roles and privileges

- An API to extract metering and chargeback data

- Integration with billing applications

This set of features can be used by enterprise IT to implement chargeback or showback for a private cloud. Furthermore, APIs that allow the exporting of metering data to billing solutions such as Oracle Billing and Revenue Management (BRM) provide a solution for the creation of chargeback and billing solutions for public clouds. Public clouds use the metering data to produce an actual bill for their customers.

Metering for Oracle Enterprise Manager Targets

To begin using Oracle Enterprise Manager's chargeback feature, the administrator needs to enable metering (instrumentation) on cloud resources. These resources may be commodity servers running various operating systems, Oracle Database or Oracle Fusion Middleware components, or engineered systems such as Oracle Exadata and Oracle Exalogic. Cloud resources being managed are represented as "targets" within the Oracle Enterprise Manager console. To enable metering, these targets are added to the chargeback application within Oracle Enterprise Manager. The target types that are supported for metering and chargeback are

- Host (operating system)

- Guest Virtual Machine (Guest VM)

- Oracle Database Instance

- Oracle Cluster Database

- Oracle WebLogic Server

- Oracle WebLogic Cluster

- Oracle WebLogic Domain

Aggregate Targets:

- Oracle VM Server Pool
- Oracle VM Zone
- PaaS Infrastructure Zone
- Group
- Generic System

When adding a composite target such as a Zone, Cluster Database, Group, or System, all chargeable entities within the composite target will be enabled for metering. Figure 7-1 shows a few targets added to the chargeback application to enable metering.

Subsequent to adding a target to the chargeback application, a daily job will collect target usage and configuration data from the Oracle Enterprise Manager monitoring and configuration tables. This data is the basis of metering in Oracle Enterprise Manager. The chargeable entities and associated metrics that are collected are summarized in Figure 7-2.

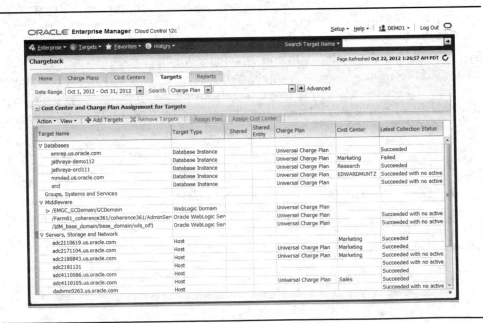

FIGURE 7-1. *Adding targets in Oracle Enterprise Manager for metering*

	Chargeable Entity			
	Host	VM	Dedicated Database	Dedicated Web Logic
Configuration	OS	Allocated Memory	Edition	Nodes of Cluster
	CPU Count	Allocated Storage	Memory Usage	Version
	CPU SPECInt Rate*	HA	Option	
	Disk Space	IP Address	Storage Usage	
	Memory	vCPU Count	Version	
	Software Installed	Size		
Usage	CPU Time	CPU Utilization (%)	CPU Time	CPU Utilization (%)
	CPU Utilization (%)	CPU Utilization (SPECInt)*	CPU Utilization (%)	CPU Utilization (SPECInt)*
	CPU Utilization (SPECInt)*		CPU Utilization (SPECInt)*	Memory Usage
	Disk Space Utilization (%)		Network IO	User Requests
	Disk Usage			Active Sessions
	Memory Used			Request Execution Time
	Memory Utilization (%)			
	Network IO			

* Metric derived using SPEC benchmark results and CPU configuration/utilization

FIGURE 7-2. *Various supported target types and related metrics*

While the metrics in Figure 7-2 provide metering for resource consumption associated with any Host, VM, Database, or WebLogic Server, the assumption here is that each resource (represented as a target) is owned by either a single cloud user or a group of users. There may, however, be situations where more granular metering is required—for example, if a single database or WebLogic Server is shared by multiple cloud users or groups of users. To support this requirement, both Database and WebLogic targets can be added to the chargeback application in a shared mode. When added in the shared mode, a set of metrics is collected for each application that is sharing the Database or the WebLogic Server.

It's important to understand how an OracleDatabase can be used as a shared resource by using multiple Oracle Database services. Database services are logical abstractions for managing workloads in Oracle Database. Services divide database workloads into mutually disjoint groupings. Each service represents a workload with common attributes, service-level thresholds, and priorities. The grouping is based on attributes of work, which might include the application function to be used, the priority of execution for the application function, the job class to be managed, or the data range used in the application function or job class. For example, an application such as Oracle E-Business Suite defines a service for each responsibility, such as general ledger, accounts receivable, order entry, and so on. Each database service has a unique name. Connection requests to the database can include a database service name. If no service name is included and the Net Services file listener.ora designates a default service, the connection uses the default service.

Services are built into Oracle Database, providing a single system image for workloads, prioritization for workloads, performance measures for real transactions, and alerts and actions when performance goals are violated. Services enable database administrators to configure a workload, administer it, enable and disable it, and measure the workload as a single entity. Database administrators can do these tasks using standard tools such as the Database Configuration Assistant (DBCA), Net Configuration Assistant (NetCA), and Oracle Enterprise Manager.

Similarly, Real Application Clusters (RAC) databases also have the concept of services. In a RAC, a service can span one or more instances and facilitate real workload balancing based on real transaction performance. This provides end-to-end unattended recovery, rolling changes by workload, and full location transparency. RAC also enables the management of a number of service features with Oracle Enterprise Manager, the DBCA, and the Server Control Utility (SRVCTL).

For both single-instance and RAC databases, Oracle Enterprise Manager collects resource usage metrics per database service, which allows metering of a shared database resource on a per-service basis.

Similar to Oracle Databases, WebLogic Server resources can also be shared among various application deployments. Oracle Enterprise Manager collects resource usage metrics per application deployment, thus allowing costs for each application deployment to be allocated to a particular cloud user or cloud user group. The table in Figure 7-3 shows various metrics collected by Oracle Enterprise Manager for shared targets.

Enabling target metering through manual addition of each target to the chargeback application works well when targets are added infrequently. However, when managing a cloud, targets can be rapidly provisioned and destroyed by self-service cloud users. This makes the task of manually adding cloud targets to the chargeback application impractical for the administrator. This is addressed in the chargeback application with the use of Zones. To enable chargeback automatically for cloud resources (databases, middleware, and virtual machines) that will be provisioned using the Oracle Enterprise

	Chargeable Entity	
	Database Service	WebLogic Application Deployment
Configuration	Option	
	Edition	
Usage	CPU Time per Service	User Requests per Application
	CPU Utilization per Service	Active Sessions per Application
	CPU Utilization per Service (SPECInt)*	Request Execution Time per Application
	DB Time per Service	
	Disk Read (Physical) Operations per Service	
	Disk Write (Physical) Operations per Service	
	SQL Executes per Service	
	User Transactions per Service	

FIGURE 7-3. *Metrics for metering for shared targets*

Manager self-service application, the administrator simply needs to add the Database Zone, Middleware Zone, or Oracle VM Zone target to the chargeback application. This will ensure that any databases, middleware, or virtual machines created within the Zone in the future are automatically enabled for chargeback.

Oracle Enterprise Manager provides a role-based access control (RBAC) model for cloud security. Only administrators with appropriate target privileges can perform corresponding operations on targets. To add targets to the chargeback application for metering, an administrator needs to have VIEW privilege on those targets. For more information on Oracle Enterprise Manager's security model, refer to the *Oracle Enterprise Manager Administrator's Guide*.

Pricing Model: Assignment of Rates

Subsequent to enabling metering for the Oracle Enterprise Manager targets, the chargeback administrator must identify the resources that will be used for chargeback and set the rates for those resources. These resources and their associated rates are stored in a charge plan. For example, an administrator may want to charge for a Guest Virtual Machine (Guest VM) target based on the number of CPUs and memory allocated to it.

Charge Plans

A charge plan, which is created by the chargeback administrator, defines the metered resources that should be charged for (charge items) and their associated rates. Once defined, a charge plan can be assigned to a target. For example, a charge plan may have a "number of CPUs" charge item associated with the rate of "50 centers per CPU per day." Furthermore, this charge plan may be associated with the Guest Virtual Machine (Guest VM) targets. It is important to note that a target can be assigned only one charge plan at any time.

Oracle Enterprise Manager allows two types of charge plans: the Universal Charge Plan and Extended Charge Plans.

Universal Charge Plan

The Universal Charge Plan is the simplest way to enable chargeback and can be used for chargeback across a wide range of chargeback targets. The Universal Charge Plan contains the following three metrics, and no further metrics can be added:

- CPU Usage
- Memory Allocation
- Storage Allocation

Within the Universal Charge Plan, a chargeback administrator can set the rates (cost per period of time) that they want to charge for each of these resources. For example, they may wish to charge $1 per day per CPU, $0.20 per day per gigabyte of memory, and $0.01 per day per gigabyte of storage. The time period for these rates can be defined as Hourly, Daily, Weekly, Quarterly, or Yearly.

The Universal Charge Plan also enables the administrator to set different rates for different CPU architectures that may be present in their enterprise. For example, they might decide to charge a higher rate for PA-RISC or Itanium processors than for x86 due to the different costs involved. Figure 7-4 shows the Universal Charge Plan with sample values.

The rates used in charge calculations may vary from month to month, but rates may only be modified for the current (active) month. It is not possible to modify the rates associated with a previous month. If rates are modified, the updated rates will be used to recalculate the charges for all days from the first of the current month onward. Each monthly period is known as the Reporting Cycle.

Extended Charge Plans

The Universal Charge Plan provides a simple plan based on CPU Usage, Memory Allocation, and Storage Allocation that can be used with any type of chargeback target. There may, however, be situations where the chargeback

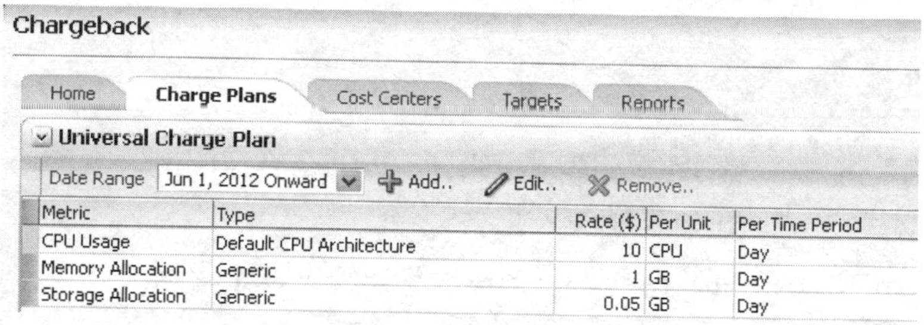

FIGURE 7-4. *Universal Charge Plan*

administrator wishes to apply target type–specific charges. Some examples of target type–specific charges could be a charge for an Oracle VM based on the VM Size attribute, a charge based on the number of WebLogic User Requests processed, or a charge for use of a Database Option.

To implement target type–specific charges, the chargeback administrator can create an Extended Charge Plan and add target type–specific charges to this plan. The Extended Charge Plan can contain charge items for a variety of target types, and the charges that prevail will be determined by the type of target that is metered. The Extended Charge Plan provides greater flexibility to chargeback administrators, enabling them to

- Define target type–specific charges

- Define fixed rates, configuration-based rates, and usage-based rates

- Override or adjust universal plan rates

It is also possible to create additional conditions on the charges that get applied to a particular type of target. For example, as shown in the Extended Charge Plan in Figure 7-5, the chargeback administrator can configure distinct groups of charges for VMs depending on whether the Machine Size attribute equals Small, Medium, or Large. In this case, the Machine Size attribute of each metered VM is used to automatically determine which rates should be applied.

Charge items that can be added to an Extended Charge Plan include fixed charges, configuration-based charges, and usage-based charges. Fixed charges enable the administrator to apply a flat rate to a target regardless of

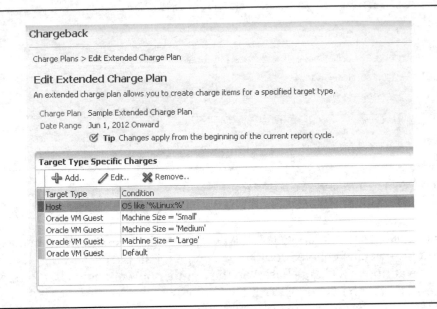

FIGURE 7-5. *A sample Extended Charge Plan*

its configuration or usage. This is useful for accounting for fixed costs such as datacenter space and IT staff. The configuration-based charge is applied only if a particular configuration is detected in a target. For example, because the configuration information collected by Oracle Enterprise Manager includes the Host OS, the chargeback administrator can use this information to create a charge plan such that a charge is applied only if the operating system is of a certain type. For example, as shown in Figure 7-5, an administrator can use an Extended Charge Plan to create a charge for any operating system (Host) with a fixed charge of $50/month and another $10/month charge specifically for a Linux Host. Similarly, the administrator can configure fixed charges based on expected service levels (i.e., availability), such as $2000 per month if running on Exadata and $1000 per month if running on a non-Exadata infrastructure.

The final step in configuring an Extended Charge Plan is to specify a Universal Rate Adjustment, which enables the chargeback administrator to specify a "multiplier" for the rates specified for resources in the Universal

Charge Plan. For example, if the administrator wants to create an Extended Charge Plan that excludes memory and storage (that is, the administrator wants no charges for these), the administrator can specify a Universal Rate Adjustment of 0 for memory and storage in the Extended Charge Plan. This ensures that the rates specified in the Universal Charge Plan for memory and storage are multiplied by 0, thus excluding them from the Extended Charge Plan.

Oracle Enterprise Manager allows the chargeback administrator to choose between reservation-based charging (no adjustment for uptime) or uptime-adjusted charging. The Uptime metric can be used to adjust fixed charges and configuration-based charges so that the end consumers do not pay for periods when the target is down. For example, suppose a database is up for 10 hours in a 24-hour period and is charged for the usage of the Partitioning option on a daily basis. If the charge is uptime adjusted, the usage of Partitioning will be accounted for only 10/24th of the period. Figure 7-6 shows Oracle Enterprise Manager's settings for uptime adjustment.

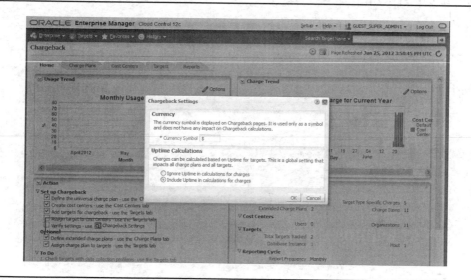

FIGURE 7-6. *Uptime-adjusted charging*

Management of Cost Hierarchy

The users of the metered IT resources need to be represented in a cost center structure to determine where the chargeback is assigned. These cost centers represent the different consumers who use the resources, and the chargeback administrator uses the cost centers to assign the chargeback ownership. The cost centers are typically organized in a hierarchical fashion for aggregation and for drilldown in tasks such as cost analysis of an organization's bill. A sample cost center hierarchy definition in the chargeback application is shown in Figure 7-7.

LDAP Integration for Cost Center Hierarchy

In a large organization, the cost center hierarchy may be large and complex, and to enter this structure manually would require significant effort on the part of the chargeback administrator. Chargeback is able to synchronize and maintain this hierarchy if it is already present in a corporate LDAP server. The LDAP synchronization can be set up to include up to five hierarchical levels.

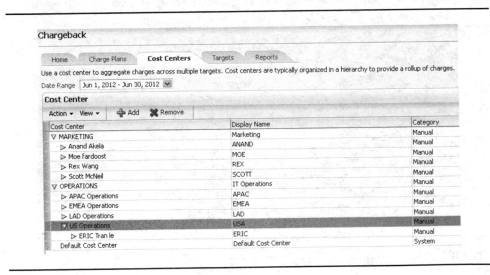

FIGURE 7-7.   *Cost center hierarchy*

When administering a self-service cloud, it is necessary to meter the consumption for each self-service user, and also to roll this up into the higher-level cost centers. In Oracle Enterprise Manager, the self-service users who create cloud targets such as databases and virtual machines appear on the Cost Centers page (refer to Figure 7-7) so that the chargeback administrator can assign them to an appropriate higher-level cost center. By incorporating self-service users into the cost center hierarchy, the chargeback administrator can see the data for each self-service user and can aggregate this data for self-service users within a particular department. The assignment of cloud consumers to higher-level cost centers can be automated if LDAP synchronization has been configured. As shown in Figure 7-8, Oracle Enterprise Manager supports LDAP servers such as Oracle Internet Directory (OID), Microsoft Active Directory, Open LDAP Server, Novell EDirectory, and Sun IPlanet Directory.

Because a cost center hierarchy may be subject to frequent updates, the chargeback application uses the most recent version of the hierarchy. Any updates made to the hierarchy will be applied from the start of the current reporting cycle up to the present date. It will have no impact on prior reporting cycles.

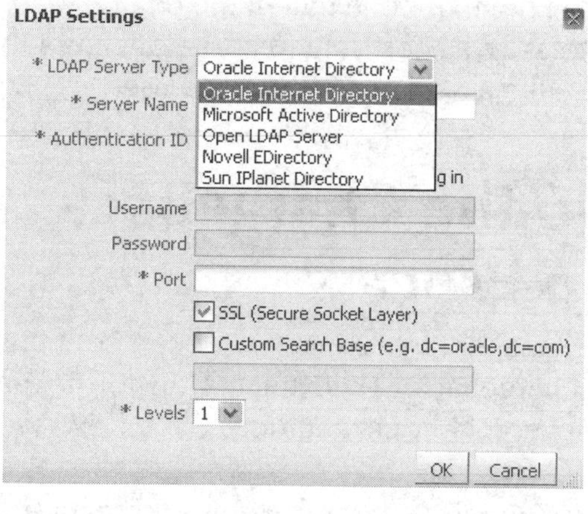

FIGURE 7-8. *LDAP server configuration*

Assigning Charge Plans to Cost Centers

The final stage in the setup of chargeback is a two-step process that determines

- The charge plan used for calculation of charges for a chargeback target
- The cost center the calculated charges should be allocated to

For each chargeback target, the administrator is able to assign a charge plan to a target and assign a target to a cost center.

Any changes made to charge plan or cost center assignment will be effective from the start of the current month (reporting cycle), and all previous charge calculations for the affected targets during the current month will be invalidated. This change will have no impact on the charges for prior months.

Because chargeback targets are often part of a hierarchy (for example, Oracle VM Guest > Oracle VM Server > Oracle VM Zone), the charge plan and cost center can be assigned to a parent. In this case, any children that do not have a direct assignment will inherit the settings from the parent.

This inheritance model is typically used for assignment of the charge plan to targets that have been created via the cloud Self Service Portal. A charge plan is assigned to a Zone, and any resources (databases, middleware, virtual machines) created within that Zone inherit the charge plan. For these targets, it is not necessary to assign a cost center, as the owner of the cloud target is already known to be the associated self-service user.

Setting Up the Chargeback Collection Process

Oracle Enterprise Manager targets that have been configured for chargeback will be part of the chargeback ETL (Extract, Transform, Load) process. This process runs once every 24 hours and does the following:

- Extracts the Configuration and Monitoring data from the Oracle Enterprise Manager repository tables
- Performs transformations and aggregations so that the data can be used for chargeback

- Loads the data into separate chargeback tables within the Oracle Enterprise Manager repository

- Calculates the charges for the cost centers based on the assigned plans

Following modifications to the chargeback setup (for example, charge plan change, cost center hierarchy change, target cost center change or plan assignment change), the ETL process must run in order for the reports to show the results as per the updated configuration.

Running the ETL Process

The ETL job is scheduled to run on a 24-hour schedule. To check when the job will next run, the system administrator can navigate to Enterprise | Job | Activity | Advanced Search and search for the Job Type called Chargeback Data Loader with a Target Type value of Targetless.

It is possible to force a manual execution of the chargeback ETL job by executing the following PL/SQL block as SYSMAN:

```
BEGIN emct_cba_loader.submit_cba_etl_job('test'); END;
```

After submitting this PL/SQL block, the ETL job will run in the background.

Usage and Charge Reporting

Any chargeback solution involves reporting so that users can understand how their use of resources translates to charges. Oracle Enterprise Manager provides reports that show both resource usage and charge information.

Summary Reports

Chargeback summary reports show information related to charge or resource utilization broken down by Cost Center, Target Type, and Resource. They enable the viewer to quickly assess the targets or cost centers with the greatest charges or resource utilization. Summary reports are primarily useful for drill-down purposes. Figure 7-9 shows a sample summary report.

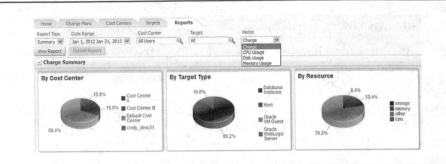

FIGURE 7-9. *Sample summary report*

Trending Reports

Trending reports show metric or charge trends over a defined period of time and are useful to end users who want to see how their charges have changed over time. They are also useful to the IT department for capacity planning purposes. Figure 7-10 shows a sample trending report.

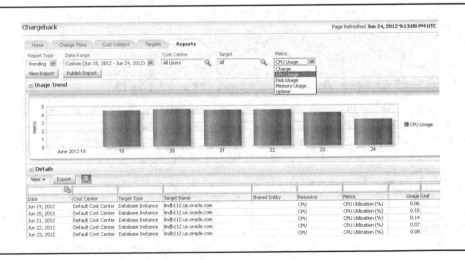

FIGURE 7-10. *Sample trending report*

Reporting Interfaces

There are a variety of audiences for chargeback reports:

- A chargeback administrator who requires a global view of all chargeback activity

- Self Service Portal users who would like to view their own chargeback information within the Self Service Portal

- Business users who need to receive chargeback information related to the systems they use

To accommodate these different types of user, the Oracle Enterprise Manager reports are available through a variety of interfaces, as described next.

Chargeback Administrator Reports

As previously shown in Figures 7-9 and 7-10, both summary and trending reports can be accessed from the Reports page in the chargeback application. From the Reports page, the chargeback administrator can get a consolidated view of charge and metric information and is able to drill down by date range, cost center, target, target type, or Resource.

The usage and charge data can also been seen in a tabular format with a variety of out-of-the-box aggregations:

- **All**   Shows every selected target and metric for each day. This is the finest level of granularity that is available in the reports.

- **Target**   Aggregates the selected data for the selected period by target.

- **Resource**   Aggregates the selected data for each target in the selected period by resource (CPU, Memory, Storage, Other).

- **Metric**   Aggregates the selected data for each target in the selected period by metric.

- **Date**   Aggregates the selected data for each target for each day in the selected period.

These views allow the chargeback administrator to filter and sort data. The administrator can also determine at a glance which charge plan, metric, and rate have been used to calculate each charge. An Export to Excel feature is also available.

Self Service Portal Reports
Chargeback information is available for individual self-service users from within the Self Service Portal, where they can see the daily charges they have incurred across various types of resources.

Oracle BI Publisher Reports
Providing reports to other stakeholders, such as business users, is a key requirement of chargeback. These recipients would not typically be defined as Oracle Enterprise Manager users. Oracle Enterprise Manager Cloud Control 12*c* provides out-of-the-box integration with Oracle BI Publisher. This enables the chargeback administrator to define external recipients for chargeback reports and chose from a variety of formats, such as HTML, PDF, RTF, Excel, and PowerPoint. Oracle BI Publisher can be configured to publish these reports to a website/portal or to e-mail them directly to the recipients.

Oracle Enterprise Manager EMCLI API for Chargeback

Oracle Enterprise Manager provides metering for resources within the cloud. In a private cloud, this is generally useful as a "showback" solution, as issuing a bill in not always a requirement. However, this is not the case with a public cloud. To meet the requirements of service providers to implement sophisticated pricing plans, or to issue bills to consumers, Oracle Enterprise Manager provides a mechanism to export usage and charge information in the CSV format using the Enterprise Manager Command Line Interface (EMCLI).

Using EMCLI, either the metering data or both the metering and charge data can be extracted from Oracle Enterprise Manager for use in external billing applications such as Oracle Billing and Revenue Management (BRM). Following could be some of the reasons of using the EMCLI API:

- To integrate with a billing system with different rate plans for small, medium, and large configurations

- To calculate chargeback for a flexible time period (for example, months starting from the 15th and ending on the 15th)

- To rationalize chargeback based on other attributes that are not captured by Oracle Enterprise Manager

- To adjust or round up chargeback based on usage (for example, charge is calculated for the full day even if the usage is for the partial day)

The process of retrieving metering data using the API involves an EMCLI call using the get_metering_data verb. The EMCLI enables administrators to access Oracle Enterprise Manager Cloud Control functionality from text-based consoles (shells and command windows) for a variety of operating systems. An administrator can call into Oracle Enterprise Manager using custom scripts, thus easily integrating Oracle Enterprise Manager features with the company's IT processes. Using EMCLI, an administrator can perform Oracle Enterprise Manager Cloud Control console-based operations, such as monitoring and managing targets, jobs, groups, and blackouts.

EMCLI is intended for use by enterprise or system administrators writing scripts, such as shell/batch files or Perl, TCL, or PHP scripts, that provide workflow in the customer's business process. They can can also use EMCLI commands interactively from an operating system console. EMCLI is fully integrated with Oracle Enterprise Manager's security and user administration functions, enabling administrators to carry out operations using EMCLI with the same security and confidentiality as the Oracle Enterprise Manager Cloud Control console. For example, they can only see and operate on targets for which they are authorized.

A verb can perform its operations locally, but most of the verbs included with the EMCLI are covered by the remote verb in the EMCLI Client. The remote verb contacts the EMCLI OMS Extension in the Oracle Enterprise Manager Oracle Management Service (OMS) Console through HTTP/HTTPS and sends the command line through HTTP to the OMS for processing.

EMCLI Syntax and Usage

The verb for retrieving metering data generates comma-separated output, with each row or line containing usage (and optionally charge) information for the specified parameters. The verb syntax is

```
emcli get_metering_data [-start_date=<start date in mmddyyyy>
[-end_date=<end_date in mmddyyyy>]]
[ -target_type=<target type> [-target_name= <target name> ] ]
[ -cost_center=<cost center name> ]
[ -charge]
```

All the parameters of this verb are optional. If no parameters are specified, default values are used. The parameters are as follows:

■ **start_date**   The value for this parameter must be specified in mmddyyyy format. If the start_date is not specified, the start date for the current report cycle is used by default. In this scenario, the start_ date means midnight on the start date.

■ **end_date**   This parameter must be used along with the start_date parameter. The value for this parameter must be given in mmddyyyy format. If the end_date is not specified, the end date for the current report cycle is used by default. In this scenario, the end_date means midnight on the end date.

■ **target_type**   In Oracle Enterprise Manager release 12.1.0.2, you can specify the target_type as oracle_databases, oracle_vm_guest, host, or weblogic_j2eeserver. If the targets of the specified target_ type have been enabled within the specified date range, appropriate metering or charge data (data for all targets of the specified target_ type) will be retrieved. If this parameter is not specified, all supported target types will be included by default.

■ **target_name**   If a target type is specified in the target_type field, the name of the target has to be specified here. If the target_name is not valid, or if the specified target has not been enabled in the given date range, then no data is generated. If this parameter is not specified, all targets for the specified target type will be included.

- **cost_center** If specified, the value of this parameter must be the same as the internal cost center (as displayed on the Cost Center tab in the chargeback application). If the specified value is a valid cost center in the given date range, appropriate metering/charge data will be retrieved. If not, then no data will be generated. If this option is not specified, the default value for the parameter is the logged-in user. To retrieve metering/charge information for all cost centers, "All Users" has to specified, including the quote marks.

- **charge** If this parameter is not specified, by default, only the metering data will be retrieved. If this option is specified, both metering and charge information will be retrieved.

The following are the privileges required to view target information in the chargeback application:

- **VIEW_CAT_TARGET** Allows the users to view information for a specific target (active or inactive)

- **VIEW_ANY_CAT_TARGET** Allows the users to view information for any chargeback target (active or inactive)

The following are a few usage examples:

- **emcli get_metering_data** Returns metering information for all targets (active or enabled in the chargeback application) for the current report cycle for the logged-in user.

- **emcli get_metering_data-charge** Returns metering and charge information for all targets (active or enabled in the chargeback application) for the current report cycle for the logged-in user.

- **emcli get_metering_data-start_date=01202011-cost_center= ORG1** Returns metering information for all targets (active or enabled in the chargeback application) starting from January 20, 2011 until the end of the month for the ORG1 cost center.

■ **emcli get_metering_data-start_date=01152011-end_date= 02152011 -target_type=oracle_database**   Returns metering information for all Oracle DB targets (active or enabled in the chargeback application) that are owned by the logged-in user, starting January 15, 2011 and ending February 15, 2011.

■ **emcli get_metering_data-target_type=host target_name=my_host -cost_center=organization1**   Returns metering and charge information for the my_host target (of type host) for the current report cycle for the organization1 cost center.

■ **emcli get_metering_data-cost_center="All Users"**   Returns metering and charge information for all targets (active or enabled in the chargeback application) in the current report cycle for all cost centers.

Log in as **cba_admin_user** (the chargeback administrator) and enter the following commands:

■ **emcli get_metering_data**   Returns metering information for all targets (active or enabled in the chargeback application) for the current report cycle for the cba_admin_user.

■ **emcli get_metering_data-cost_center=ssa_user1**   Returns metering information for all targets (active or enabled in the chargeback application) that are owned by ssa_user1 in the cost center in the current report cycle.

If the value specified for the cost center, target type, and/or target name is incorrect, no data will be generated.

EMCLI Output

This get_metering_data EMCLI generates the following output:

CONSUMER_NAME   Name of the cost center.

TARGET_TYPE   Type of target.

TARGET_NAME   Name of the target.

ITEM_TYPE Type of the item or metric. Possible values are config, fixed, metric, property, and usage.

CATEGORY_NAME Possible values are cpu, memory, storage, activity, instance, network, service, and software.

ENTITY_NAME Name of the shared entity (valid when the target is enabled in chargeback in shared mode).

ITEM_DISPLAY_NAME Display name of the item or metric (in English language). Note: Translation support is currently not available.

VALUE_AVERAGE Average value for the metric on the given date (valid for numeric metrics).

STRING_VALUE Value for the metric data (valid for string-based metrics).

DATA_TYPE Data type of the metric. This can be string or number.

UNIT Unit of the metric data (for example, GB).

COLLECTION_DATE Date on which the data is collected from the Oracle Enterprise Manager metric or configuration tables.

PLAN_NAME Name of the charge plan associated with the particular target.

CHARGE Charge value for the specific metric of the target on the particular date.

DEFINED_RATE Charge rate defined in the charge plan associated with the target.

RATE_TYPE Type of the rate. Possible values are No value (blank), flat, config, and usage.

RATE_FACTOR Adjustment rate for universal metrics, as defined in the associated Extended Charge Plan.

CHARGE_RATE_UNIT Unit, corresponding to the metric or item, as defined in the charge plan for the specific rate. For example, for an item or metric named CPU Utilization (%) or CPU Utilization (%) per service, the value will be "CPU." For a metric or item named Base Charge, the value will be "instance," a metric named "User Requests," the value will be "req"). If the rate defined in the charge plan is $1 per MB per Day, the value for this column will be "MB."

CHARGE_TIME_UNIT Time unit as defined in the charge plan for the specific rate (such as hourly, daily, weekly, monthly, or yearly). For example, if the rate defined in the charge plan is $1 per MB per day, the value for this column will be daily.

Sample Output

```
"CONSUMER_NAME","TARGET_TYPE","TARGET_NAME","ITEM_TYPE",
"CATEGORY_NAME","ENTITY_NAME","ITEM_DISPLAY_NAME",
"STRING_VALUE","PLAN_NAME","COLLECTION_DATE","CHARGE",
"VALUE_AVERAGE","DEFINED_RATE","RATE_TYPE","RATE_FACTOR",
"CHARGE_RATE_UNIT","CHARGE_TIME_UNIT","NORMALIZE_RATE",
"ADJUST_RATE","DATA_TYPE","UNIT"

    "linbo","oracle_vm_guest","mySite/myWls/
AdminServer:agent_push","fixed","instance"," ","Base
Charge","","zone_plan",15-OCT-11
00:00:00,72,1,"3","flat",1,"instance","hourly",1,1,"number",""

    "linbo","oracle_vm_guest","mySite/myWls/
AdminServer:agent_push","fixed","instance"," ","Base
Charge","","zone_plan",16-OCT-11
00:00:00,72,1,"3","flat",1,"instance","hourly",1,1,"number",""

    "linbo","oracle_vm_guest","mySite/myWls/
AdminServer:agent_push","fixed","instance"," ","Base
Charge","","zone_plan",17-OCT-11
00:00:00,72,1,"3","flat",1,"instance","hourly",1,1,"number",""

    "linbo","oracle_vm_guest","mySite/myWls/
AdminServer:agent_push","fixed","instance"," ","Base
Charge","","zone_plan",18-OCT-11
00:00:00,72,1,"3","flat",1,"instance","hourly",1,1,"number",""

    "linbo","oracle_vm_guest","mySite/myWls/Cluster-0_
vm0:assembly1","fixed","instance"," ","Base
Charge","","zone_plan",15-OCT-11
00:00:00,72,1,"3","flat",1,"instance","hourly",1,1,"number",""
```

Summary

The growing number of applications deployed on shared infrastructure and the emergence of cloud computing have resulted in a new interest in IT chargeback. Oracle Enterprise Manager Cloud Control 12c leverages the rich monitoring and configuration data to provide a simple-to-use metering and chargeback solution. The highlight of the Oracle Enterprise Manager solution lies in its flexibility that enables it to adapt to different models. This solution enables administrators to meter resources, assign costing rates to the metered resources, manage cost centers, and issue usage and charge reports to consumers. The solution can also be integrated with enterprise billing engines such as Oracle Billing and Revenue Management (BRM). More examples of metering and chargeback are provided in Chapter 8 in the context of self-service.

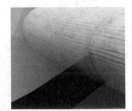

CHAPTER
8

Managing the Cloud:
Monitoring, Configuration
Management, and
Compliance

he previous chapters discussed how the cloud can be modeled to provide metered, self-service facilities to end consumers. While self-service eliminates IT as a gating factor in the resource provisioning process, the role of IT is actually of greater significance in the management of a cloud. Ultimately, IT administrators have the role of managing the cloud and making sure that the lights are on and that the service levels of the cloud are being met. Their role is even greater in case of public clouds, where the assets are large in number and the concurrent usage is high.

This chapter looks at some of the operational aspects of clouds for the cloud administrator. The list of cloud management operations can be broadly classified into the following disciplines:

■ **Large-scale monitoring**   An enterprise cloud typically consists of hundreds or thousands of servers and related targets. Large-scale monitoring implies monitoring the cloud and making sure that all those enterprise components that make up the cloud are working properly.

   With single-pane-of-glass visibility into the physical, virtual, OS, and application environments, Oracle Enterprise Manager's monitoring capabilities enable administrators to quickly and easily identify and remediate outages. Oracle Enterprise Manager can detect events as they happen in the data center and can publish them to other ticketing systems.

■ **Performance and service-level management**   For the cloud to be functional, it is not adequate to simply make sure it's operational. It is also important to ensure that the performance levels are maintained, so that the quality of service (QoS) promised in SLAs can be guaranteed. The SLAs are typically defined in terms of business continuity, which translates to availability and performance goals for the application. For example, 99.999% availability is a goal commonly used for mission-critical applications.

   Oracle Enterprise Manager provides industry's most comprehensive performance management capabilities, especially for the Oracle ecosystem. With deep tuning and diagnostic capabilities that span the operating system, database, middleware, and application layers, it lets administrators quickly diagnose performance bottlenecks in the cloud and remediate them.

■ **Configuration management and compliance**   A typical cloud has thousands of hardware and software assets. For ongoing operations, it is very important to track them and make sure that they are compliant with established best practices and standards. Some examples of best practices include security best practices and PCI compliance.

Oracle Enterprise Manager comes with out-of-the-box configuration management capabilities for discovery, inventory tracking, configuration drift control, and configuration compliance management that facilitate the need for administrators to track these assets even at a detailed level.

■ **Automation of repetitive administrative tasks**   Finally, on a day-to-day basis, administrators need to perform repetitive tasks such as backup, patching, log cleanup, and so on.

Oracle Enterprise Manager comes with an automation framework comprising Jobs and Deployment Procedures (discussed in Chapter 3) that let administrators define these repetitive actions and schedule them as needed.

For large-scale cloud operations, Oracle Enterprise Manager has been explicitly tested and certified, such that it

■ Scales to hundreds of thousands of managed targets

■ Accommodates hundreds of concurrent users

■ Runs hundreds of concurrent jobs in the cloud

■ Offers water-tight security and integrates with Oracle Access Manager and Identity Management systems

■ Offers a command-line interface for large-scale customized automation

Large-Scale Monitoring

When it comes to monitoring the cloud, it's important to recognize that in large organizations, there are different roles involved and the monitoring has to be tailored for each specific role. For example, in a typical public cloud, there are self-service users (often part of a larger tenant group), tenant administrators, operations support personnel, and cloud administrators. The self-service users are more interested in monitoring their own requests and usage; the tenant administrators are interested in monitoring the services for the entire group; the support personnel are only interested in looking for targets with reported problems; and cloud administrators are interested in monitoring the health and growth of the entire cloud. Since this chapter is mainly about operational aspects of the cloud from a provider's perspective, it primarily focuses on monitoring from the perspective of the cloud administrator.

Monitoring by Exception

It is not practical to attend to and visually monitor an enterprise cloud 24 hours a day, 7 days a week, so the principle of *management by exception* needs to be followed. In Oracle Enterprise Manager parlance, an *exception* is represented by an event. An event is a significant occurrence on a managed target that typically indicates something has occurred outside normal operating conditions. Examples of events include: database target down, performance threshold violation, change in application configuration files, or job failure. An event can also be raised to signal successful operations or a job successfully completed.

However, not all events need equal attention. With the numerous IT components that constitute the cloud, there could be a significant amount of "noise" that is generated. It is, therefore, important to weed out the unimportant events from the events that need attention. To manage this significant subset of events, Oracle Enterprise Manager provides incident management features. An *incident* is a significant event or a set of related significant events that needs to be managed because it can potentially impact your business applications.

Managing incidents is carried out through Incident Manager, shown in Figure 8-1, which provides you with a central location from which to view, manage, diagnose, and resolve incidents as well as identify, resolve, and eliminate the root cause of disruptions. Incidents allow administrators to manage many discrete event types by providing an intuitive way to combine them into meaningful issues that they can act upon.

When an incident is created, Oracle Enterprise Manager makes available a rich set of incident management workflow features that enable you to

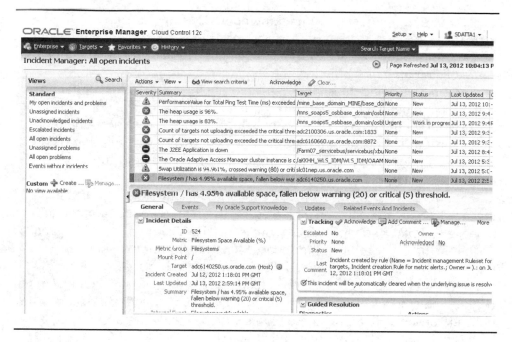

FIGURE 8-1. *Incident Manager console*

manage and track the incident through its complete life cycle. Incident management functions allow you to

- Assign incident ownership

- Track the incident resolution status

- Set an incident priority

- Set an incident escalation level

- Access (in context) My Oracle Support knowledge base articles and other Oracle documentation to help resolve the incident

- Access direct, in-context diagnostic/action links to relevant Oracle Enterprise Manager features, allowing you to quickly diagnose or resolve the incident

All incident management/tracking operations are carried out from Incident Manager. Creation of incidents for events, assignment of incidents to administrators, setting priority, sending notifications, and other actions can be automated using (incident) rules.

The simplest incident is composed of a single event. For example, if you want to be notified whenever any production target is down, you can create an incident for the target down event, which is raised by Oracle Enterprise Manager if it detects the monitored target is down. Once the incident is created, you will have available all incident management functionality required to track and manage its resolution.

Situations of interest may involve more than a single event. It is an incident's ability to contain multiple events that allows you to monitor and manage complex and more meaningful issues. For example, if a monitored system is running out of storage space, separate, multiple events may be raised, such as tablespace full and filesystem full. Both, however, are related to running out of space. Another machine resource monitoring example might be the simultaneous raising of CPU utilization, memory utilization, and swap utilization events. Together, these events form an incident indicating extreme load is being placed on a monitored host.

When working in a large enterprise, it is conceivable that when systems are under heavy load, an extraordinarily large number of incidents and events will be generated. All of these need to be processed in a timely and efficient manner in accordance with your business priorities. Having them processed sequentially can result in long waits before incidents can be resolved, which is problematic because high-priority events/incidents need to be addressed before those of low priority.

In order to determine which event/incidents are of high priority, Oracle Enterprise Manager uses a prioritization protocol based on two incident/event attributes: Lifecycle Status of the target and the Incident/Event Type. Lifecycle Status is a target property that specifies a target's operational status. You can set the Lifecycle Status either through the GUI or through the Enterprise Manager Command Line Interface (EMCLI). In cloud parlance, you can set the Lifecycle Status at the zone level for the infrastructure and the platform components that constitute the zone. So, all targets belonging to the Production Zone, for example, could have a Lifecycle Status of Production, while those belonging to the Development Zone could have a Development Lifecycle Status.

An integral aspect of management by exceptions is the ability to notify based on exceptions. Oracle Enterprise Manager notifications not only can send messages to e-mail addresses and pagers, but can also perform actions such as executing operating system commands (including scripts) and PL/SQL procedures when specific incidents, events, or problems occur. In previous versions of Oracle Enterprise Manager, you had to use notification rules to choose the individual targets and conditions for which you wanted to perform actions and/or receive notifications (send an e-mail, send a page, or open a trouble ticket) from Oracle Enterprise Manager. In Oracle Enterprise Manager 12c, the concept and function of notification rules has been replaced with rules and rule sets.

- **Rules**   A rule instructs Oracle Enterprise Manager to take specific actions, such as send notifications, when incidents, events, or problems occur. Beyond notifications, rules can also instruct Oracle Enterprise Manager to perform specific actions, such as raising additional incidents.

- **Rule set**   A rule set is a grouping of one or more rules that apply to a common set of objects such as targets (hosts, databases, groups), jobs, metric extensions, or self-updates. A rule set allows you to logically combine different rules relating to the common set of objects (such as jobs, targets, and applications) into a single manageable unit. Operationally, individual rules within a rule set are executed in a specified order, as are the rule sets themselves. By default, the execution order for both rules and rule sets is the order in which they are created, but you can reorder them from within the Incident Manager UI.

Most enterprise IT organizations have some ticketing system, such as Remedy or HP Service Manager, that manages the tickets and assigns them to administrators. The intergration between Enterprise Manager and such third-party ticketing system is achieved through Connetors, that leverage the notification mechanism previously described, to automatically open a ticket when the incident is created, add then track the ticket ID and query the status of the ticket. This provides administrators with a way to check the status of the ticket from within Incident Manager. Oracle Enterprise Manager also allows you to link out to a web-based, third-party console directly from the ticket so that you can launch the console in context directly from the ticket, as shown in Figure 8-2.

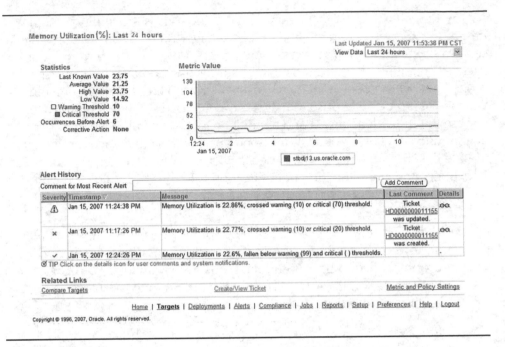

FIGURE 8-2. *Notification via Remedy Connector*

Administration Groups are a special type of group used to fully automate the application of monitoring and other management settings to targets, upon joining the group. When a target is added to the group, Oracle Enterprise Manager applies these settings using a Template Collection consisting of Monitoring Templates, Compliance Standards, and cloud policies. This completely eliminates the need for administrator intervention. With the preparatory work complete, you are ready to begin the four-step process of creating an Administration Group hierarchy and the Template Collections. The Administration Group user interface is organized to guide you through the creation process, with each tab containing the requisite operations to perform each step.

This process involves

■ Creating the Administration Group hierarchy

■ Creating Template Collections

■ Associating Template Collections to Administration Group

■ Synchronizing the targets with the selected items

Monitoring Self-Service Requests

The preceding concepts of monitoring are also used by Oracle Enterprise Manager for monitoring the self-service requests via specific administration pages. As self-service users start consuming the cloud, the cloud administrators need greater transparency about how the requests are getting satisfied and how the resources are being utilized. Certain aspects of this monitoring are of paramount importance:

- The ability to monitor the request rates

- The ability to see the target flux (that is, the rate of creation vs. the rate of retirement)

- Capacity of the individual zones in terms of resources

- Top consumers of the cloud

- Any incidents and policy violations that have happened in the past 24 hours

Monitoring the preceding elements enables cloud administrators to be cognizant of any issues that may potentially disrupt the ability to serve requests from cloud consumers. The Cloud target is available out of the box and represents the entire cloud infrastructure monitored by Oracle Enterprise Manager Cloud Control. You can view and monitor the various targets in the data center from the Infrastructure Cloud home page or the Middleware and Database Cloud home page. From the Cloud home page, you can drill down into the home pages of the constituent targets. For example, in case of IaaS, you can drill down into the Oracle VM hypervisor's home page and view the related metrics, as shown in Figure 8-3. Similarly, in case of PaaS, you can drill down into the Oracle Middleware and Database Cloud Home page of the target and review the patches applied, as shown in Figure 8-4. The monitoring aspects of IaaS and PaaS are described in detail in their respective chapters.

Since engineering systems offer a ready-to-use cloud infrastructure, they deserve a special mention in the context of monitoring. The management of engineered systems is indeed special, because they are managed vertically as a unit by administrators with specialized skills in managing multiple-stack

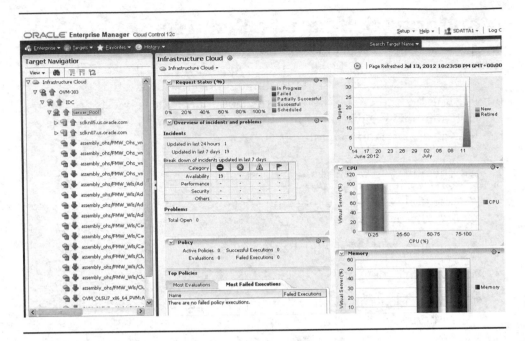

FIGURE 8-3. *IaaS cloud administration home page*

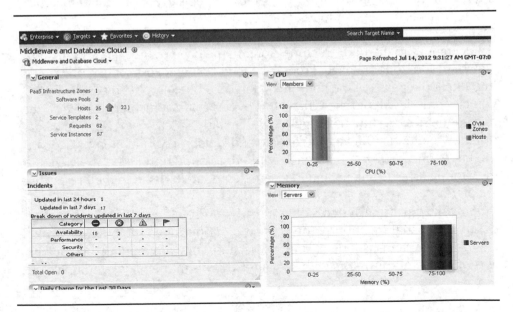

FIGURE 8-4. *PaaS (database and middleware) cloud administration home page*

components. The Exadata Database Machine home page (shown in Figure 8-5) includes the following components:

- The hardware schematic allows you to view hardware components of the Database Machine (for example, compute nodes, Exadata cells, and InfiniBand switches), monitor critical hardware metrics, and view aggregated alerts and faults from all components.

- Alerts sourced from hardware components.

- Easily accessible links and flows to other key features, such as viewing the topology or modifying the schematic.

- Underlying components of the DB Machine. The DB Machine monitors all subcomponent targets, whether hardware or software. This includes the database, ASM, CRS, hosts, Exadata, and the InfiniBand network.

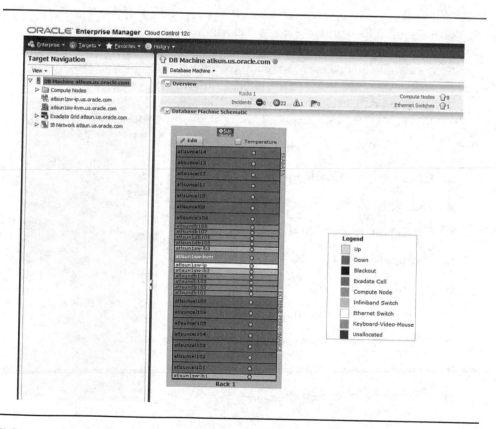

FIGURE 8-5. *Exadata hardware schematic*

- The two targets specifically available to facilitate Exadata Database Machine monitoring are

  - Exadata Storage Server

  - InfiniBand Network Fabric

Similarly, the Oracle Exalogic home page displays status information that included alerts and key performance metrics of the following targets in the Oracle Exalogic Elastic Cloud:

- Application deployments

- WebLogic domains

- Coherence clusters

- Hosts with underlying hardware and hardware schematic

For managing the Oracle Exalogic Elastic Cloud infrastructure, Oracle Enterprise Manager offers contextual drill-downs into Exalogic Control, an instance of Oracle Enterprise Manager Ops Center installed with each Exalogic rack for managing the hardware. Exalogic Control provides management of the Oracle VM Servers, ZFS Storage Appliance, and network fabric.

The following lists some of the Exalogic machine management features offered by Exalogic Control:

- Hardware schematic visualization

- Exalogic machine rack as a top-level asset

- Exalogic fabric and multirack relationship

- Physical fabric or network (see Figure 8-6)

- Monitoring and alerting (see Figure 8-7)

- Fault detection and management

- Support request management with My Oracle Support

- Hardware replacement life cycle

- Exalogic system reports

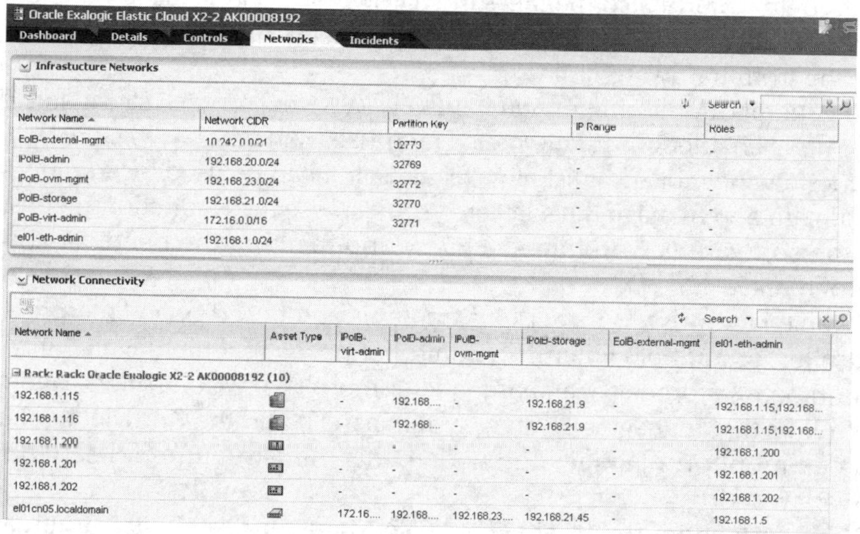

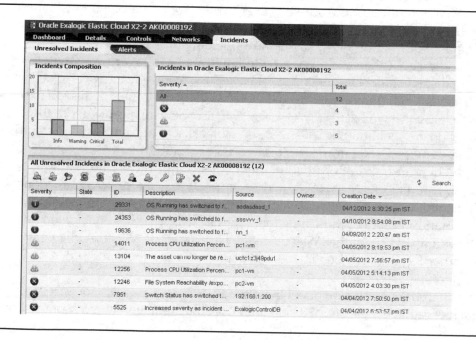

FIGURE 8-6. *Exalogic network configuration captured in Exalogic Control*

FIGURE 8-7. *Hardware faults detection in Exalogic Control*

Exalogic Control also manages the hardware-level events and incidents and automatically creates the Service Requests (SRs) in case of incidents resulting from hardware faults.

In general, monitoring of Sun hardware systems (servers, storage, and network) is enabled through Oracle Enterprise Manager Ops Center, which includes a variety of administrative features that can be used by administrators to maintain and manage the software. You can use these functions to ensure that the software is working effectively and meeting the needs of your environment.

Oracle Enterprise Manager Ops Center is composed of an Enterprise Controller (or multiple Enterprise Controller nodes in a high-availability environment), a product database, one or more Proxy Controllers, Agent Controllers that manage operating system assets, and the Knowledge Base. You can monitor, manage, and update this infrastructure to keep the software working.

You can configure Oracle Enterprise Manager Ops Center to create Automated Service Requests (ASRs) for qualified assets when certain incidents occur. An ASR can only be generated for an asset if a set of valid My Oracle Support (MOS) credentials have been provided. The asset must be present in MOS, and the credentials must be associated with a Customer Service Identifier (CSI) with rights over the asset. Service Request Creation rights are required to create new SRs, and Admin rights are required if the contact information for the asset must be updated.

When ASRs are enabled, Oracle Enterprise Manager Ops Center periodically launches a job to activate assets for ASRs, and attempts to activate all assets when they are discovered. You can view the details of this job to see which assets have been activated. You can also view an asset's ASR status. You can add the serial number of an asset to a blacklist to prevent Oracle Enterprise Manager Ops Center from enabling that asset for ASRs.

When a qualified critical incident causes an ASR creation attempt, a job is run to create the ASR, and an annotation is added to the incident to indicate the ASR creation attempt. If the ASR creation is successful, another annotation is added, indicating that the ASR was successfully created and providing a URL for the ASR. Once they are created, ASRs are identical to other SRs and can be viewed and managed using the same processes and tools.

For more information about the assets that can be activated for ASRs and the incidents that can create ASRs, see the ASR documentation at www.oracle.com.

Ops Center can publish events in Oracle Enterprise Manager Cloud Control through the Ops Center Connector.

For a complete understanding of monitoring with Oracle Enterprise Manager, the following official documentation can offer more details:

- Oracle Enterprise Manager Framework, Host, and Services Metric Reference Manual

- Oracle Enterprise Manager Cloud Control Administrator's Guide

- Oracle Enterprise Manager Connectors Integration Guide

- Oracle Enterprise Manager Exadata Management Getting Started Guide

- Oracle Enterprise Manager Ops Center Administration Guide

Performance and Service-Level Management

In order for a cloud to be functional for its end users, it has to adhere to strict service levels, comprising performance and availability criteria. In this section, we will discuss how Enterprise Manager 12c helps in performance and service-level management of the cloud. We will first start with the detail, on how Enterprise Manager aids in component-level performance management at the infrastructure and platform layers, and then see how those component-level metrics can be rolled up to define higher service levels.

Diagnosing Component-Level Problems

Now that you know the relationship between events, incidents, and notifications, you need to understand that the events themselves do not offer a diagnosis of the underlying problem. Diagnosing the problem requires a deeper inspection of what's going on. That is provided by deep diagnostic tools instrumented into each target type that Oracle Enterprise Manager supports. For the database layer, for example, Oracle Enterprise Manager includes a self-diagnostic engine built right into the Oracle Database kernel, called Automatic Database Diagnostic Monitor (ADDM), that completely liberates administrators from the complex and arduous task of diagnosing performance problems. Similarly, for the Java components, Oracle Enterprise Manager includes JVM Diagnostics (JVMD) capabilities to detect performance bottlenecks and resource contention.

Some common database performance problems include

- CPU bottlenecks
- Undersized memory structures
- I/O capacity issues
- Suboptimal use of Oracle Database by the application, such as SQL parsing
- Concurrency issues
- Database configuration issues
- Short-lived performance problems
- Degradation of database performance over time
- Inefficient or high-load SQL statements
- SQL statements using excessive system resources that impact the system
- Object contention
- Unexpected performance regression after tuning SQL statements

ADDM starts its analysis by focusing on the activities that the database is spending the most time on and then drills down through a sophisticated problem classification tree to determine the root cause of problems. ADDM's ability to discover the actual cause behind performance problems, rather than just reporting symptoms, is just one of the several factors that make it superior to any other Oracle Database performance management tool or utility. Each ADDM finding has an associated impact and benefit measure to enable prioritized handling of the most critical issues. To better understand the impact of the findings over time, each finding has a descriptive name that allows the application of filters and facilitates search, and a link to any previous occurrences of the finding in the past 24 hours.

A significant addition to Oracle Enterprise Manager is a feature called Real-Time ADDM. This feature provides an innovative way to analyze problems in unresponsive or hung databases. Real-Time ADDM (shown in Figure 8-8) uses 2 different modes of connection to the database. A normal connection and a diagnostic mode that is a lock less, latch less connection which allows only few actions. Using the diagnostic mode connection

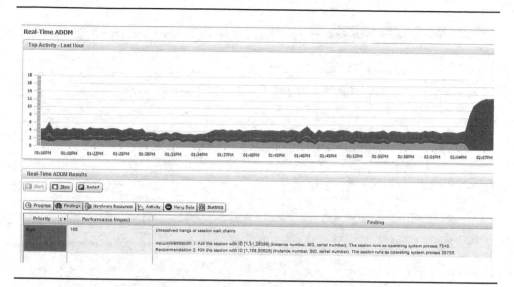

FIGURE 8-8. *Real-Time ADDM analysis of hung databases*

Real-Time ADDM performs a hang analysis and determines any blockers in the systems. This using a normal and a diagnostic mode connection helps the DBA to resolve deadlocks, hangs, shared pool contentions, and many other exceptional situations that today would force the DBA to bounce their databases, causing significant loss of business availability. Specifically, for the Exadata Database Machine, Oracle Enterprise Manager provides comprehensive monitoring and management for the entire engineered system. It provides a unified view of hardware and software that enables you to view hardware components, such as compute nodes, Exadata cells, and InfiniBand switches, and see the placement of software running on them along with their resource utilization.

DBAs can also drill down from the database to the storage layer of Exadata to identify and diagnose problems such as performance bottlenecks or hardware faults. The lights-out monitoring capability of Oracle Enterprise Manager is optimized for Exadata, where metrics and thresholds are predefined so that administrators can get timely notifications when issues arise.

ADDM's counterpart for problem diagnosis of the middleware stack is JVM Diagnostics, commonly referred to as JVMD, as shown in Figure 8-9. JVMD samples the JVM heap and gives the user detailed insight into threads, locks, memory usage, and local variable usage. Operators can utilize this tool to identify the root cause of performance and functional problems. The

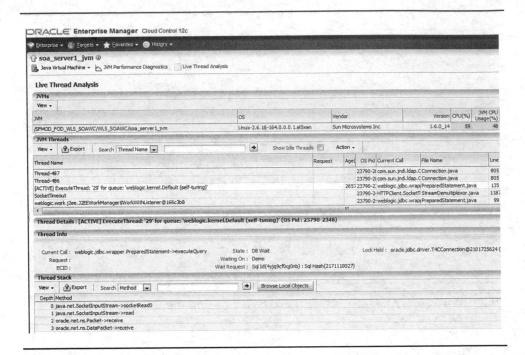

FIGURE 8-9.   *Deep JVM Diagnostics*

tool provides historical and real-time analysis, helping to solve problems on the spot. This unique capability allows operators to investigate and solve problems the first time they happen, even if the JVM is not being monitored at the time the application starts.

When a problem is raised for targets running from Oracle software, Oracle may determine that the recommended recourse is to open an SR, in order to send to support the diagnostic logs. To manage and resolve problems, it is recommended that you use Support Workbench to open an SR with the Oracle Support organization. Access to Support Workbench functionality is available through Incident Manager (Guided Resolution area) in the context of the problem. Support Workbench helps in identifying the right diagnostic information (log and trace files, typically) that need to be provided to Oracle Support for faster problem identification and resolution. Oracle Enterprise Manager provides the ability to monitor SRs as well, so that administrators are apprised of the progress.

In the latest release of Oracle Enterprise Manager 12*c*, for the customized approach to uploading diagnostic data to Oracle Support, you must first collect the data into an intermediate logical structure called an incident package (package). An *incident package* is a collection of metadata that is stored in the Automatic Diagnostic Repository (ADR) and that points to diagnostic data files and other files both in and out of the ADR. When you create a package, you select one or more problems to add to the package. Support Workbench then automatically adds the following to the package: the problem information, incident information, and diagnostic data (such as trace files and dumps) associated with the selected problems. Because a problem can have many incidents (many occurrences of the same problem), by default, only the first three and last three incidents for each problem are added to the package, excluding any incidents that are over 90 days old. You can change this default number on the Incident Packaging Configuration page of Support Workbench.

In the latest release of Oracle Enterprise Manager 12c, a Cloud Support Console is specifically tailored to facilitate support of cloud environments.

- In a cloud environment, each target can be tagged (via target properties) with some identifier, such as the subscriber ID of the tenant to which it belongs, as well as a Support identifier (CSI in case of Oracle Support).

- The Support personnel can then search the services and their incidents using business parameters (for example, customer name and subscription ID).

- The Cloud Support Console can provide launch points for deeper diagnosis. You can also drill down to topology views for impact analysis.

- If Support Workbench is configured to connect to My Oracle Support, the Support personnel can attach the diagnostics, configuration, and dependency data to the SR.

Managing Overall Cloud Service Levels

In spite of Oracle Enterprise Manager's deep capabilities in problem diagnosis and resolution for individual layers of the stack, it needs to be understood that those aspects managed in silos are not adequate to manage the overall service levels of the cloud. Traditional system monitoring does not provide an answer to the one question an application owner is most concerned with: Is my application working right now? System monitoring can tell you a server is out of disk space, but that doesn't mean that the application is down. From a provider's point of view, the performance and availability of business applications of the consumers are essential to the delivery of the cloud service. A poorly performing business application can have a negative effect on revenue, customer satisfaction, and availability, thereby negating all the benefits of the cloud. Agile application development approaches, and the increased rate of application changes, are leading organizations to rethink application performance management from the usual development and operations silos, to new approaches based on the DevOps model.

NOTE
DevOps is a new interaction model where Development and IT Operations work with shared responsibility that largely eliminates finger pointing and project delays. DevOps involves more than just software deployments: it is a set of processes and methods for thinking about communication and collaboration between departments. The reason Ops is so often worried when Dev is deploying new apps is that Dev doesn't really care how secure their apps are, how hard they are to deploy, how hard they are to keep running, or how many times they have to be restarted—because Ops pays the price for those mistakes, not Dev. DevOps may just be emerging as a concept, but many organizations are adopting it.

System monitoring might find no errors and no threshold violations, but the application still may be nonfunctioning. User Experience Monitoring is the first step to overcome this problem. Regardless of the availability of the cloud, the SLA has little impact on the overall business unless the end users are satisfied. Oracle Enterprise Manager's User Experience Management offers a common solution for monitoring the real user experience of all web applications. The User Experience Monitoring products capture very rich

RAFT (Response, Availability, Fault, Throughput) data about applications, application components (pages, objects, and queries), and user-initiated transactions. You can monitor the interaction experience by real end users—you can see the top pages and objects, i.e., the pages with the worst performance in terms of average latency and error count. You can also see the top users, i.e., users with worst satisfaction score. By default, the satisfaction score is based on average latency and error count and can also be configured to be based on content such as "Product not available." It also offers contextual drill-downs into the user session details and into the diagnostic details of the JVM heap that may be running the application.

As long as real users can use the application, the business application is generally assumed to be working. Still, it is possible that the user interaction is working well but the back-end transactions are not performing. For example, the user can submit a purchase request, and may even receive a confirmation page, but the purchase transaction fails to execute or to be committed on the back-end environment. To complete this coverage, Business Transaction Management monitors the back-end transactions. Now, with System monitoring, End User monitoring, and Business Transaction monitoring, all working together, the business owner can determine whether his or her application is working well. Once a culprit component is identified, domain expertise may be required to solve the problem. Deep-dive diagnostics tools can help the expert identify the root cause of the problem. For these tools to be effective, they must be available at the time the problem occurs (eliminating the time and effort it takes to reproduce the problem in a staging environment). This requires that the tools be able to continuously monitor the component 24×7, with minimal overhead.

Business Application is a new target type in Oracle Enterprise Manager. It is a logical entity that represents one business application. A business application such as a Purchasing application comprises one or more business transactions. Business transactions are the back-end transactions invoked by the user activity (the "purchase" transaction is invoked by the "submit purchase request" step, for example). They represent a sequence of operations made by the end users (for example, the three operations "search catalog," "add to cart," and "submit purchase request" can be one user flow). Cross-tier and cross-application transactions are modeled and traced end to end with the Oracle Business Transaction Management (BTM) product in a nonintrusive manner (that is, no changes are made to the messages themselves). The transactions are automatically discovered by utilizing a patent-pending fingerprinting algorithm or can be manually stitched together by leveraging custom properties in the message header or payload. These end-to-end transactions are then monitored in real time, along with business key performance indicators (KPIs) extracted from the payload. Transactions can then be searched for and aggregated to better trace, track, and troubleshoot problems.

By modeling the business transactions and the underlying systems involved in the transactions, Oracle Enterprise Manager can monitor the service levels of the cloud and compare them against the SLA that was agreed upon between the cloud provider and the end users. Using the DSS Fusion CRM Service Dashboard, users can see cumulative KPIs and statuses for all the underlying entities, as shown in Figure 8-10. These status entries can represent the current, long-term, and future status of the business application:

■ The combination of the user flows and the business transaction status entries represents the current status.

■ Long-term status can be concluded from the sum of the SLA calculations.

■ Future status can be indicated by the System status.

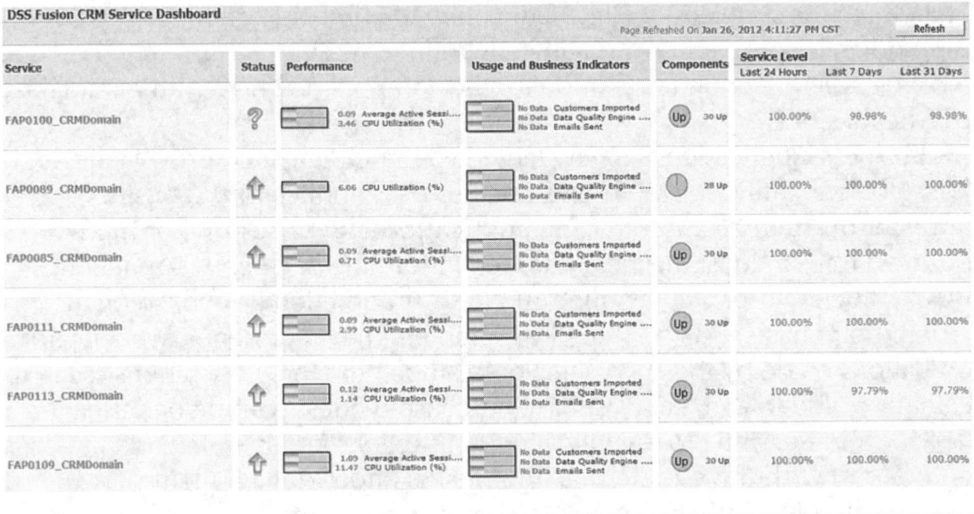

FIGURE 8-10. *Service Level Management Dashboard*

Both Real User Experience Monitoring and SLM Service Level Management are also integrated with Oracle's Application Testing Suite (ATS). The tests can be reused for production monitoring, and production application activities can be captured from actual users and can subsequently be used to generate functional and load testing scripts to support ongoing application development.

Configuration Management and Compliance

The basic need for any cloud administrator is to know what resources are out there. Often this information spans multiple data centers across multiple geographies. In the past, lengthy spreadsheets would be the administrators' only means to capture and maintain those asset records. Over time, as configuration management became an important IT discipline, administrators have automated methods of dealing with the same.

Oracle Enterprise Manager discovers and collects configuration information for all managed targets across the enterprise. Collected configuration information is periodically sent to the Management Repository over HTTP or HTTPS, allowing cloud administrators to access up-to-date configuration information for the entire enterprise. Once this information is collected, it can be used by the other Oracle Enterprise Manager facilities, such as Inventory, Search, Compare, and Compliance.

The Inventory and Usage Details page of Oracle Enterprise Manager provides a summary view of the discovered targets and allows you to drill down to view details on each target (see Figure 8-11). The inventory can be sliced and diced based on target properties, such as location or cost center. The inventory page also provides trends in the flux of IT assets within the

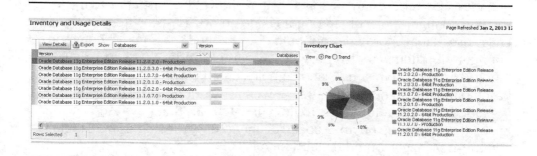

FIGURE 8-11.   *Inventory and Usage details page showing database installations*

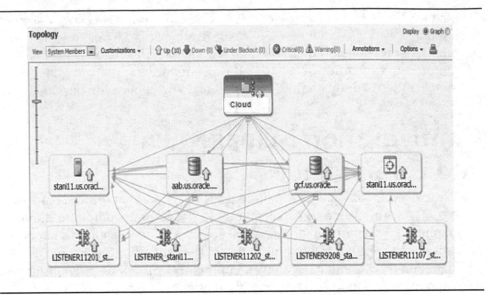

FIGURE 8-12. *Topology Viewer*

data center. Since the cloud typically has thousands of fast-changing assets, it is important to follow the trends. While it is important to provide this inventory of assets, it is also important for administrators to understand the interdependencies between those assets. Oracle Enterprise Manager provides out-of-the-box relationships to map the dependencies between these assets. For example, an application server may be *connected to* a database *deployed on* a host *running on* a virtual machine. The Topology Viewer (see Figure 8-12) provides a rich visualization of these dependencies and helps administrators to perform impact analysis.

To supplement the inventory reporting, Oracle Enterprise Manager also provides a powerful Search capability that allows administrators to track specific configurations on an ongoing and ad hoc basis. While Oracle Enterprise Manager provides out-of-the-box canned searches for common configuration items, it also provides a Search Builder that helps define reports based on both simple and complex criteria. You can define a search based on configuration properties as well as relationships. For example, if a cloud administrator wants to find all databases that have Audit Vault enabled and running on an Exadata, defining such a search using Oracle Enterprise Manager would be fairly simple.

To most enterprises, the cloud is significantly about standardization. Without standardization, the benefits of automation will be limited. Therefore, it is simply not adequate to track the inventory in a cloud. Changes to configuration data invariably happen, typically because of common events like patches and upgrades. At some point, a change to one component can affect the overall system in a negative way. Detecting the root cause in these cases becomes paramount. But, even for seasoned administrators, finding these differences is like finding a needle in a haystack. The comparison feature enables you to compare configurations of a target with configurations of another target of the same type. The comparisons can be done on the current configuration or on configurations previously saved (perhaps, for example, just before applying a patch or doing an upgrade). The comparison feature allows you to do the following:

■ Compare configurations against live targets or against a stored snapshot

■ Ignore certain attributes during a comparison

■ Design and share Comparison Templates with other administrators

■ Schedule a comparison to run on a recurring basis and notify administrators when a drift is detected

■ Compare complete target systems; match target system members automatically or manually

■ Compare configuration file data as raw file content or in a parsed format

■ Reconcile differences by synchronizing at a file level

A Comparison Template is an exemplar for fine-tuning a comparison of like configurations. A Comparison Template is associated with a specific target type, which determines the configuration item types, items, and properties to be compared. Oracle Enterprise Manager provides a number of out-of-the-box Comparison Templates that enable administrators to establish certain constants to take into account when comparing configurations of the given target type; for example, which property differences to ignore, and which property differences trigger an alert. Certain constraints, such as allowable values, can also be specified.

In a DBaaS environment, Comparison Templates can be used to compare two Exadata Database Machines or its subcomponents, such as the Exadata Storage Servers, as shown in Figure 8-13 In a PaaS environment, a Comparison Template can be defined, for example, to compare all managed servers and keep them the same while ignoring URLs containing hostnames and so forth.

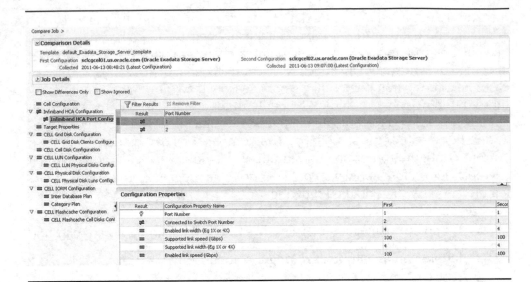

FIGURE 8-13. *Stack comparison of Exadata Storage Servers with a saved golden standard*

In an SaaS environment, the comparison feature can be used to find discrepancies among application PoDs (Points of Delivery).

Comparison Templates can be used as is or as a guideline. For example, the Comparison Template for comparing the database platform for hosting a Production cloud could be different from the Comparison Template for comparing the database platform for hosting a Development cloud. Or, a WebLogic platform for hosting business applications can use a different Comparison Template from that used by a WebLogic platform for hosting custom applications.

Of the several items in the preceding bulleted list, the ability to schedule comparison jobs deserves special mention. In an enterprise-class cloud, it is not practical to do manual comparisons. Administrators can schedule the comparison jobs based on Comparison Templates and associate the results to one of the notification methods such as e-mail.

Configuration compliance is another very important aspect of managing the cloud. We often see news reports about how the security of clouds has been breached. The security breaches often happen as a result of a faulty configuration, such as a relaxed file permission, an exceedingly simple password, or an open port. Compliance inherently demands certain disciplines that may get submerged in the entropy of a cloud. Oracle Enterprise Manager recognizes this and provides a single interface for managing configuration compliance for the entire cloud. The Compliance

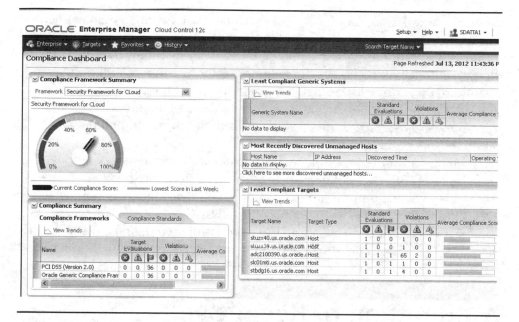

FIGURE 8-14. *Security Compliance Dashboard*

Framework in Oracle Enterprise Manager (see Figure 8-14) is hierarchical in nature, allowing for ease of management and reuse. Starting from the top level, the hierarchy contains Compliance Frameworks, Compliance Standards, and Compliance Rules. Compliance Frameworks aggregate the compliance scores of Compliance Standards, which may be for different target types. Compliance Standards contain one or more Compliance Rules, but are specific to a single target type. Compliance Rules are responsible for executing a single, specific validation of a target and reporting the conformance.

A perfect example of *monitoring by exception* is Compliance Rule which is based on real-time observations. Observations are the actions that were seen on a host or target that were configured to be monitored through real-time monitoring rules. Observations help Oracle Enterprise Manager determine in near real time *who* did *what* and *when*. Each distinct user action results in one observation. Observations are additionally bundled if there are multiple observations done in a short period of time by the same user on the same target and against the same real-time monitoring rule. For example, there could be an observation that the listener.ora file in a database cloud platform should not be tampered with. The observation can be then marked as an incident and reconciled with a change management system, such as Remedy, to determine if it was authorized or unauthorized. Multiple observations can be combined into an observation bundle. Even though an observation is part of group, the determination of authorized vs. unauthorized is done for a single observation, not at the group level. If a group has at least one observation that is marked as "unauthorized," then the group is considered to be a "violation" and an event or incident can be raised for this group violation.

There are around 40 Compliance Standards and hundreds of Compliance Rules that are shipped with the product. They are stored in the Compliance Library. However, administrators can define their own rules and standards. If a configuration item is not already collected by Oracle Enterprise Manager, administrators can define a Custom Collection and then define a rule against that collection. They can also assign to the rules severity levels that influence the overall Compliance Score and can be referenced by auditors.

Automation of Repetitive Administrative Tasks

Had it not been for automation tools, the bulk of time in managing a cloud would be spent behind mundane, repetitive, administrative tasks such as patching. Experiences from customers indicate, for example, that without Oracle Enterprise Manager, administrators spend hundreds of person-hours to apply quarterly patches to databases.

Some of the repetitive administrative tasks include the following:

- Backups
- Patching and upgrading
- Regular housekeeping tasks, such as log file cleanup and so forth
- Account creation
- Ongoing reporting

Oracle Enterprise Manager comes with a sophisticated task-automation framework comprising Jobs and Deployment Procedures. Jobs serve such purposes as the following:

- Automating many administrative tasks, such as backup, cloning, and patching

- Executing OS and SQL scripts

A job is a unit of work that you define to automate commonly run tasks either immediately or on a predefined schedule. You can also run the job once or at a specific interval, such as three times every month. Deployment Procedures utilize the Job System underneath and are typically used for multistep operations that span targets. Deployment Procedures additionally have flow control between the steps. (A detailed description of Deployment Procedures is provided in Chapter 6, in the context of DBaaS.)

While the automation framework provides a generic capability to schedule and execute repetitive tasks, Oracle Enterprise Manager comes with a library of out-of-the-box tasks in which it leverages a deep understanding of targets. One such example is Patch Automation. To make the cloud experience predictable, the cloud platform needs to be up to date with the latest patches. The following is a quick overview of Oracle's patches.

Chapter 5, which covers Database as a Service, provides a good overview of the database pool built on the PaaS Infrastructure Zone. The patch levels for the cloud platform should be chosen such that the homogeneity of the members is not breached. The pool, as per this definition, would be based on a patch level (typically the fourth digit of the database version). All the members should be patched together so that homogeneity is preserved. Similarly, when upgrading the members of an Oracle VM zone, all of them should be upgraded together. Performing major upgrades to the database pool or middleware pool is not recommended. Major upgrades are typically out-of-place; that is, they create a new Oracle Home, which would necessitate the creation of a new pool. The consumers can then migrate to the new pool as their own requirements allow.

For applying one-off patches to multiple members of the cloud in a single session under limited down time, Oracle Enterprise Manager has introduced

Overview of Oracle Patches

The primary mechanism for the release of fixes for security vulnerabilities in Oracle products is the quarterly Critical Patch Updates (CPUs). CPUs are released on dates announced a year in advance. As much as possible, Oracle tries to make CPUs cumulative; that is, each CPU contains the security fixes from all previous CPUs. In practical terms, for those products that receive cumulative fixes, the latest CPU is the only one that needs to be applied when solely using these products, as it contains all required fixes. Fixes for the other products that do not receive cumulative fixes are released as one-off patches.

Oracle also releases patch bundles in the form of Patch Set Updates (PSUs). The PSUs contain critical patches for major features, in addition to the security fixes. Oracle recommends application of these patch bundles periodically to ensure that the databases are healthy. Similarly, for Oracle WebLogic Server (and other Oracle Fusion Middleware components), Oracle releases one-off patches, security fixes, and Patch Set Updates. For Linux, Oracle releases the updates via the Unbreakable Linux Network (ULN) channels. In addition to regular updates delivered as RPMs, ULN also releases periodic Errata for critical fixes such as security fixes.

For Solaris 11, Oracle customers with an active Oracle Support plan have access to the support package repository so that they can routinely update their Oracle Solaris 11 systems:

- **Support Repository Updates (SRUs)** Updates from the Oracle Solaris 11 support repository are available as SRUs, which are released on a regular basis. SRUs take the place of maintenance updates or patch bundles that are available for Oracle Solaris 10 releases. (See "How to Configure the Oracle Solaris support Repository" at http://docs.oracle.com/cd/E23824_01/html/E24456/gljrq.html#installmain-1.)

- **Future Oracle Solaris 11 releases** Future Oracle Solaris 11 releases are made available in the support repository or a release repository that provides the currently available OS.

the concept of Patch Plans and Patch Templates (see Figure 8-15 for the lifecycle of a Patch Plan, described later):

■ **Patch Plans**   Help administrators create a consolidated list of patches to apply as a group to one or more targets. Patch Plans have states (or statuses) that map to key steps in the configuration change management process. Any administrator or role that has view privileges can access a Patch Plan.

■ **Patch Templates**   Help administrators create predesigned plans based on an existing successfully analyzed or deployable Patch Plan, but without any targets selected. This makes the Patch Templates reusable over different groups of targets.

Most large enterprises have a separation of duties when it comes to patching. Patch designers are typically IT staff who decide which patches to apply and how. Patch operators, on the other hand, are staff who deploy the patches at a scheduled time. Using the Oracle Enterprise Manager features, as a patch designer, you can create a Patch Plan with a set of patches, test them in your environment, save the successfully analyzed Patch Plan as a

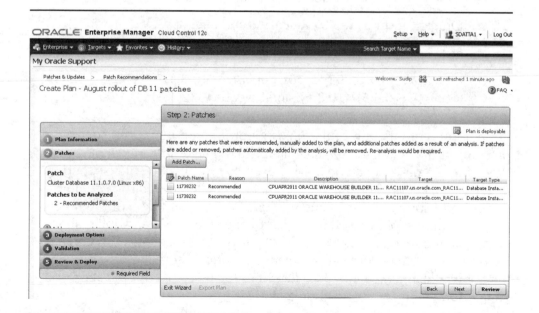

FIGURE 8-15.   *Patch Plan*

Patch Template, and publish it to patch operators. The patch operator can create Patch Plans out of the templates, add another set of targets, and roll out the patches to the production environment in a recursive manner. As a best practice, it is recommended to run the Patch Plan in Analyze mode to perform a preflight check on the patching process. If there are some configuration problems that can cause patching to fail, those can be captured ahead of time, thereby avoiding unnecessary downtime.

The following list (which is by no means intended to be exhaustive) mentions some of the Oracle Enterprise Manager 12.1 supported target types for patching:

- Oracle Database (standalone) 10*g* Release 1 and later

- Oracle Automated Storage Management (Oracle ASM) 10*g* Release 1 and later

- Oracle Real Application Clusters (Oracle RAC) 10*g* Release 1 and later

- Oracle Exadata RAC Databases 11*g* Release 2 (11.2.0.1, 11.2.0.2, and 11.2.0.3) and later

- Oracle Restart 10*g* Release 1 and later

- Oracle Clusterware 10*g* Release 1 and later

- Oracle Grid Infrastructure 11*g* Release 2

- Oracle WebLogic Server 10*g* Release 3 (10.3.1), (10.3.2), (10.3.3), (10.3.4), (10.3.5), (10.3.6), and Release 1 (12.1.1)

In addition to the out-of-the-box support for common tasks such as patching and backup, the Oracle Enterprise Manager Job and Deployment Procedure framework can be used to execute tasks like log file cleanups or OS user creation. For simple tasks that do not need sophisticated flow control and software library integration, Jobs can suffice. For the tasks that do require sophisticated flow control and software library integration, Deployment Procedures are needed. Deployment Procedures can contain steps that execute either host commands or scripts, stored as directives in the Software Library. Figure 8-16 describes the types of customization you can perform with Deployment Procedures.

Type 1	Type 2
Editing Custom Deployment Procedures	**Creating a User Defined Deployment Procedures**
You can edit an existing custom Deployment Procedure that is offered by Cloud Control to add new phases and steps. However, for patching the steps that can be added are restricted to either a Directive step or a Host command step.	You can create your own Deployment Procedure with new steps, phases, privilege levels, and so on.
You can perform the following tasks:	You can perform the following tasks:
• Add your own phases and steps to the pre-defined blocks of the procedure structure.	• Add your own phases and steps to the pre-defined **Default phase** of the procedure structure.
• Enable and disable phases and steps	• Enable and disable phases and steps
• Delete phases and steps	• Change privilege levels
• Change privilege levels	• Change error handling modes
• Change error handling modes	• Enable e-mail notifications
• Enable e-mail notifications	
	Note: For steps to Create a User Defined Deployment Procedure, see Creating an User Defined Deployment Procedure (UDDP).
Note: You can not edit an Oracle-owned deployment procedure. To do so, you must clone the Oracle-owned procedure and then edit the copy to include your changes.	For an example about Creating a User Defined Deployment Procedure, see

FIGURE 8-16. *Customization options for Deployment Procedures*

For large-scale automation in the cloud, it is not always feasible to use the GUI. All the Deployment Procedures and jobs are supported through the command-line interface (EMCLI). Some of the EMCLI verbs available with Oracle Enterprise Manager are

- describe_procedure_input
- save_procedure_input
- update_procedure_input
- get_executions
- get_instance_data (replaces get_instance_data_xml)
- submit procedure

The verbs help in describing the procedure parameters, executing them, and getting their status. These verbs can be easily incorporated as a part of scripts or another orchestration tool.

Finally, ongoing reporting on SLAs, configuration, and compliance is usually required to keep administrators and executives aware of the state of the cloud. Oracle Enterprise Manager comes with out-of-the-box reports on monitoring, configuration, patching, and compliance. The Information Publisher in Oracle Enterprise Manager can also be used to write custom reports against the Enterprise Manager MGMT views. Writing reports on underlying tables is not recommended because they are subject to change across major upgrades. To supplement these reports, there is a prebuilt integration with Oracle BI Publisher. The Oracle BI Publisher reports can be scheduled to run at periodic intervals and send the information to non-Oracle Enterprise Manager users such as IT executives.

For more information on lifecycle management and configuration management, refer to the *Oracle Enterprise Manager Lifecycle Management Administrator's Guide*, available at http://docs.oracle.com.

Summary

Cloud computing is a fascinating concept for today's CIOs. However, the benefits of the cloud can be compromised by the high cost of managing the operations. As cloud administrators wage their day-to-day struggle in keeping the cloud operational, they need sophisticated tools to aid them in this struggle. Oracle Enterprise Manager offers monitoring, cnnfiguration management, and automation capabilities that can scale to hundreds of thousands of servers, thereby helping administrators manage real enterprise-scale clouds.

CHAPTER
9

Real-Life Case Studies

his chapter presents some real-life examples of cloud implementation and employs the architectural models described in the preceding chapters. The most important thing to recognize while implementing a cloud is that there is no single design that fits all situations. The design choice is driven by application requirements, such as performance, security, and availability requirements, and the roles and responsibilities of end users.

Case Study 1: Private Infrastructure as a Service

Acme Corporation has 1045 software developers who need vanilla Oracle Linux 6 environments for their design and development activities. IT is entrusted with providing the hosts to the developers as and when they need them. The developers usually need 2GB of RAM and two vCPUs for running their workgroup version, and 4GB of RAM and four vCPUs for their Enterprise version. Because the cost of providing physical assets to the developers is prohibitive, IT has to look at alternative technologies. Also, because the development group is divided into two subgroups, Acme, Boston Center and Acme, Bangalore Center, IT needs a way to distinguish between these development groups and identify which requests came from which group.

In this case study, the first thing the administrators need to think about is what kind of service this is. The fact that the developers are interested only in hosts (servers with a Linux operating system) suggests that this is an IaaS, as per the definition in Chapter 1. This can be implemented using Oracle VM technology.

Second, the administrators need to determine how many physical servers they need. If 1045 software developers hold two hosts concurrently on average, the infrastructure would need to support 2090 VMs. Assuming that each physical server can support eight VMs, the infrastructure needs around 260 physical servers.

Third, the administrators need to decide how to segregate the physical servers so that the Boston Center and Bangalore Center can be accounted for separately. The actual distribution would depend on the employee distribution (and hence, requests) between these two centers. Therefore, the IaaS should have two zones (as described in Chapter 4).

The administrators then need to worry about access control. They can create roles for Boston employees and Bangalore employees and give them access to their respective zones. That way, the administrators can ensure that developers of the Boston Center cannot deploy into the Bangalore infrastructure zone, and vice versa.

Finally, the administrators need to create two Oracle VM templates with different configurations—one designated as "Small," with 2GB of RAM and two vCPUs, and another designated as "Large," with 4GB of RAM and four vCPUs—and publish them in the self-service catalog. The developers can choose the right configuration for the zone and deploy the Oracle VM templates.

Case Study 2: Assembly-Based Private Platform as a Service

Maximus Healthcare, a large healthcare company, uses a CRM application for its call center operations. The deployment consists of the CRM application, Oracle WebLogic Application Server, and an Oracle Database, all running in their individual tiers. The system is complex and is patched and customized every quarter. The QA engineers need a quick way to create the system from their last baseline and deploy it in a couple of hours for functional testing. The application needs seven inputs to be fully configured, and the QA engineers are not familiar with the inputs. All that they need is a fully baked environment in which to carry out their functional testing. IT must design a custom portal where the engineers can request this environment.

The first task is to map Maximus's case study to the right service model and the right underlying technology. Maximus wants to deploy a full application stack. The best way to deploy this platform would be via Oracle VM Assemblies, as described in Chapters 2–5.

The application integrators first need to create these Assemblies. They can do so by using Oracle Virtual Assembly Builder Studio as described in Chapters 2–5. The output of that exercise would be an Assembly that can be staged directly in the Oracle Enterprise Manager Software Library from OVAB itself. During the Assembly creation process, the integrators can define the seven inputs needed for full configuration of the stack.

Once the Assemblies are staged in the Software Library, the platform administrator can make the Assembly available to the QA organization for functional testing via the Oracle Enterprise Manager self-service user interface. However, the requirement here is to integrate the self-service application with the custom portal. This can be achieved using the RESTful APIs, described in Chapter 4.

Case Study 3: Metering and Showback

Acme's Marketing and Human Resources departments are demanding more servers for their operations. Both departments complain that the current IT budget allocated to them is inadequate to run operations like campaigns, recruitment, and so forth. IT has no idea what the current usage of computing resources is by these respective groups, though IT is aware that both groups run Oracle 10g Database on Solaris. The CIO wants to get this resolved in an expedited manner for the coming fiscal year so that IT has visibility into the usage and, hence, can plan the budgetary allocations.

Over time, Acme's CIO wants to operate IT like a services unit that charges its consumers. He wants the Marketing, HR, and Sales units to pay for their usage at the rate of 5 cents an hour of CPU used. For databases that are running more securely (using features such as Data Vault), he wants a higher payback. IT has been asked to design the system.

This requirement is more for metering and showback than for self-service. The CIO does mention that he wants to operate IT like a services organization, but that does not necessarily mean that he wants IT to implement self-service. He wants a way to offer compute and database services and meter the consumption so that the metering data can be used for planning and budgeting of resources for the respective departments, Marketing and HR.

Using Oracle Enterprise Manager 12*c*, this can be implemented on brownfield resources without massive redeployment of the IT infrastructure. Chapter 7 explored how metering and showback can be implemented based on the metrics that Oracle Enterprise Manager collects. To accomplish this, the Oracle Enterprise Manager 12*c* agent has to be deployed on all the hosts, and the charge plan has to be created on the collected data. In this specific example, IT needs to implement two kinds of charge plans:

- **Universal Charge Plan**   For the CPU consumption
- **Extended Charge Plan**   For defining additional charges for the usage of Data Vault

The hourly metering data can be extracted via EMCLI and fed into the reporting and billing systems. So, if Acme wants to associate the usage to a costing model in the future, it can easily do so.

Case Study 4: Private Database as a Service

The DBAs at Maximus are weary of waiting for resources to create databases for load testing. Each time they ask for a database environment, whether single instance or Real Application Clusters (RAC), they are provided a VM. This has two major problems. First, the VM environment does not represent their production environment, which is on an Exadata appliance, and hence this type of load testing serves little purpose. Second, all the individual DBAs have to keep their database stack patched on their own. They are looking for a database platform on which they can create databases and use them for load testing. There is some spare capacity in a half-rack Exadata that can be used for this.

This is a classic case of Database as a Service, where the DBAs want to provision databases on demand. The Chapter 6 explanation of DBaaS covers the architectural details on how to set up the servers in the PaaS Infrastructure Zone.

First, the lead DBA, acting as the self-service administrator, needs to create a PaaS Infrastructure Zone on the compute nodes of the Exadata. The DBA has to identify the compute nodes to be used for single instances and RAC, respectively. Based on the preceding requirements, two pools of resources are needed, one for RAC and one for single instances. For single instances, the Oracle Home has to be provisioned, and for RAC, the Grid

Infrastructure and Oracle Home have to be provisioned *beforehand*. The self-service administrator has to select the right version of the database stack so that minimal, incremental one-off patching is needed.

Once the zones are set up, the Service Templates that tie the respective Deployment Procedures to the self-service process are defined. The Service Templates then have to be associated with the pools. The Service Templates can be tagged as Single Instance or RAC for simpler identification.

Case Study 5: Java Platform as a Service

The application developers at eDevelopers are in the business of providing J2EE applications for clients in the financial sector. They need a Java platform for deploying and testing their custom apps. They have explored the possibility of deploying into public clouds, but their databases carry proprietary information and are deployed on an in-house Exadata platform. The architects at eDevelopers have, therefore, been asked to develop a Heroku-like platform, primarily focused on ease of deployment.

The application developers in this case study are essentially looking for a deployment platform or a runtime platform for their Java applications. They can use the platform for performance analysis, testing, and so forth. This is a classic case where they would use a Google-, Amazon-, or Heroku-style cloud, but a public cloud comes with its own security challenges and limitations. Moreover, the application has to use the in-house Exadata platform as a data source.

The PaaS models described in Chapter 5 provides the right technical details for implementing this. Based on whether eDevelopers uses Oracle VM technology, it can choose either an Assembly PaaS or a Java PaaS. The Assembly PaaS will deploy a full middleware stack along with the application, while the Java PaaS will allow deployment of a Java application on a preexisting WebLogic platform, exposed as a zone. In either of these cases, the data source can be a preexisting database deployed via DBaaS or otherwise. Oracle Enterprise Manager 12*c* provides a tailored home page for the application itself, with the ability to start it up, shut it down, scale it, and monitor it. The developers can monitor the application, modify it, and redeploy it if needed.

Case Study 6:
Public Infrastructure as a Service

A telecom provider in Asia that offers compute services wants to offer VMs via its catalog. It wants a custom portal where tenants can sign up and request compute resources. It also wants to charge 10 cents an hour for the compute resources used; extract the data on actual usage and feed that into its billing system; and allow prorated monthly billing (that is, the month is counted from the day of joining).

This case is different from the previous cases because it pertains to offering a public cloud. From Oracle Enterprise Manager's perspective, there is not much difference between a private cloud deployment model and a public cloud deployment model because the VM provisioning use cases described in Case Studies 1 and 2 can easily be applied to public cloud deployment models. There are a few nuances, however.

First of all, public cloud providers need to have their own branded console. For this, they can't invoke Oracle Enterprise Manager programmatically from the console. Oracle Enterprise Manager 12c offers RESTful APIs to integrate the provisioning process with a public cloud offering's branded console.

The networking requirements for a public cloud may entail some additional nuances, like the usage of security groups. That can be implemented using network profiles, described in Chapter 4.

The additional requirements in this case are about billing, where the hourly metering data has to be extracted into a billing system, such as Oracle Billing and Revenue Management (BRM). Public cloud providers can have varying billing requirements. They may want to do a partial-month billing or a prorated-month billing. Oracle Enterprise Manager 12c does not have out-of-the-box billing models, but the hourly data, once extracted, can be used with any of these models.

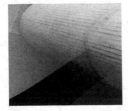

Index

P

Reach More than 700,000 Oracle Customers with Oracle Publishing Group

Connect with the Audience that Matters Most to Your Business

Oracle Magazine
The Largest IT Publication in the World
Circulation: 550,000
Audience: IT Managers, DBAs, Programmers, and Developers

Profit
Business Insight for Enterprise-Class Business Leaders to Help Them Build a Better Business Using Oracle Technology
Circulation: 100,000
Audience: Top Executives and Line of Business Managers

Java Magazine
The Essential Source on Java Technology, the Java Programming Language, and Java-Based Applications
Circulation: 125,000 and Growing Steady
Audience: Corporate and Independent Java Developers, Programmers, and Architects

For more information or to sign up for a FREE subscription:
Scan the QR code to visit Oracle Publishing online.